PRIMARY DINOSAUR INVESTIGATIONS

PRIMARY DINOSAUR INVESTIGATIONS

How We Know What We Know

Craig A. Munsart

Karen Alonzi Van Gundy

1995

Teacher Ideas Press

A Division of Libraries Unlimited, Inc.

Englewood, Colorado

Teacher Ideas Press
A Division of Libraries Unlimited, Inc.
P.O. Box 6633
Englewood, CO 80155-6633
1-800-237-6124

Production Editor: Kevin W. Perizzolo
Copy Editor: Deborah W. Korte
Proofreader: Eileen Bartlett
Typesetter: Kay Minnis
Indexer: Nancy Fulton

Library of Congress Cataloging-in-Publication Data

Munsart, Craig A.
    Primary dinosaur investigations : how we know what we know / Craig
A. Munsart and Karen Alonzi Van Gundy.
    xxi, 293 p. 22x28 cm.
    Includes bibliographical references (p. 283-86) and index.
    ISBN 1-56308-246-2
    1. Dinosaurs--Study and teaching (Primary) 2. Science--
Methodology. I. Van Gundy, Karen Alonzi. II. Title.
QE862.D5M86   1995
372.3'5--dc20   94-47105
                                                                    CIP

This book is dedicated to my parents, Eva and Samuel, who first introduced me to dinosaurs at the American Museum of Natural History and to my daughters, Carolyn and Gayle, who provided me with a firsthand appreciation of how children love dinosaurs and who have been giving me grief ever since I did not mention them in my first book.

——Craig A. Munsart

Dedicated to the memory of my grandfather, Charles Beauchamp Beall, Sr., whose love of Colorado and passion for history will live in my heart forever. And to all the children in my life, most especially Brittany, Matthew, Vincent, Megan, Nicole, Louis, Jesse, and Christopher.

——Karen Alonzi Van Gundy

Contents

Part 3: The Emerging Picture

Acknowledgments

Craig Munsart

This book was possible only through the assistance of a great many people. Any thank yous must begin with all the elementary school students in primary grades whose wide-eyed interest during dinosaur lessons told us classroom dinosaur activities had to reach beyond spelling long names and assembling puzzles. Many primary grade teachers have taken Dinosaur Ridge training classes in Morrison, Colorado, and have indicated the need for a classroom resource that would provide teacher-ready lessons about the science of dinosaurs; their comments have been very helpful. David Loertscher of Libraries Unlimited was responsible for the initiation of the project and was an ardent supporter during its preparation. A special thank you to our production editor Kevin W. Perizzolo who worked hard to make this book a reality and for getting the book on track and keeping it there. Deborah Korte's rigorous editing has made this a much better book. My editor and friend, Suzanne Barchers, provided valuable assistance during the preparation of the manuscript. John Taylor of Rockley Music in Lakewood, Colorado, provided assistance during preparation of chapter 10, "Sounds." Krista Henke helped with the research. My wife silently (almost) endured my mounds of papers and general clutter around the house during preparation of the manuscript. A special thanks must be extended to all those whose discoveries made it possible for us to write this book, from Dr. and Mrs. Gideon Mantell and William Buckland to those paleontologists and researchers in the field and laboratory today; their insight and perseverance have made dinosaur science a reality. My friends in The Friends of Dinosaur Ridge have provided much encouragement. A special thanks and apology to Bob Raynolds, president of the Friends, who has been an ardent supporter and whose name I spelled wrong in an earlier work. Others who provided encouragement were Norb Cygan, Bob O'Donnell, and the Denver Museum of Natural History's Jack Murphy. This book would not have been possible without the creative efforts and teaching expertise of my coauthor Karen Alonzi Van Gundy; she deserves the lion's share of the credit for any success of this book in the elementary school classroom.

Karen Alonzi Van Gundy

For me this book is a dream come true. I thank my friend and coauthor Craig A. Munsart for inviting me to collaborate with him on this project. I will cherish this opportunity for life. To my mother, Dorothy Alonzi, I say thanks for being such a great kid's mom. Our summer treks to the "Hogback" (now Dinosaur Ridge, west of Denver) will always be a fond memory. Sadly, many of the beautiful tracks I marveled at as a child have disappeared forever. Fortunately, The Friends of Dinosaur Ridge have rescued and preserved remaining tracks for future generations. Thank you to my father, Louis Alonzi, who holds the philosophy that hard work and vigilance pave the road to success. Dad, this ethic certainly has paid off on this project. I appreciate my daughter Brittany's sharing computer time and household responsibilities so that I could concentrate on my writing. My husband Bruce's quiet, caring support allowed me to maintain my focus this past year. To my colleagues Jamie Hawkins-Fink, Dedre Hubbard, and Rosalyn Munsart, I extend an appreciation for trying and critiquing activities. To Jamie, an extra thanks for being patient and listening to more information about dinosaurs than you ever thought you'd want to hear. Finally, I extend professional thanks to Merrillyn Brooks Kloefkorn, who has helped me move to the exciting practice of integrating literature across the curriculum.

Introduction

The present wave of dinosaur mania makes it easy to utilize a student's interest in the former masters of the earth to introduce a wide variety of concepts. Students are already familiar with the names and habits of many of the animals, but familiarity with dinosaurs can accomplish much more. Stephen Jay Gould (1991, 102) asks, "Could we not immediately subvert more of the dinosaur craze from crass commercialism to educational value? . . . Dinosaur facts and figures can inspire visceral interest and lead to greater wonder about science. Dinosaur theories and reconstructions can illustrate the rudiments of scientific reasoning." We fervently share Gould's tenet that dinosaurs can be used as a medium not only to teach students about the way science works but to introduce a broad range of thinking skills as well. That tenet is the foundation of this book.

This is not a textbook. It is a collection of teacher-friendly, classroom-ready lessons and activities that will allow students to better understand the workings of science through the vehicle of dinosaurs. We are both classroom teachers and appreciate the time and energy requirements of day-to-day classroom survival. To that end we have tried to make the lessons user-friendly with minimal teacher setup. Each lesson contains a short introductory text to familiarize the teacher with the science contained and several activities that allow students to investigate the world of science through dinosaurs. The book moves from the process of discovery to details of those discoveries and on to the conclusions and speculations drawn from the discoveries.

An eight-year-old child from Colorado walking along a Florida beach on vacation picks up a seashell and wonders where it came from. A 40-year-old marine biologist from California (with three college degrees and 15 years of experience) walks along the same beach, picks up the same shell, and asks the same question. They have both begun the process of scientific investigation. Obviously, the methods and results of that investigation may be quite different for the two beach visitors, but the initial inquiry is identical. Despite what many believe, there is nothing magical about science.

Much is made of the scientific method as some obscure, magical procedure that only Nobel Prize winners or people who wear long white coats and spend much of their lives sequestered in laboratories can ever hope to understand. The reality is that we all exercise the scientific method every day, whether in selecting the appropriate wardrobe for the weather or determining the cooking sequence of ingredients while preparing dinner. Weather reports and cookbooks were the reference materials used, and our own experiences provided the experimentation. We don't document what we do, but the scientific method is being used nonetheless.

The method of scientific inquiry can be considered a five-part process:

1. **Asking**. Wondering why something happens or what makes something work starts the process. Asking logically leads to investigating.

2. **Investigating**. Investigation will provide the framework where possible answers to the questions will be found. Frequent offshoots of investigations of an original question are additional questions or solutions to other problems. Investigation will most often provide several possibilities rather than a single, definitive answer to a problem. Determination of the correct answer will require the investigator to try different solutions.

3. **Trying.** Trying to narrow down the possibilities the investigation process produced may require multiple steps, such as prediction and experimentation. Trying to determine the correct answer is both the most rewarding and frustrating part of science. Trying to find the correct answer is matched in importance by the need to record what was done.

4. **Recording.** As the testing of possible correct answers continues, it is important to document or record what was done and what methods were followed. The purpose of recording is twofold. First and foremost, if the trial is successful, careful documentation will allow it to be repeated both by the investigator and other investigators as well. Second, if the trial is unsuccessful, it is possible to modify the procedure so that success may ultimately be achieved. All results must be evaluated to verify success.

5. **Evaluating.** Scientific truth is a discovery that must survive careful evaluation. Any successful scientific investigation can withstand careful scrutiny by peers of the original investigator; peer scrutiny is the most cherished guardian of scientific truth. Evaluation may identify flaws in the initial trials, indicating why they failed, or it may identify ways the trials may be streamlined or improved.

This five-part paradigm is used as a frame of reference for all activities within the book. The student icon guide (see pages xv and xvi) will serve as a reminder of the steps of the scientific method. When introducing an activity refer to the icons on the student icon guide and ask students to determine which step is the focus of the activity. Students will become aware of the sequential approach to scientific investigation and where they are within that sequence.

We mentioned before that successful scientific investigation can withstand careful scrutiny by peers. To that end, we recommend many of the activities be done in peer group settings (appendix A provides suggestions on how to divide students into groups). Peer scrutiny begins when young children learn to accept and provide meaningful criticism. Gone are the days of sit-in-your-seats-and-listen education. Research supports interactive, cooperative, and collaborative learning.

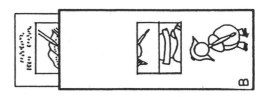

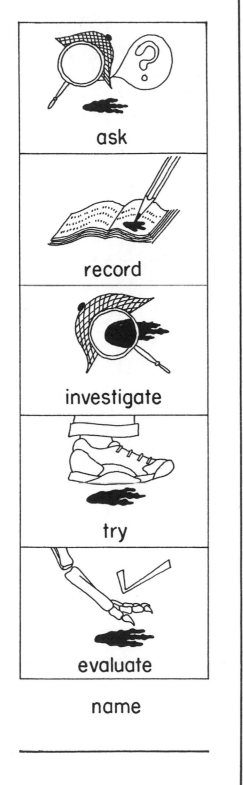

STUDENT
ICON GUIDE

ask

record

investigate

try

evaluate

name

_____

Student icon guide assembly instructions.

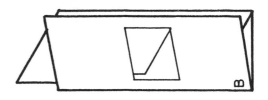

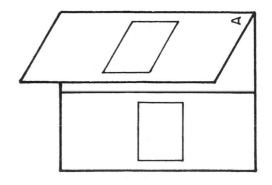

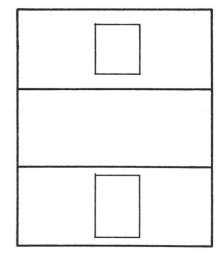

PRIMARY DINOSAUR INVESTIGATIONS

remove

B

A

remove

As science is the primary focus of this book, we are fortunate that there are a number of excellent children's authors who provide us with wonderful resources appropriate to the age level and interests of primary-school-age children. All of the materials recommended for use in these lessons are in print as of 1995. Ideally, a personal library is every teacher's dream. Realistically, you will probably want to work closely with your school librarian and the public library to have resources available for your students. The annotated book list (appendix B) provides a limited list of specific resources. New things are coming out all the time. Add to your collection as you desire.

Each activity lists the required time, materials, and student grouping. The time requirement is classroom time only and does not include preparation time for making copies, cutting, or laminating.

Science can be fantastically exciting or horribly boring. We have all taken science classes in which much of the curriculum was based on memorization of as many facts or vocabulary words as possible, with tests once a week to confirm our memorization abilities. Problem-solving and critical-thinking skills were either an afterthought or were ignored completely. We recently observed an inner-city science class where students were asked weekly to memorize 10 facts about trees. After a week, only a few of the 28 students could successfully repeat the definitions they should have committed to memory; even worse, none of the students knew anything about how a tree functions or why trees are important.

Science is not about memorization. Albert Einstein never knew his own phone number. Because we have only a certain amount of brain capacity available, he felt it was a waste to memorize information that was easily available from a reference source. Information is not an end unto itself; the ability to organize and analyze the information available is the goal of science.

Barry K. Boyer (1991, xv) notes that "integrating the teaching of thinking skills with subject matter teaching leads to improved student thinking *and* more meaningful content learning," and he goes on to list the following grade-appropriate thinking skills (1991, 10):

Grades K-2	*Grades 3-6*
Observing	Classifying
Comparing	Sequencing
Sorting (classifying)	Summarizing
Ordering (sequencing)	Decision making
Predicting	Problem solving
	Hypothesizing
	Drawing conclusions
	Identifying facts and value claims
	Identifying relevant information
	Determining the accuracy of a claim
	Identifying reliable sources

Because this book is designed for use in primary classrooms (grades K-3), not all activities will work equally well with all children. Once again, you are the professional in your classroom, and only you know what your students can do. We believe that Boyer's list will help in making activity selections. The activities in each part are designed to support the science of that part. Some of the activities can stand alone; other activities are dependent on each other. You will have to determine which are appropriate for your class.

We strongly recommend that classrooms have at least a globe and world map (see appendix C). Geographic literacy seems to be a victim of reductions in school budgets and ever-increasing curricula demands: by the time students enter high school, they seem to know less geography than they did in the primary grades. Students need a strong foundation in geography in the primary and intermediate grades. Unfortunately, searching for an absolutely accurate representation of the earth for use in the classroom is a waste of time: it does not exist.

The most accurate representation of the earth is a globe. All globes are spherical, portraying the earth in a perfect ball shape. In fact, the earth is not perfectly spherical, but the representation comes close enough. Most schools have political globes that indicate political boundaries by representing different countries in different colors. The problems with political globes are that (a) the earth really doesn't look like a colored mosaic from space and (b) changing political situations make such globes obsolete very quickly (the National Geographic Society updates its map products several times each year to keep up with changes). Look at your globe. More than likely, Russia is shown as the Soviet Union.

Physical globes show the mountains, deserts, and oceans; these change, too, but slowly enough so that physical globes will generally be accurate within our lifetimes. Physical globes are also available showing the mountains and trenches of the ocean floor rather than simply showing the oceans as water. Some physical globes have a relief surface: mountains are raised and basins are depressed so that a student can literally feel the topography of the earth's surface. These relief surfaces can be misleading, however. Mount Everest projects less than six miles from the surface of a "sphere" that is approximately 7,900 miles in diameter. The earth's surface is really relatively smooth. The irregularities on the surface of an orange represent a surface with similar bumpiness to that of the earth. If a 12-inch globe with raised relief projects Mount Everest 1/4-inch above the surface, the globe is actually showing the mountain to be more than 164 miles high, or approximately 869,000 feet above sea level. Sir Edmund Hillary would still be climbing! This discussion is not an indictment against globes. It is merely a caution that the only accurate representation of the earth is the earth itself, and students and teachers should be aware that all others are flawed.

Globes may have their problems, but maps are even worse. A map is man's attempt to accurately represent a nearly spherical object on a flat piece of paper. Not surprisingly, these attempts are not completely successful. In your classroom you probably have a map of the world. In most cases it is a world map based on what is called a Mercator projection. Mercator was a Dutch navigator in the 1500s who designed his map so that directions from one place to another would be shown correctly for sailors navigating at sea. Lines of longitude run up and down, and lines of latitude run side to side, forming a convenient grid. It was never meant to accurately depict the relative sizes of landmasses and bodies of water, and it was certainly not intended for teaching geography to young students. Take a second to look at the map and compare it with a globe. The only area where sizes are correctly represented is at the equator. As the projection moves north and south toward the poles, it distorts areas and looks progressively less like the globe. Also, because of the way the projection is laid out, it is impossible to show the north and south poles. Following are two examples of the shortcomings of the Mercator projection:

1. The Mercator projection map of the world prepared by the United States Geological Survey does not display the areas north of 84 degrees north latitude or south of 70 degrees south latitude: 26 degrees of a possible 180 degrees of latitude are not shown. More than 14 percent of the earth's latitudes are missing!

2. Greenland is distorted. Have you ever wondered why so many students believe Greenland is a continent? That's right—the Mercator projection. Because landmasses become stretched and distorted near the poles, Greenland appears to be three or four times larger than Australia; in reality, just the opposite is true (Australia is 2,968,000 square miles, whereas Greenland is only 837,000 square miles).

Each type of map will have its own flaws when compared to a globe. Before the map is put on the wall for students to see, those discrepancies should be explained and understood. Your students will remember what they see. How long was it before you finally found out that Greenland is not considered a continent? There is no perfect way to show the earth in the classroom, but it is important that you be aware of the problems with any representation you use and perhaps more importantly, that you share the problems with the students. If you live in or plan to visit the Denver metropolitan area, maps can be obtained over-the-counter at the Map Sales Office in the Denver Federal Center, located just west of Denver in Lakewood, Colorado.

Many of the activities will be enriched if you can show the students actual fossils, rather than drawings. Fossils, and fossil collectors, are more common than you might think. A search for local fossil sources might begin with state geological surveys, local universities, high school science departments, or amateur clubs of collectors. Many collectors would be delighted to "strut their stuff" in front of a group of interested students. Local rock and mineral shops have fossils they might be willing to loan for educational purposes. The United States Geological Survey has large, hands-on fossil sets available free of charge for loan. The sets contain hundreds of specimens representing a broad range of organisms, including insects, plants, and dinosaurs. The sets also come with a detailed guide to the collection. These sets are available from earth science centers, called Geocenters, at three libraries of the USGS. For information, contact the center nearest you (see appendix D).

Geologic time is the framework within which all earth history is discussed and can sometimes be overwhelming. Appendix E provides a short background into the development of, and names used on the time scale. For the readers' convenience the glossary contains 1) definitions of words possibly unfamiliar to some readers and 2) a listing of names, descriptors, and pronunciation guide for animals and plants discussed in the text.

We both believe that classroom learning experiences should be enhanced by field trips—with any study involving dinosaurs this is almost a necessity. Appendix F provides some hints about the effective use of field resources, such as the zoo or museum.

At the conclusion of several chapters, we have included drawings of dinosaur bones taken from original discoveries at Como Bluff in southeastern Wyoming in the late 1800s. Beneath the drawings are quotations from those involved in the discoveries. We hope these will provide a sense of what it was like at the time. All are taken from *Marsh's Dinosaurs: The Collections at Como Bluff* by John Ostrom and John McIntosh (1966). Take note of the spelling as you read and share these quotes with your students and colleagues. Some nineteenth-century teachers must be spinning in their graves. Here is proof that students have been making interesting spelling approximations since time immemorial!

We now invite you and your students to enjoy science with the help of the masters of the Mesozoic Era.

REFERENCES

Boyer, Barry K. 1991. *Teaching Thinking Skills: A Handbook for Elementary Teachers*. Boston: Allyn & Bacon.

Gould, Stephen Jay. 1991. *Bully for Brontosaurus*. New York: W. W. Norton.

Ostrom, John H., and John S. McIntosh. 1966. *Marsh's Dinosaurs: The Collections at Como Bluff*. New Haven, Connecticut: Yale University Press.

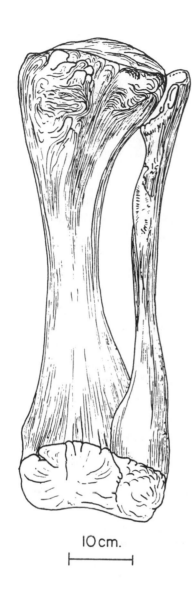

Stegosaurus ungulatas

tibia/fibula
(lower leg)

10 cm.

"I have had the worst time finding a good quary that a man ever had but now I wish you wer here to see the bones roll out and they are beauties to I think this quary eaqual no. 1 for good bones and quanity it outcrops for X80 feet length there is more than one animal it would astonish you to see the holes we have dug since we left no. 3 I think I took up ten ton of bones."

March, 1878

"A heavy thunderstorm and rain occurred in afternoon in evening our tents were inundated with *Siredons* {=*Amblystoma*} who swarmed in such numbers insinuating themselves under every box and bed that although we threw out and killed dozens it became useless to stop the horde of slimy lizards that waddled liesurely into the tents as if they had a perfect right to them and resenting any attempt at interference by a vigorous curling up of their tails. What with the noise of these creatures working their way under our boxes papers and bed, the baying of wild geese on the lake, the gnawing of mice at our furbiture and the roar of the thunder, the voices of the night were not conducive to slumber."

August 11, 1879

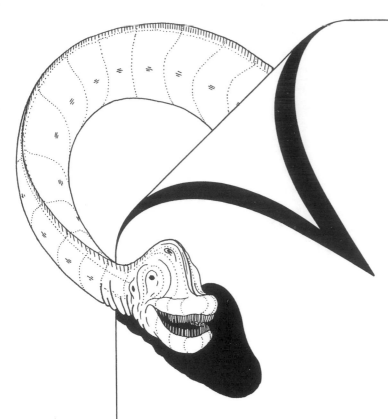

BEGINNING THE INVESTIGATION

Younger students already know about dinosaurs. They know the sizes; they know the names; they know the spelling of the names; they know the carnivores; and they know the herbivores. They can probably name as many dinosaurs as they can animals in the zoo. What the students don't know is how we know about dinosaurs. Zoo animals can be observed in the zoo. What they look like, how tall they are, what they eat, what sounds they make, how they move, whether they live alone or in groups: these things are all readily observable even on a casual visit. With dinosaurs no such observations are possible. None of the animals we call dinosaurs have ever been seen by a human being, yet we believe we know what they looked like, what animal class they belonged to, and how they moved. Everything we know (or think we know) about dinosaurs has been determined by application of asking, investigating, trying, recording, and evaluating: in short, the scientific method. Students may know a lot about dinosaurs; they know very little of the science applied to their study.

The process of scientific investigation is much like the children's game 20 Questions. In this game, an answer to the question, What is it? is sought by posing a series of questions that can be answered "yes" or "no," always narrowing choices until the correct solution is obtained. The often ballyhooed scientific method is merely a rigorous application of the same technique. An idea is proposed, tested against various criteria, evaluated, and tested again if necessary, the entire process accompanied by strict documentation and always exposed to the scrutiny of the investigator's peers.

In 20 Questions the answer already exists. Somewhere in the convoluted recesses of the brain, the answer is waiting to be discovered. All other options must be eliminated until only that single answer satisfies all criteria. If we were to play 20 Questions and *Stegosaurus* was the answer, the sequence of questions might be that in figure 1.

1.	Is it a vegetable?	Answer: No.
2.	Is it an animal?	Answer: Yes.
3.	Is it a large animal?	Answer: Yes.
4.	Does it swim?	Answer: No.
5.	Does it fly?	Answer: No.
6.	Does it have two legs?	Answer: No.
7.	Is it a carnivore?	Answer: No.
8.	Can I see it in a zoo?	Answer: No.
9.	Does it live in Africa?	Answer: No.
10.	Does it live in Australia?	Answer: No.
11.	Does it live in Asia?	Answer: No.
12.	Does it live in Europe?	Answer: No.
13.	Does it live on earth today?	Answer: No.
14.	Did it live a long time ago and is now extinct?	Answer: Yes.
15.	Is it a woolly mammoth?	Answer: No.
16.	Is it older than mammoths?	Answer: Yes.
17.	Is it a dinosaur?	Answer: Yes.
18.	Did it have very tall legs?	Answer: No.
19.	Did it have plates on its back?	Answer: Yes.
20.	Is it a *Stegosaurus*?	Answer: Yes!

Fig. 1. S*tegosaurus* 20 Questions.

Unfortunately, scientific investigation is not quite this easy. The big problem is that we do not know the answer before we begin the investigation, and the search for answers is often obstructed by time-, resource-, and energy-consuming dead-ends. The simple "yes" or "no" of 20 Questions is often replaced by "maybe," followed by a host of conditions. Dealing with the frustrations of not having all the necessary information and being wrong most of the time constantly tests the mettle of scientists. In 20 Questions there are only 20 opportunities to be wrong. In science the possible errors are infinite.

Do scientists enjoy their work because they thrive on disappointment and rejection? None that we know of. Certainly, scientists enjoy success as much as anyone else, but in science the search is an integral part of that success. Scientific investigation means persevering to find the solution that best satisfies all known criteria, even though the scientist knows full well that new information available the next day could refute lifelong efforts.

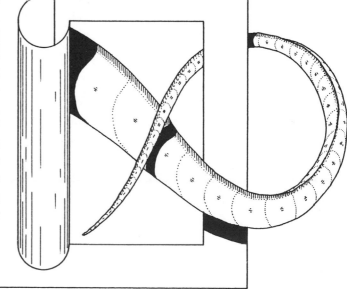

Are scientists smarter than other people? Not usually. They may be more focused on what they are trying to accomplish; they may learn more from their failures; and they may become discouraged less easily than other people; but they are not necessarily smarter.

1

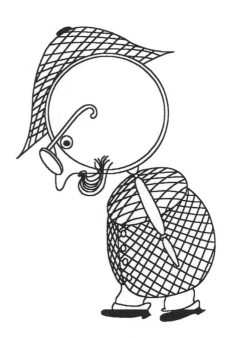

The Process of Dinosaur Discoveries

INTRODUCTION

The scientific discovery process is typically associated with the dramatic and instantaneous "Eureka!" of Archimedes, who arrived at the solution to how to measure the volume of an irregular object as he sat in an overfilled bath and watched the water spill over the top. Discovery, however, is more often the result of a methodical approach to a problem, the collection and analysis of many different pieces of data (often seemingly unrelated), and a final synthesis of the results into a resolution to the problem. Often, the discovery process takes years rather than minutes.

It is an unfortunate reality of the discovery process that failures far outnumber successes. When Thomas Edison was experimenting with the filament for the incandescent bulb, he tried thousands of materials before his ultimate success with a carbon filament in a vacuum (*New Standard Encyclopedia*, 1992, E-52). Medical research creates volumes and volumes of procedures that ultimately lead to failure, yet only a few pages in a prestigious medical journal alert society to a successful discovery.

It is important for students to be aware that perseverance and dedication to an idea are more critical to the discovery process than having a brainstorm in the shower. Some of the problems faced by science teachers even in younger grades are that students are

a. unwilling to take risks to determine solutions,

b. want instant answers, and

c. are unable or unwilling to follow a trail of information to a conclusion.

As teachers, it is important for us to provide students with an understanding of the discovery process so they can:

a. apply themselves for the duration of the investigative process,

b. have the confidence to be wrong and still continue the process,

c. understand that some pieces of information may be more important than others, and

d. analyze the critical information.

The activities in this chapter will provide an introduction to the discovery process. They are based on an actual investigation that began in the late 1970s in the northern Rocky Mountains.

ACTIVITY: A PREHISTORIC DREAM

Students will participate in an imaginary dig in Montana. The strategy suggested for this activity is *guided imagery*. Vacca and Vacca (1989, 141–142) suggest using this strategy as a means for "building an experience base for inquiry, discussion, and group work." In guided imagery, the teacher structures a daydream for students. In this daydream, the students imagine sights, sounds, and feelings. This strategy is effective for prereading because the daydream will preview the actual story.

There is a 10-minute period for drawing images of the daydream following each of the three guided imagery readings. The discussion and drawing period is an important time for processing the given information.

REQUIREMENTS

Time

One 45-minute session

Materials

- One large piece of white drawing paper for each group of three children

- Pencils, markers, or crayons for each student (all materials should be set aside until it is time to draw)

- One copy of the guided imagery "Digging for *Maiasaurus*" (for teacher use)

- A minute timer

Grouping

Three children per group (assign each group a number), then entire class for the guided imagery session

DIRECTIONS

1. Before reading the guided imagery lesson, assign each group a work space.

2. Place one piece of white drawing paper and all pencils, markers, or crayons for the group in the assigned space.

3. Gather all students together in front of you to begin the guided imagery lesson.

4. Read the guided imagery "Digging for *Maiasaurus*." (This title is for teacher information only. Do not tell students the title, as it will encourage them to focus on a specific animal rather than drawing their own conclusions.)

5. Follow up with the questions and directions for each section of the guided imagery.

"Digging for *Maiasaurus*"
Guided Imagery
(Title is for teacher information only)

GUIDED IMAGERY

Close your eyes. Tell all of your muscles to relax. *(PAUSE)* It is 1978. The famous paleontologist John Horner has invited you to join him on an exploration. You are walking across the vast grasslands of Montana. It is a very hot day, and you have been walking for a long time. John Horner always keeps his eyes on the ground. He has told you to do the same. *(STOP)* Open your eyes. Think about what you have just experienced.

Directions:

Tell students that based on the limited information they have been given, each group will begin to draw a picture of what the area might have looked like. Remind children to be sure to draw the picture *using only the information they have been given so far.*

Before students begin to draw, ask them some leading questions. What kind of a day was it? What did the landscape look like? Set a timer and allow 10 minutes for planning and drawing time. *(The timing is important because it will encourage the children to focus on the assignment.)*

When 10 minutes are up, gather students together again. Direct them to leave all materials at their work space. Continue the guided imagery.

GUIDED IMAGERY

Close your eyes. Tell all your muscles to relax. *(PAUSE)* Suddenly, you trip over something hard sticking out of the ground. John Horner is very interested in whatever it is that you tripped over. Carefully, he kneels near the object and tells you to do the same. John Horner takes out a small hand spade, a chisel, and a hammer. He hands you a small paintbrush and explains that your job will be very important. You are responsible for brushing away the dust as John Horner digs out the object that you tripped over. As the two of you work, it becomes apparent that the object is oval-shaped. Surprisingly, you discover that there are more of these objects in the same area. *(STOP)*

Open your eyes. Think about the experience you have just had. Do you have more information? How will this additional information help your group?

Directions:

Tell students to return to their group work spaces, where they will continue to add to the original drawing. Before students begin drawing, make sure they understand the terms *hand spade, chisel,* and *hammer.* Give students the following instructions: Add the new information to your drawing, showing what you imagined happened. Think about the tools, the shape of the object, and where you and John Horner are working.

Set a timer and allow 10 minutes for drawing. When the 10 minutes are over, return to the guided imagery.

GUIDED IMAGERY

Close your eyes. Tell all your muscles to relax once again. *(PAUSE)* The day is getting hotter, but you and John Horner are anxious to see what it is that you have found. You pick up your canteen for a drink of water. In the spot where your canteen was lying, there is another interesting-looking object. You tell John Horner, and he begins to dig around this new find. As you brush away the specks of dust, a recognizable shape becomes apparent. This time you have come upon a skull of some small animal. You ask John Horner, "What do you think it is?" Horner examines the skull closely and describes it as having an interestingly shaped mouth. Excitedly, John Horner exclaims, "I believe we have come upon a nest of hadrosaurs—duck-billed dinosaurs!" *(STOP)*

Open your eyes. Think about the experience you have just had.

Directions:

Once again, ask students to return to their original drawings. This will be the final addition to this drawing exercise. Give students the following instructions: Think about all the information you have about the trip. Discuss with your partners and make decisions about what to include in this picture.

Set timer and allow 10 minutes for students to complete the drawings. Collect the drawings and save them, or if space allows, display them to provide a quick reference for the follow-up activity "Was the Dream Real?"

ACTIVITY: WAS THE DREAM REAL?

This is the follow-up activity to the "Digging for *Maiasaurus*" guided imagery. The importance of facts for the development of scientific theory will be further reinforced. The core literature for this lesson is *Maia: A Dinosaur Grows Up* by John R. Horner and James Gorman (1989). In addition, a KWL (Know, Want to know, Learned) chart will be employed to build on prior knowledge and encourage connections between the scientific information presented in this book and background experiences that the children have had with present-day animals (see the sample KWL chart in fig. 1.1, p. 8).

REQUIREMENTS

Time

Approximately two 45-minute sessions

Materials

- The book *Maia: A Dinosaur Grows Up* by John R. Horner and James Gorman

- Enlarged KWL chart (fig. 1.1). This chart may be copied to a large piece of butcher paper or to a piece of poster board. If possible, laminate the chart so that it may be used again in future lessons.

Grouping

Whole class

DIRECTIONS

1. Begin to fill in the KWL chart by accessing knowledge from the children. They may refer to the guided imagery experience and the pictures in the book *Maia: A Dinosaur Grows Up*. Explain to the students that they will be looking at the pictures in the book and predicting what John Horner and James Gorman could tell about the dinosaurs in the story. That information will be recorded in the K section of the KWL chart. The K section of the chart is reserved for information that students already know or information they are able to obtain from a body of material (see fig. 1.2, p. 9).

2. Begin the prediction process with page 8 of *Maia: A Dinosaur Grows Up*. You may choose to have students make predictions from all of the picture pages or skip through the book and use only those pictures you believe are most significant to your students.

3. Next, you will be concentrating on the W section of the KWL chart. In the W section of the chart, students will focus on what they would like to find out or learn (see fig. 1.3, p. 10). Brainstorm and, in the W section of the KWL chart, record questions that the students may have about the material they have seen so far.

(Text continues on page 11.)

What we think we KNOW. K	What we WANT to learn. W	What we LEARNED. L

student names _____ , _____

Fig. 1.1. Know, Want to know, Learned (KWL) chart.

student names _____ , _____		
What we think we <u>know</u>. **K**	What we <u>want</u> to learn. **W**	What we <u>learned</u>. **L**
The area was flat and grassy. The animals built nests.		

Fig. 1.2. KWL chart with K column partially filled in.

student names _____, _____		
What we think we <u>know</u>. **K**	What we <u>want</u> to learn. **W**	What we <u>learned</u>. **L**
The area was flat and grassy. The animals built nests.	Where is Montana? How many eggs were in one nest?	

Fig. 1.3. KWL chart with K and W columns partially filled in.

ACTIVITY: MEET MAIA

This activity will complete the KWL chart begun in the activity "Was the Dream Real?" The L section of the chart is reserved for facts that the students have learned after exploring a body of material.

REQUIREMENTS

Time

Approximately two 30-minute sessions (20 minutes of reading and 10 minutes to add information to the KWL chart)

Materials

- *Maia: A Dinosaur Grows Up* by John R. Horner and James Gorman
- Partially completed KWL chart from "Was the Dream Real?" activity
- Marker

Grouping

Whole class

DIRECTIONS

Session 1

1. Begin the session by reviewing the entries in the K and W sections of the chart. Explain to students that in this lesson they will gather information to add to the L section of the KWL chart. The L section of the chart is reserved for information gleaned from a body of material.
2. Next, read aloud pages 7-31 of *Maia: A Dinosaur Grows Up.*
3. After reading the selection, refer to the L section of the KWL chart (see fig. 1.4, p. 12).

Session 2

Session 2 will follow the same format as Session 1. Read pages 32-55 aloud and continue to add information to the L section of the KWL chart.

Save all material on the KWL chart to be used in a culminating activity ("What We Learned About Maia").

student names _____ , _____		
What we think we know. **K**	What we want to learn. **W**	What we learned. **L**
The area was flat and grassy. The animals built nests.	Where is Montana? How many eggs were in one nest?	Eighty million years ago Duckbill dinosaurs lived in Montana.

Fig. 1.4. KWL chart with K, W, and L columns partially filled in.

ACTIVITY: WHAT WE LEARNED ABOUT MAIA

Students will refer to the information on the KWL chart and the book *Maia: A Dinosaur Grows Up* to create specific categories to be used as an outline for a group or class science report. The categories will be recorded on a large piece of butcher paper divided as in figure 1.5, page 14.

REQUIREMENTS

Time

- One 30-40-minute session

Materials

- Butcher paper divided as in figure 1.5 to show categories
- Markers (five colors)
- Completed KWL chart from previous activity

Grouping

Whole class

DIRECTIONS

1. Using the KWL chart as a resource, children will identify categories that can be used to prepare an outline for the group research paper. Typically, when working with information about animals, there are four apparent categories: the animal's name, its habitat, its food, and its enemies. In addition, children may want to add a fifth category for interesting facts; these frequently include the animal's habits and behaviors. These categories might be used on the butcher paper chart or students may generate their own.

2. Assign a marker color to each category (for example, red for the animal's name, blue for its food, yellow for its enemies, and green for its habitat).

3. Look through the entries on the KWL chart completed in the previous activity and color code them according to the key you have created with the children.

4. Place the color-coded information in the corresponding categories on the butcher paper chart. By doing this, the students will have created an outline for the paragraphs of the report.

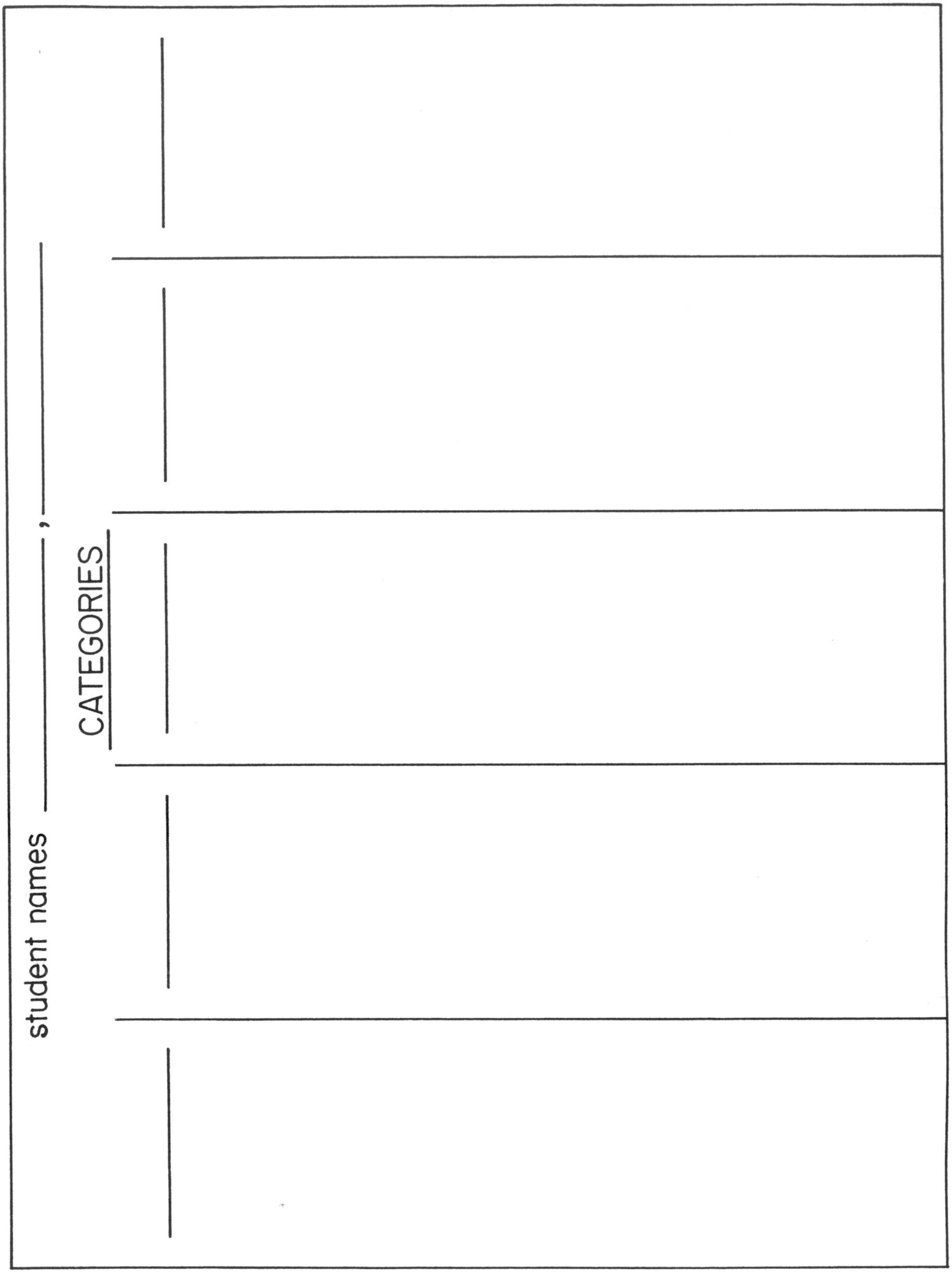

student names

CATEGORIES

Fig. 1.5. Layout of butcher paper chart with categories.

ACTIVITY: IMAGINATION DEVELOPS FROM EVIDENCE

This alternate culminating activity asks students to examine the illustrations in the book to determine which parts show evidence and which parts were the authors' imaginations.

REQUIREMENTS

Time

One 20–30 minute session

Materials

- *Maia: A Dinosaur Grows Up*
- Butcher paper chart divided as in figure 1.6, page 16
- Marker

Grouping

Whole class

DIRECTIONS

1. Use any teacher-selected or student-selected page from the book for discussion.

2. Teacher and students examine the page and select evidence from the text to put in the "Evidence" section of the butcher paper chart. Then examine the illustration and record the authors' elaboration in the "Author's Imagination" section of the chart (see fig. 1.7, p. 17).

3. The number of times #2 is repeated will be dictated by the students' enthusiasm for the activity.

EXTENSIONS

Give students an opportunity to exercise their report-writing skills by visiting the library and checking out books about dinosaurs or other animals of interest. Work with the library media specialist to have helpful books or suggestions for subjects available. Working independently or in pairs, students will create their own KWL chart and outline for a report about their chosen animal.

(Text continues on page 18.)

page number _____

AUTHOR'S IMAGINATION

EVIDENCE

Fig. 1.6. Chart layout to be used in Activity: Imagination Develops from Evidence.

page number _7,10,11_

AUTHOR'S IMAGINATION

The authors imagined that

the Maiasaur adults took good

care of their young. They

imagined that the big animals

laid close by to protect the

young.

EVIDENCE

Eighty million years ago,

duck-billed dinosaurs built

nests and laid eggs in what

is now Montana.

Fig. 1.7. Example of filled-in Figure 1.6.

REFERENCES

Horner, John R., and James Gorman. 1989. *Maia: A Dinosaur Grows Up.* Philadelphia, Pennsylvania: Running Press.

Murphy, Jim. 1992. *Dinosaur for a Day.* New York: Scholastic.

New Standard Encyclopedia, 1992. Chicago: Standard Education.

Vacca, Richard T., and Jo Anne L. Vacca. 1989. *Content Area Reading.* Glenview, Illinois: Scott, Foresman.

SUGGESTED READING

Horner, John R., and James Gorman. 1988. *Digging Dinosaurs.* New York: Workman.

Fossils

INTRODUCTION

We are all familiar with book illustrations, posters, and even wall murals depicting the earth at the time the dinosaurs lived. Artists depict forests, ferns, swampy areas, insects alighting on plants, small mammals crawling along the ground, and flying reptiles that coexisted with the dinosaurs. Are these merely products of the artists' imagination? How could such information be known? There are no photographs. There are no drawings by primitive people because humans did not coexist with the dinosaurs. The information required to create such factual recreations is available only from fossils. The word *fossil* (from the Latin *fossilis*, or "dug up") was first used in the Middle Ages to describe anything of interest removed from the ground, including rocks and minerals (Adams 1954, 137). Its meaning underwent a series of changes (see Adams 1954, 250-263), but during the seventeenth century, *fossil* arrived at its current meaning: "a remnant or trace of an organism of a past geologic age" (*American Heritage Dictionary* 1982, 527).

Refer to appendix D for fossil collections available on loan for classroom use.

Fossils are classified either as body fossils or trace fossils. *Body fossils* are remnants of the organism itself. Bones and teeth of animals, and leaves, pollen, and seeds of plants are examples of body fossils. So are molds and casts, which are impressions found in rock that are made by these pieces of the original organism. *Trace fossils* result from an organism's activities and include footprints made by dinosaurs or burrows dug by clams.

Fossils are often considered mere collectibles, but they are much more. They are powerful tools that provide a window into the geologic past. Like detectives trying to re-create a crime scene with the evidence available, geologists and paleontologists use fossil data to determine earth history. When information from fossils is added to the information yielded by the rocks themselves, strong clues are provided that allow detailed reconstruction of what the earth was like in the distant past. For example, scientists can determine who ate what or whom; what the climate was like (mild or cold, wet or dry); whether or not there was wind, and if so, from what direction and how strong; whether bodies of water were present, and if so, were they salty or fresh, deep or shallow?

ACTIVITY: FOSSIL HUNTERS

This activity is paired with the "Fossil Classification" activity that follows. In this first fossil activity, students will have an opportunity to think about the fossils that a fossil hunter is finding in the deserts of the southwestern United States. The accompanying text is *If You Are a Hunter of Fossils* by Byrd Baylor (1980). The comprehension strategy that accompanies the book is a structured overview, set down on a graphic organizer. This graphic organizer (see fig. 2.1, p. 23) will help students categorize the fossils into body fossils and trace fossils.

REQUIREMENTS

Time

Two 30-minute sessions

Materials

- *If You Are a Hunter of Fossils* by Byrd Baylor
- Two 3-x-3-foot pieces of chart paper or butcher paper
- Marker for writing on the chart paper
- Wall map of the United States (other than Mercator projection)

Grouping

Whole class for a storytime

Advance Preparation

Make a list of the following fossil finds (from *If You Are a Hunter of Fossils*) on one of the sheets of chart paper: fish in a stone, trilobite, dinosaur track, seed fern, rhinoceros bone, sponges in rock, seashells in rocks, *exogyra*, brachiopod, mollusk, sea urchin, signs of tiny clams plowing through the mud, sea lilies. Set this list aside to be used after the book has been read to the students.

DIRECTIONS

1. Introduce students to the term *fossil*. Give them an opportunity to define *fossil* in their own words.
2. From the students' background knowledge, formulate a working definition for *fossil* and write it on the second piece of chart paper.
3. Under the definition of *fossil*, write the words *Body Fossils* and *Trace Fossils* as headings for two lists.

4. Encourage discussion about the meanings of these two terms. Students will probably be able to come up with many body fossils, but the teacher may need to help with the trace fossils by asking leading questions such as, "Is the evidence of an animal's home a fossil?" Formulate definitions of the two terms, using the students' own words.

5. As the students name different fossils, write them down on the fossil classifications chart without making a distinction between body fossils and trace fossils. Save this list for the next activity ("Fossil Classification").

6. Introduce the book *If You Are a Hunter of Fossils*.

7. Tell the students that they are going to hear about the experiences of a Native American child who lives in a desert of the southwestern United States. Using a map, show them the desert area of west Texas. It might be interesting to tell the students that the author, Byrd Baylor, lives in this desert and that she knows it very well. A word of caution: Byrd Baylor's books are beautifully written lyric prose. They do need to be rehearsed to be effective when read to a group of children.

8. Read the book *If You are a Hunter of Fossils* to the students. This reading will take approximately 15-20 minutes. Take time to examine all of the illustrations.

9. After reading the book to the students, direct their attention to the list of fossil evidence that was prepared earlier. Post this list on the wall or board for easy viewing.

10. As a class, decide whether each of the words on this list is a body fossil or a trace fossil. Mark a B next to body fossils and a T next to trace fossils. Save this list for the fossil classification activity that follows.

ACTIVITY: FOSSIL CLASSIFICATION

The class will continue to identify body fossils and trace fossils. They will be using the list of fossil finds and the brainstorming list developed in the "Fossil Hunters" activity.

REQUIREMENTS

Time

One 30-minute session

Materials

- List of fossil finds prepared in "Fossil Hunters" activity
- Brainstorming list from "Fossil Hunters" activity
- Transparency of the graphic organizer (fig. 2.1)
- Vis-à-Vis pen for writing on the transparency
- Copies of graphic organizer (one per pair of students)

- Pencils (one per student)
- Overhead projector

Grouping

Whole class for initial instruction, after which students will be grouped in pairs (see appendix A for grouping suggestions)

DIRECTIONS

1. Review the list of fossil finds prepared in "Fossil Hunters" activity.
2. Review the brainstorming list, which defines the term *fossil* and lists body fossils and trace fossils.
3. Introduce structured overview by projecting the transparency of the graphic organizer (fig. 2.1).
4. Label graphic organizer as shown in figure 2.2, page 24.
5. Refer to the list of fossil finds and work with students to fill in the graphic organizer transparency as shown in figure 2.3, page 25.
6. Explain to students that they will fill in a graphic organizer using the brainstorming list from Session 1.
7. Divide the class into pairs and give each pair one graphic organizer.
8. Instruct them to fill in the three boxes using the headings Fossils, Body Fossils, and Trace Fossils (refer to the overhead transparency).
9. Instruct students to work together to determine which heading the items from the brainstorming list belong under.
10. Be available to students who need help.
11. At the end of the work period, collect all the graphic organizers and prepare a Fossil Display Area.
12. Prepare a Fossil Display Area by hanging the students' graphic organizers and display any fossil collections available to the class.

(Text continues on page 26.)

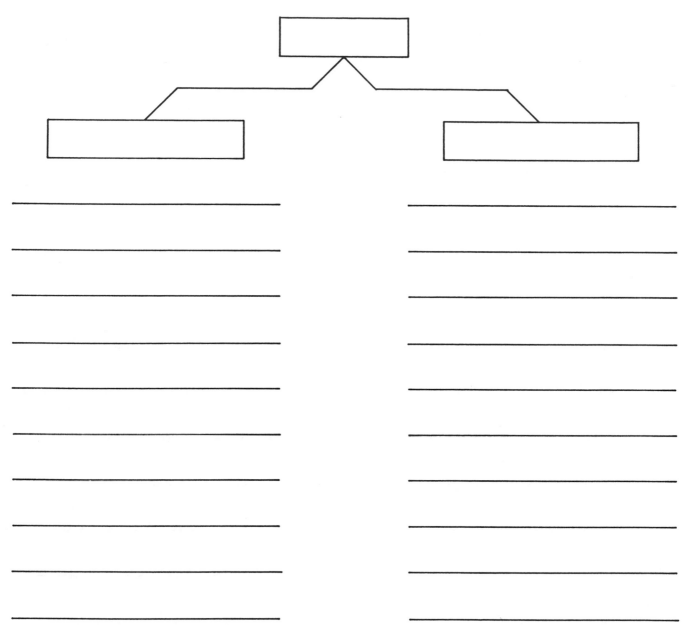

Fig. 2.1. Graphic organizer.

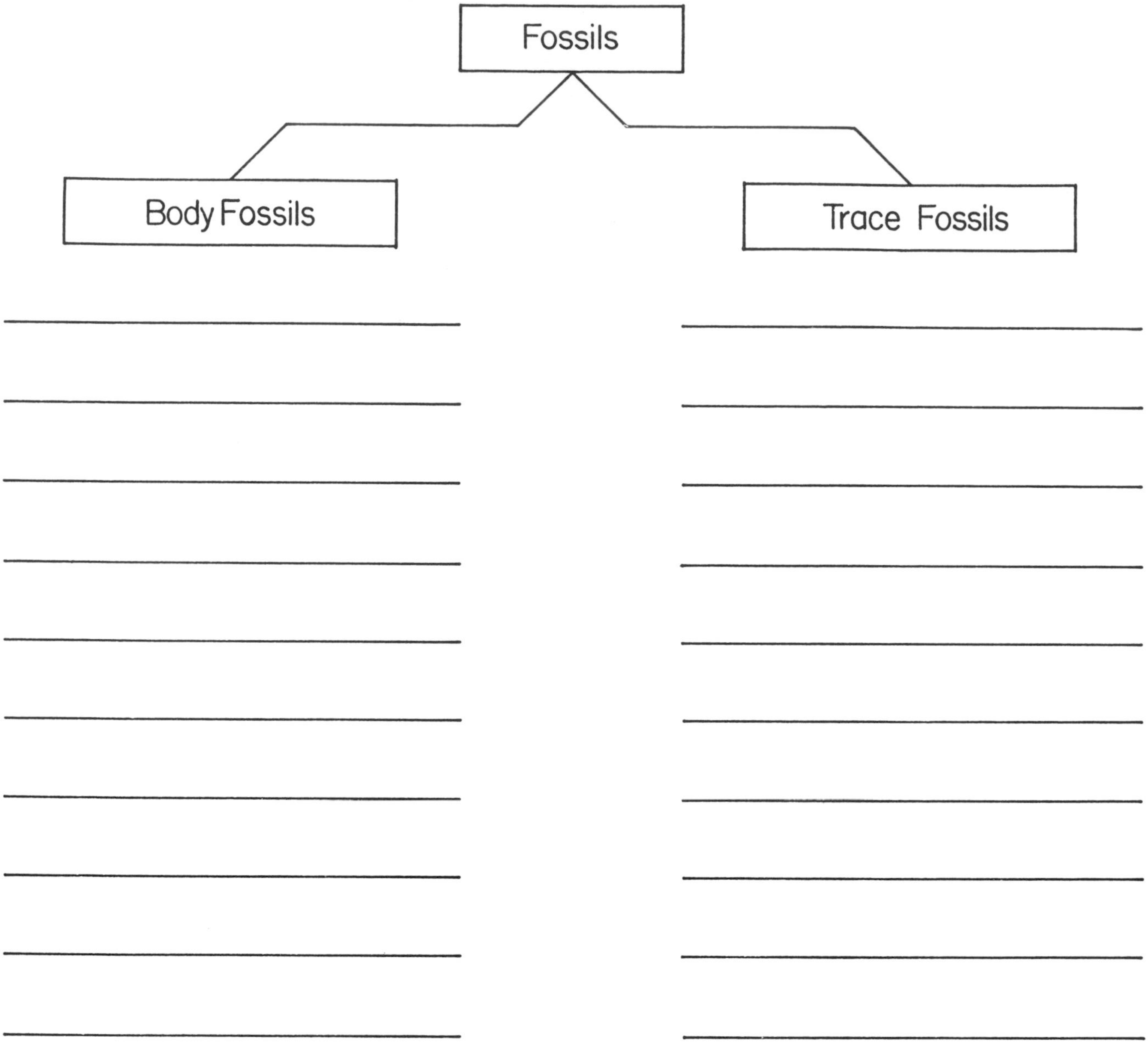

```
                    ┌─────────────────┐
                    │     Fossils     │
                    └─────────────────┘
          ┌──────────────────┐      ┌──────────────────┐
          │   Body Fossils   │      │   Trace Fossils  │
          └──────────────────┘      └──────────────────┘
```

_____   _____

_____   _____

_____   _____

_____   _____

_____   _____

_____   _____

_____   _____

_____   _____

Fig. 2.2. Graphic organizer with heads filled in.

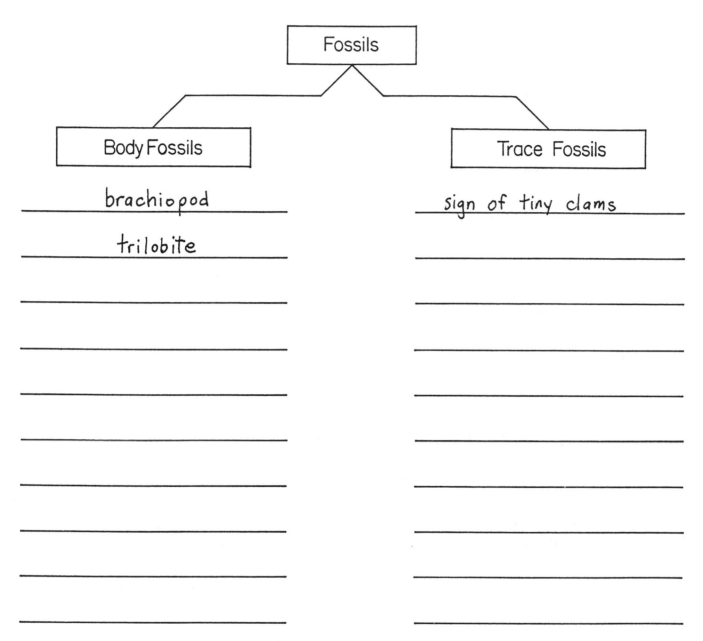

Fossils

Body Fossils

brachiopod

trilobite

Trace Fossils

sign of tiny clams

Fig. 2.3. Partially completed graphic organizer.

ACTIVITY: DO WE KNOW WHERE THEY LIVE?

Students are more familiar with organisms that exist today than they are with animals and plants of the geologic past. The following activity will involve students in looking at modern animals and their habitats. By thinking about the relationship between familiar animals and their environments, students will better understand how fossils are used to interpret the environments of the earth's past.

REQUIREMENTS

Time

One 45-minute session

Materials

- One set of "Do We Know Where They Live?" match-up game cards (see figs. 2.4-2.6, pp. 27-29). Note that each card has a letter designation (A, B, C), which will correspond to a student group.
- A world map (other than Mercator projection) or globe
- One 3-x-3-foot piece of butcher paper or chart paper
- Glue

Grouping

Whole class for initial instruction, after which students are divided into three equal teams (A,B,C) for the puzzle search game

DIRECTIONS

1. Gather students together.
2. Set the search rules that best satisfy your teaching style (have students search silently or allow them to discuss potential matches).
3. Divide the class into three equal groups (A,B,C) and have students sit or stand in a space designated for each group.
4. Distribute the appropriate puzzle sections to groups A, B, and C.
5. Have students look at their puzzle pieces to make sure that their group letter corresponds to the letter at the top of their cards.
6. Explain to the class that students in group A have the animal cards, students in group B have the environment cards, and students in group C have the geographic location cards. Students will need to search among all three groups until the appropriate animal/environment/location matches for their particular card have been found.
7. When three matching pieces have been found, the students holding them should sit down on the floor and raise their hands.
8. Gather students together in front of the world map or globe.
9. Ask for volunteers to share their puzzle pieces and tell the animal's name, environment, and geographic location.

(Text continues on page 30.)

A	B	C
penguins △	△ cold, ice △	△Antarctica

A ○	○ B ○	○ C
black bear ○	○ forest ○	North America ○

A ○	○ B ○	○ C
camel ○	○ desert ○	○ Africa

A ▢	▢ B ▢	▢ C
llama ▢	▢mountains ▢	South America ▢

A ⬆	⬆ B ⬆	⬆ C
whale	salt water	oceans

A ●	● B ●	● C
trout ●	● fresh water ●	● lakes ●

Fig. 2.4. Match-up cards.

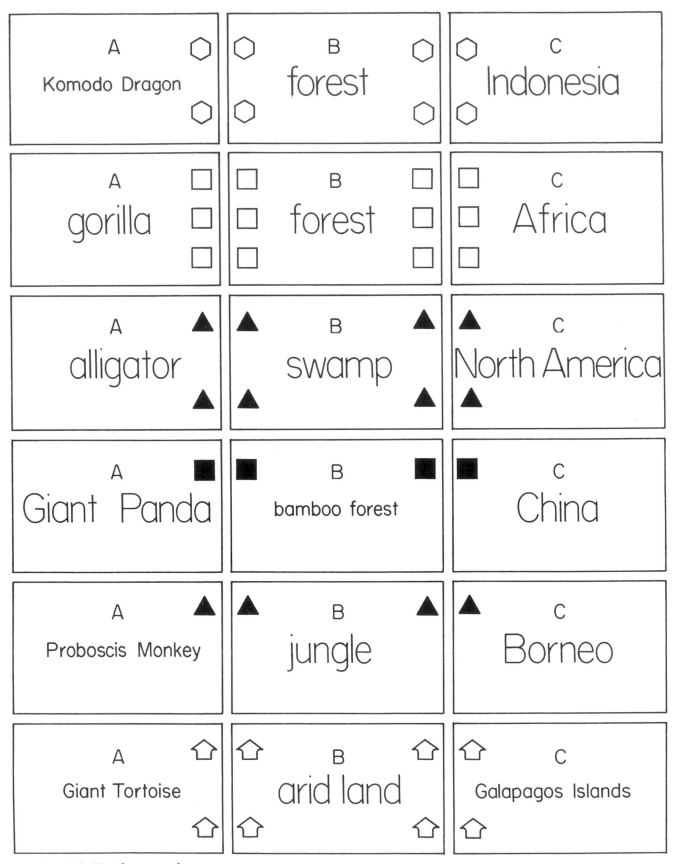

A ☆ ☆ polar bear ☆	☆ B ☆ ☆ cold, ice ☆	☆ ☆ C Arctic
A lion ☆	☆ plains B ☆	☆ C Africa
A tiger ⬡	⬡ jungle B ⬡	⬡ C Asia
A △ kangaroo △	△ B plains △	△ C △ Australia
A elephant ☐	☐ plains B ☐	☐ C Africa
A elephant ●	● jungle B ●	● C Asia

Fig. 2.6. Match-up cards.

From *Primary Dinosaur Investigations.* ©1995. Teacher Ideas Press. (800) 237-6124.

10. Glue the puzzle pieces on the butcher (chart) paper so that the appropriate pieces are connected (see fig. 2.7).

11. Locate the continents and major bodies of water on the world map or globe.

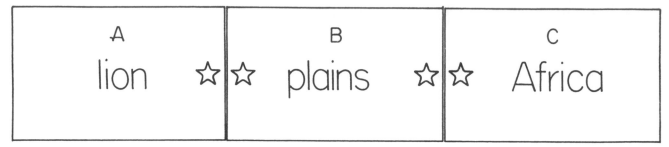

Fig. 2.7. Completed card match-up.

EXTENSIONS

Review the seven continents, the oceans, and their locations. Have students alphabetize the continents. This is a good strategy for memorization.

ACTIVITY: DIFFERENT ORGANISMS, DIFFERENT ENVIRONMENTS

Students will be determining whether the organisms presented in this activity would live in the water or on land. You will need to discuss organisms that spend time both on land and in the water. Remember that in many situations there will be more than one correct answer. Encourage students to defend their thinking.

REQUIREMENTS

Time

One 45-minute session

Materials

- For each pair of students:
    —One enlarged (11-x-17-inch) copy of a environmental cross section (see fig. 2.8)
    —Magazines
    —Glue

- For each student:
    —Scissors
    —Crayons, colored pencils, or markers
    —One pencil

- For the teacher:
    —Transparency of the environmental cross section (fig. 2.8)
    —Sample animal pictures taken from magazines or other resources
    —Vis-à-Vis pen
    —Overhead projector

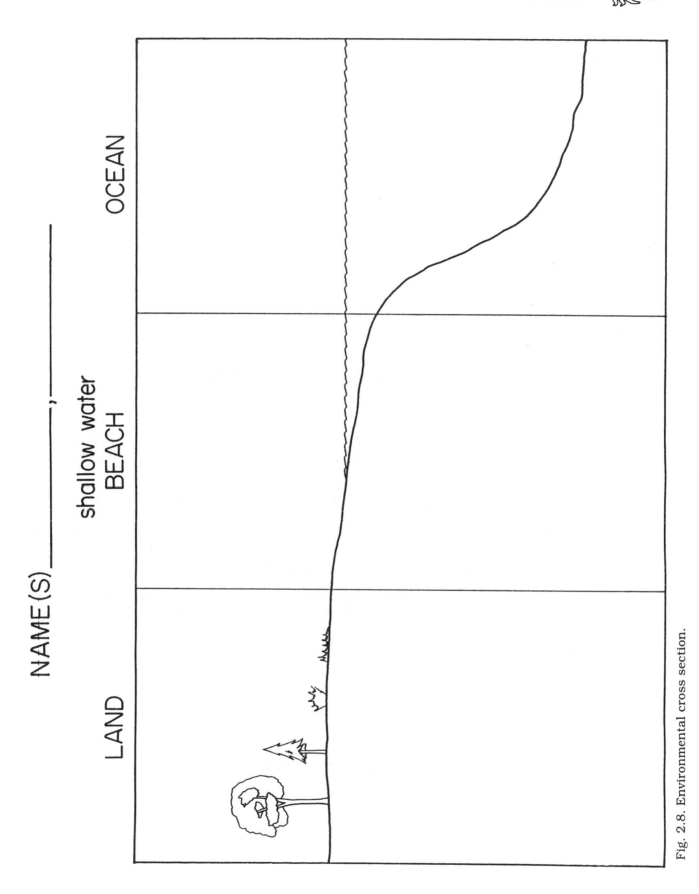

NAME(S) _____ , _____

OCEAN   shallow water   LAND
         BEACH

Fig. 2.8. Environmental cross section.

Grouping

Whole class for initial instruction, after which students will work in pairs to complete the project

Advance Preparation

Ask students to bring in magazines from home, or you can visit the school library or public library and ask them to donate old magazines. Outdated *National Geographic, Ranger Rick,* or any wildlife publications will work well for this activity. If you obtain magazines from a library, make sure the media specialist understands that the magazines will be cut up.

DIRECTIONS

1. Gather students together as a class.

2. Project the environmental cross section transparency.

3. Ask students where some of the sample animals might live and mark the suggested habitat for each animal on the environmental cross section transparency.

4. Show students the enlarged 11-x-17-inch environmental cross section they will be working on.

5. Divide students into pairs.

6. Give each pair of students an 11-x-17-inch environmental cross section and some magazines. Have students select small pictures of animals from the magazines.

7. Have students collect glue, scissors, pencils, and coloring materials.

8. Ask students to color the areas of the environmental cross section—land, beach, shallow water, and ocean—appropriately.

9. Have students cut out the animal pictures from the magazines.

10. Tell students to glue the animal pictures to the appropriate environment on the cross section (e.g., a seal may be glued on the beach or in the ocean).

11. Collect completed cross sections and save them for the next session on fossils (you may also display them or send them home with students).

ACTIVITY: LET'S LOOK AT THE PAST

Students will place fossil drawings in an appropriate position on an enlarged wall-sized environmental cross section. Students and teacher can work together to complete this wall-sized picture of the past.

REQUIREMENTS

Time

One 30-minute session

Materials

- Wall chart of the environmental cross section (enlarged from fig. 2.8)
- Fossil collection (figs. 2.9-2.11, pp. 34-36) run on card stock, laminated (for durability), and cut apart into individual fossil pieces
- Glue or tape

Grouping

Students and teacher will work together to complete the wall chart (completed cross sections from the previous activity provide a useful reference, although they are not required)

DIRECTIONS

1. The class will play a game of "I Spy a Fossil." Randomly distribute the fossil collection cards to students.
2. Have students lay out their individual fossil collections on a table or the floor so that all the pieces are visible.
3. The teacher will say, for example, "I spy an *allosaurus* claw," making certain to read the description of the fossil just as it is written on the fossil collection card.
4. The student with that fossil card will respond, "I have the *allosaurus* claw."
5. The student will then tape or glue the fossil card in its appropriate place on the wall chart so that the rest of the class can see it.

EXTENSIONS

Using the fossil collection cards or fossils from a loaned fossil collection, students may choose a fossil they would like to further research and report on. These reports may be done by groups, pairs, or individuals. When young children are writing reports, it is helpful for them to have adult supervision and a structured format. We suggest a format similar to that presented in figure 2.12, page 37.

See appendix D for addresses of resources for fossil collections that can be borrowed for classroom use.

All of these activities would be enhanced by trips to a fossil site, zoo, aquarium, botanical garden, natural history museum, circus, or pet store. If field trips are impractical, library resources and catalogs from biological supply companies (contact them about getting multiple copies of outdated issues) may supply pictures and information about a broad range of animals and plants that exist today or existed in the geologic past.

(Text continues on page 38.)

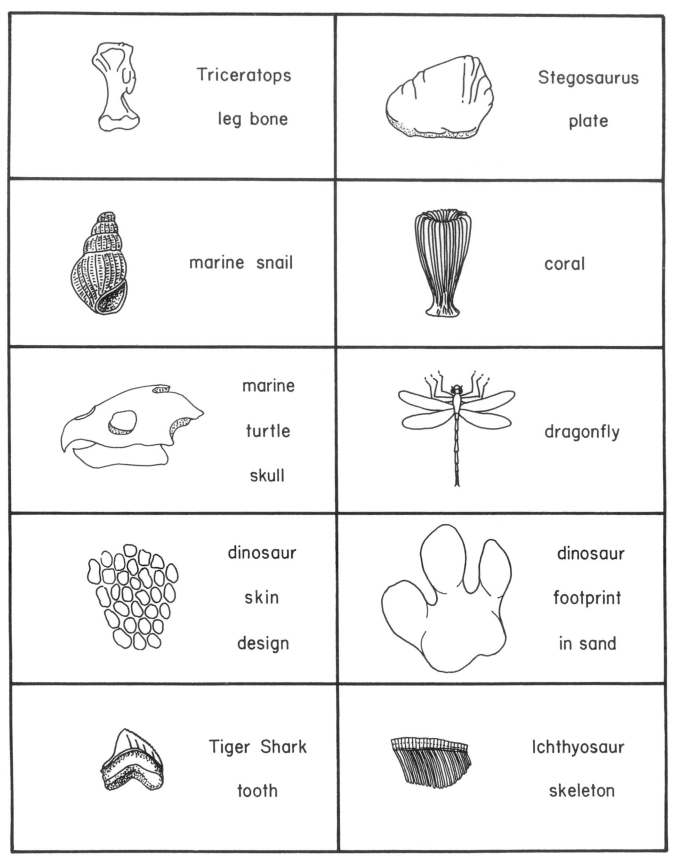

Triceratops leg bone

Stegosaurus plate

marine snail

coral

marine turtle skull

dragonfly

dinosaur skin design

dinosaur footprint in sand

Tiger Shark tooth

Ichthyosaur skeleton

Fig. 2.9. Fossil collection.

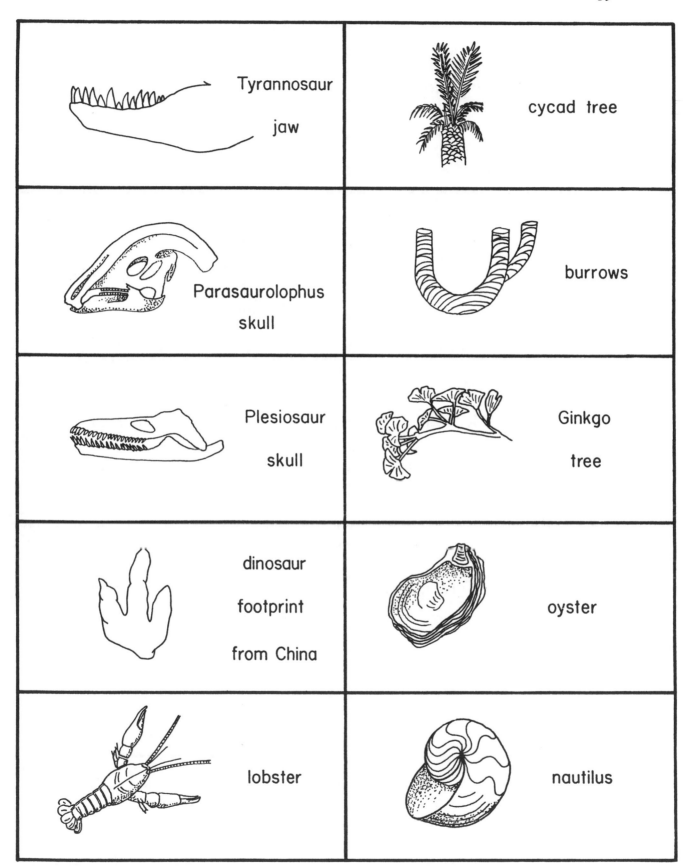

Fig. 2.10. Fossil collection.

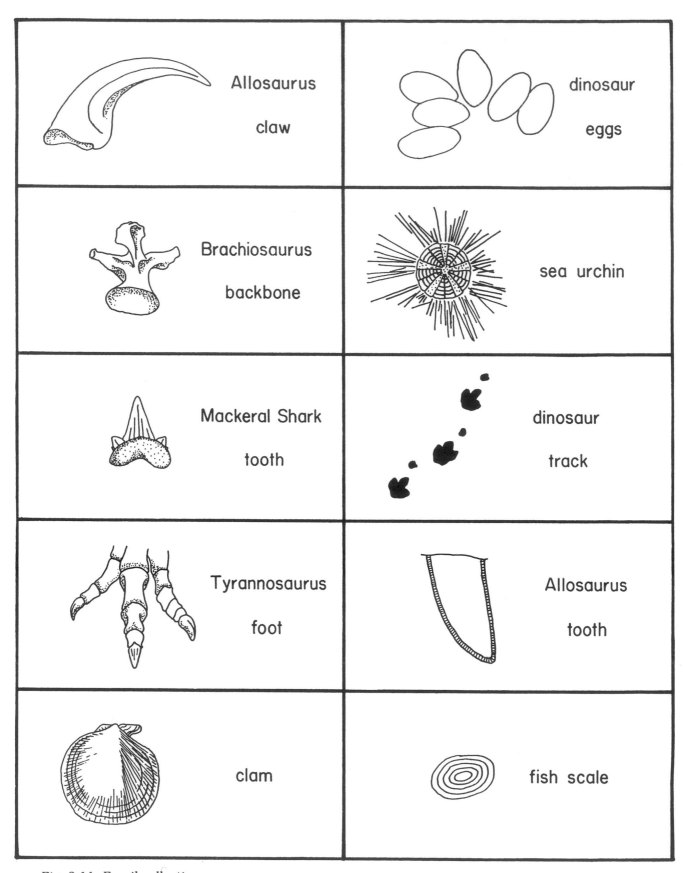

Fig. 2.11. Fossil collection.

FOSSIL   RESEARCH

Group Members (or individual name)

_____

_____

_____

_____

FOSSIL NAME_____

Some facts about the fossil you are researching.

_____

_____

_____

_____

_____

What are some surprising things that you learned about the fossil you are researching?

_____

_____

_____

_____

_____

MATERIALS USED FOR RESEARCH

AUTHOR	TITLE	PUBLISHER AND DATE
_____	_____	_____
_____	_____	_____

Fig. 2.12. Fossil research report format.

ACTIVITY: PALEO!

Students will play a fossil identification game similar to Bingo.

REQUIREMENTS

Time

40 minutes (10 minutes for card preparation and 30 minutes for actual playing time)

Materials

- For each student:
  —One PALEO grid sheet (fig. 2.13)
  —One set of 30 PALEO fossils cards (figs. 2.14-2.15, pp. 40-41)
  —Scissors
  —Glue
  —Set of 25 beans or other small markers

- For the teacher:
  —One blank PALEO grid
  —One set of 30 PALEO fossils cards

Grouping

Individuals (very young children may do better playing with a partner)

DIRECTIONS

1. Give each student a blank PALEO grid.

2. Tell students that when they receive their PALEO fossils cards, they will be cutting the fossils apart and gluing 25 of them randomly onto the PALEO grid.

3. Pass out the PALEO fossils cards.

4. Circulate among the students as they are cutting and gluing to be sure they understand the directions.

5. Explain that there are 30 fossils and only 25 squares on the PALEO grid, so every child will have five fossil pieces left over after gluing.

6. When all students have prepared their grids, begin the game. Say, for example, "L, *allosaurus* tooth" and place the teacher *Allosaurus* tooth fossil in the L column of the teacher PALEO grid. Any student who has the *allosaurus* tooth glued in the L column will place a marker in that spot.

7. Continue playing the game until someone has a winning card: five consecutive horizontal markers, five consecutive vertical markers, or five consecutive diagonal markers.

8. The winner says "PALEO!"

9. Check the student's card against your teacher card to verify a match.

NAME _____

P A L E O

Fig. 2.13. PALEO grid sheet.

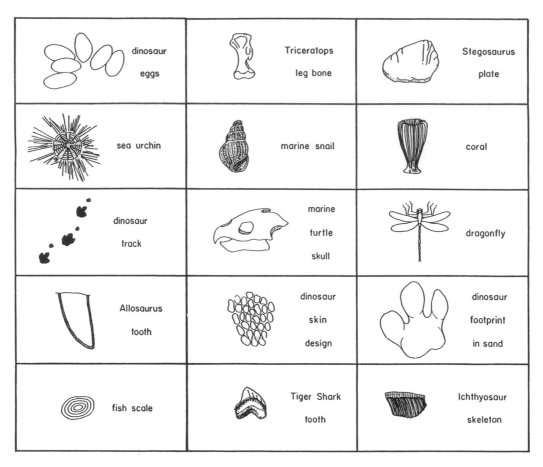

Fig. 2.14. PALEO fossils card.

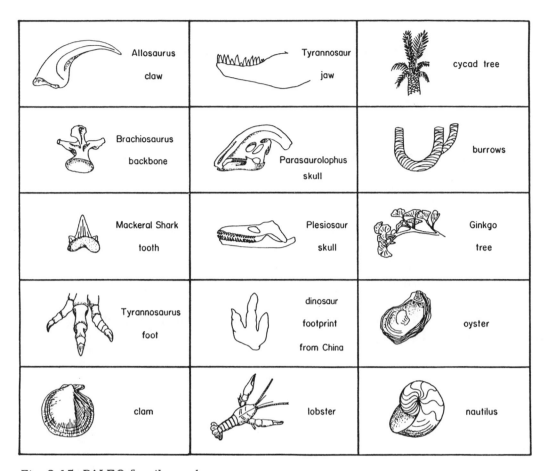

Fig. 2.15. PALEO fossils card.

REFERENCES

Adams, Frank Dawson. 1954. *The Birth and Development of the Geological Sciences.* New York: Dover.

American Heritage Dictionary, Second College Edition. 1982. Boston: Houghton Mifflin.

Baylor, Byrd. 1980. *If You Are a Hunter of Fossils.* New York: Charles Scribner's Sons.

SUGGESTED READING

Farlow, James O. 1991. *On the Tracks of Dinosaurs: A Study of Dinosaur Footprints.* New York: Franklin Watts.

Lauber, Patricia. 1987. *Dinosaurs Walked Here and Other Stories Fossils Tell.* New York: Bradbury Press.

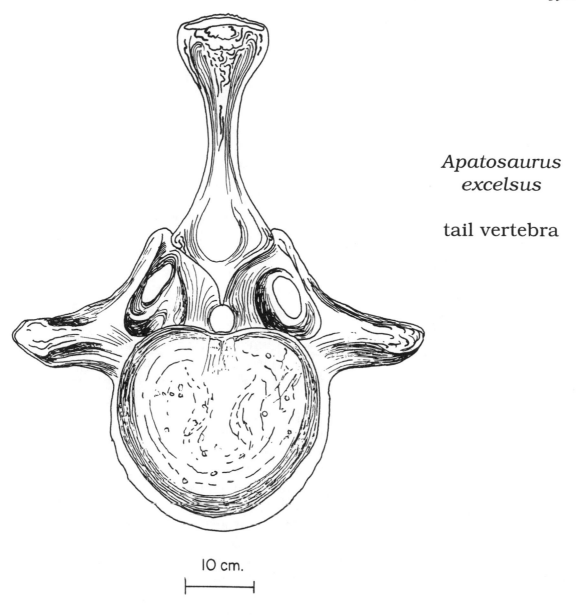

Apatosaurus excelsus

tail vertebra

10 cm.

"Collecting at this season is under many difficulties. At the bottom of a narrow pit 30 feet deep into which drift snow keeps blowing and fingers benumbed with cold from thermo between 20 and 30 below zero and snow often blowing blindingly down and covering up a bone as fast as it is unearthed."

February 5, 1880

"i shiped you 3 cans of fossils 16th and came near being my last shipment to you for a man working for you by the name of Brown assaulted me at station with two revolvers and wanted me to fight him. i Refused on account of my family and he said to agents wife before i get thear he would shoot me. he has Been my enemy since you left hear for what Reasons i don't Know and more don't care from this out."

December, 1884

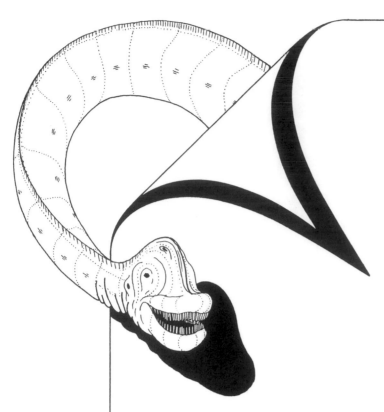

Because no one has ever recorded information about living dinosaurs, all of what we know about them has been learned from a combination of fossil evidence and analogy to modern animals. To the pessimist, this can be very frustrating and restrictive because so little is known for certain. To the optimist (and by nature, most scientists are optimists), the arena of exploration is virtually unlimited, and multiple scientific theories abound. It is important for students to understand that disagreement and divergent theory provide the energy that drives the machinery of science, and the animals we see today are important parts of that machinery. When scientists debate the cold- or warm-bloodedness of dinosaurs, the possible relationships between dinosaurs and birds and between dinosaur metabolism and that of modern animals are critical to the discussion.

Field trips to animal resource facilities (zoos and aquaria) are a part of the education of every student in the primary grades, as well they should be. Often, however, such trips are a cursory stroll through zoological gardens, giving the students a quick opportunity to see animals they have only read about and to appreciate the size of an elephant, the teeth of a tiger, or the talons of a bald eagle. Because modern animals play an important role in unraveling the mysteries of the dinosaurs, zoo trips can become a critical tool for studying dinosaurs. In the following chapters, we encourage you to include animal resource facilities in your lessons. Where appropriate, each activity will describe reinforcement available at the local zoological gardens or aquarium.

It is important for students to be able to view the living analogs of the extinct animals. Emus and ostrich, for example, are considered the best source of motion data for bipedal dinosaurs, including tyrannosaurs. Studying movements of living bipedal dinosaurs is impossible, and examining ostriches or emus in the wild is impractical; the zoos offer an excellent alternative (see appendix G). In the eighteenth century, geologist James Hutton, "realised . . . 'the past history of our globe must be explained by what can be seen to be happening now.'" (Holmes, 1965, 43) What is true for the Earth, is true in large degree for extinct animals as well.

Combining rare fossil evidence with the study of living animals provides the clues that help scientists unravel dinosaur mysteries. Were dinosaurs warm- or cold-blooded? Clues are found in teeth, bone structure, and behavior. Did dinosaurs live alone or function in herds? Herd animals provide clues in their trackways and behavior. Did dinosaurs make sounds? Studying skull structures and speculating about the attached soft tissues provide information about what kinds of sounds the dinosaurs might have produced, and how. What functions did dinosaur tails serve? Tail structures of living animals provide analogs.

The chapters that follow examine the size, eyes, legs, feet, hands, and tails of dinosaurs. Observing animals in zoos allows students to appreciate the size of larger animals such as elephants. When these animals are related to dinosaurs, comparisons become more meaningful. Neither elephants nor dinosaurs can be fully appreciated in small photographs, posters, or models. Eye position can reveal clues about an animal's behavior: wide-set eyes can scan for predators, and close-set eyes can focus at a distance on potential prey. This holds true for dinosaurs as well as modern animals. Legs and tails operate as a system, providing balance, defense, and propulsion. Watching a tail operate is by far the best way a student can understand its function. For example, kangaroo tails provide balance while running; crocodile tails provide propulsion during swimming; bird tails act as flight control surfaces; monkey tails provide an extra hand on a high limb; beaver tails serve as an alarm; stingray and scorpion tails act as weapons. All dinosaurs had tails, and they served many different functions. Animal footprints and trackways can also provide clues to animal and dinosaur behavior. For instance, dinosaurs are often compared to modern lizards. As lizards walk, their tails leave drag marks along the ground. Many dinosaurs had large tails, but trackways do not reveal drag marks. Apparently, the structure of dinosaur legs made the tail an unnecessary appendage during walking or running.

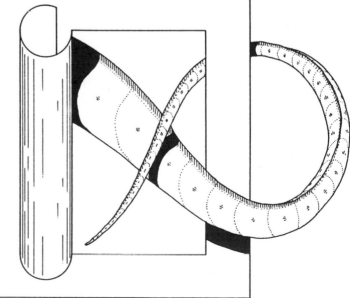

There are no animals, only skeletons and footprints to provide information about how the extinct animals functioned. Large numbers of living animals provide valuable information to supplement the fossil evidence. Is it certain that today's animals are perfect analogs for the extinct dinosaurs? No, but until additional evidence becomes available, what we know about the animals alive today is the best foundation we have for investigating the animals that died more than 65 million years ago.

3

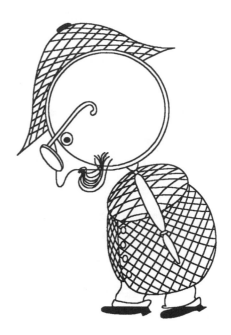

Bones, Bones, Bones

INTRODUCTION

Often when paleontologists discover remains of animals, they find several species buried together. A spectacular example of this occurrence is the 150-million-year-old sandbar exposed at Dinosaur National Monument near Vernal, Utah. The Jurassic sandstones in the monument have yielded 14 species of dinosaurs, in addition to many turtles, fish, frogs, salamanders, crocodiles, lizards, and other reptilian contemporaries of the dinosaurs. As of 1994, visitors to the Monument are able to see more than 1,600 bones (Echoes 1993–94, 11) representing many animal species. These remains have been left permanently exposed in the former sandbar so that their diversity and mode of preservation can be appreciated by even the casual tourist.

The comprehension strategy used in this chapter is a *sequence chain.* This strategy develops a linear sequence of events. It will help children see the steps a scientist must follow when a new discovery has been made.

ACTIVITY: DIG, DIG, DIG!

This activity begins with the reading of Aliki's book *Digging Up Dinosaurs* (1988). Using a sequence chain, students will develop an awareness of the difficulty of specimen collection, ponder the same questions that scientists confront as they identify and categorize bones, and learn about the sequential process scientists follow from discovery to museum presentation.

REQUIREMENTS

Time

One 45-minute session

Materials

- *Digging Up Dinosaurs* by Aliki

- Transparency of *Digging Up Dinosaurs,* page 13 (fig. 3.1)

- One copy of the sequence chain (fig. 3.2, p. 50). Note: it may be useful to enlarge this to a piece of poster board and laminate or prepare a transparency.

- Markers or Vis-à-Vis pen for writing on the sequence chain

- Overhead projector

Grouping

Entire class seated on floor for group instructions

DIRECTIONS

1. Read *Digging Up Dinosaurs* to students. The book takes approximately 15 minutes to read aloud. However, Aliki has provided a number of humorous and informative captions that intrigue students. Allow approximately 25 minutes for reading and discussion of the book and captions.

2. Direct students' attention to figure 3.1 and explain that the pictures have been organized in a linear sequence; that is, the events that occurred 80 million years ago have been arranged in the order in which they happened. Explain what Aliki means by, "Fossils are a kind of diary of the past."

3. Introduce students to the sequence chain (fig. 3.2) by placing it in clear view. The graphic either needs to be mounted in a stable position so that the teacher is able to write on it or projected on an overhead projector.

4. Review the pictures in figure 3.1 and discuss the order in which events might have occurred.

5. Have students interpret the picture sequence from figure 3.1. Record, in the children's own words, what has occurred. Complete the sequence chain (fig. 3.2).

Closure

Focus on the statement children made for the "Finally" section of the sequence chain. Explain to students that at their next session, they will be focusing on what happens when a fossil or many fossils are discovered.

Fig. 3.1. *Digging Up Dinosaurs* transparency. Copyright © 1981 by Aliki Brandenberg. Selection reprinted by permission of HarperCollins Publishers.

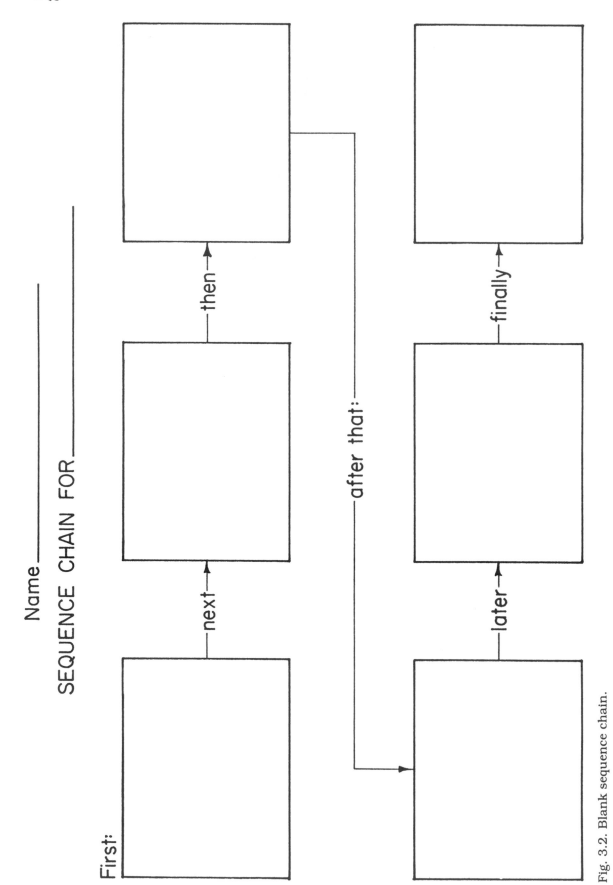

Name _____

SEQUENCE CHAIN FOR _____

First:

next

then

after that:

later

finally

Fig. 3.2. Blank sequence chain.

ACTIVITY: QUARRY QUERY

The following activity uses the Howe Bone Quarry to illustrate the discovery process that often frustrates and excites paleontologists as they begin to excavate a quarry of dinosaur bones. The scientists must identify which skeletal parts they are looking at and which dinosaur they belong to.

REQUIREMENTS

Time

One 30-45-minute session

Materials

- For teacher demonstration:
  —Transparency of Howe Bone Quarry in Wyoming (fig. 3.3, p. 52)
  —Articulated *Tyrannosaurus* skeleton with the following bones labeled: skull, torso and ribs, hind legs, front legs, tail, and neck (fig. 3.4, p. 53)
  —Markers (six different colors)
  —Overhead projector

- For each student:
  —8½-x-11-inch copy of Howe Bone Quarry (fig. 3.3)
  —Articulated *Tyrannosaurus* skeleton (fig. 3.4)
  —Crayons, markers, or colored pencils (six different colors)

DIRECTIONS

1. Gather the class together for a quick review of figure 3.1. Call attention to the last frame of the page. The picture shows a single fossil ready to be unearthed. Explain to students that this is an oversimplification of what paleontologists normally encounter when they are excavating dinosaur bones.

2. Project the transparency of the Howe Bone Quarry (fig. 3.3). Tell students that this figure more accurately portrays what paleontologists actually find in a quarry.

3. Display the articulated *Tyrannosaurus* skeleton (fig. 3.4) and identify the labeled bones.

4. Assign each of the labeled bone groups a color (e.g., red for ribs and torso, blue for the neck, yellow for the tail, brown for the skull, green for the hind legs, black for the front legs).

5. Ask for a volunteer to come forward and identify a bone in the Howe Bone Quarry and color it the appropriate color. Encourage the volunteer to look closely at the *Tyrannosaurus* skeleton to help identify the bones in the quarry.

(Text continues on page 54.)

Fig. 3.3. Dinosaur remains at the Howe Bone Quarry. Modified from Czerkas and Czerkas.

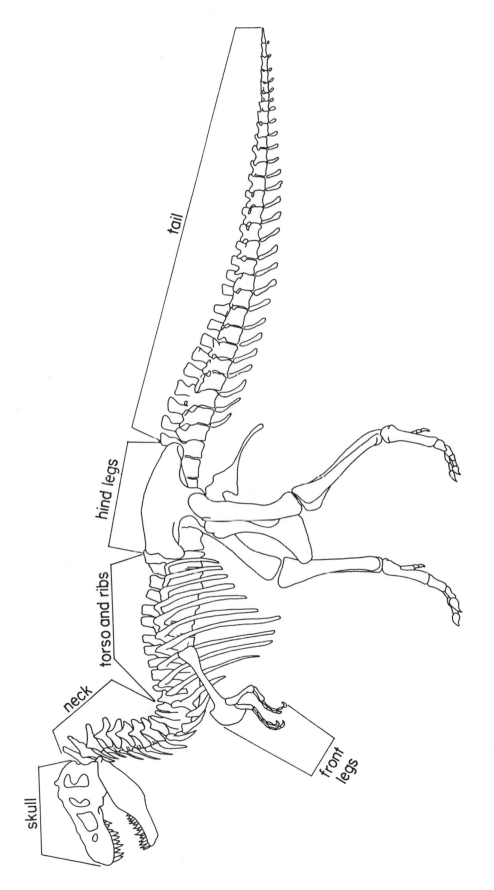

Fig. 3.4. *Tyrannosaurus* skeleton with bones labeled.

6. Repeat Step 5 several times to ensure that students understand the bone identification procedure.

7. Distribute the individual copies of the Howe Bone Quarry (fig. 3.3) and the individual *Tyrannosaurus* skeleton sheets (fig. 3.4).

8. Instruct students to follow the identification procedure demonstrated and color the bones on their individual quarry sheets.

Alternate Procedure

When working with very young children, the teacher may choose to do the quarry bone coloring activity as a whole group, calling on a number of volunteers, helping them to identify the bones, and having them color the identified bones on the transparency rather than on the individual quarry sheets. Another grouping configuration that would work well with very young children is peer partnerships, or partnerships with older students (see appendix A, #9).

ACTIVITY: JUMBLE, JUMBLE, JUMBLE

Session 1

By playing this game, students will experience some of the satisfactions of success and the frustrations of not having enough information to be totally successful. As in the "Quarry Query" activity, students will be given a collection of bones to work with. By the end of the game, each student will construct a complete skeleton.

REQUIREMENTS

Time

One 45-minute session

Materials

- For each group of four students:
  —One die
  —Laminated set of dinosaur bone cards (figs. 3.5-3.8, pp. 55-58);
      each set of 30 cards contains five dinosaurs, with six bone cards
      for each genus
  —Laminated Discovery Key (fig. 3.9, p. 59)

- For each child:
  —Discovery Sheet (fig. 3.10, p. 60)
  —Pencil
  —Legal-size envelope (with child's name on it)

(Text continues on page 61.)

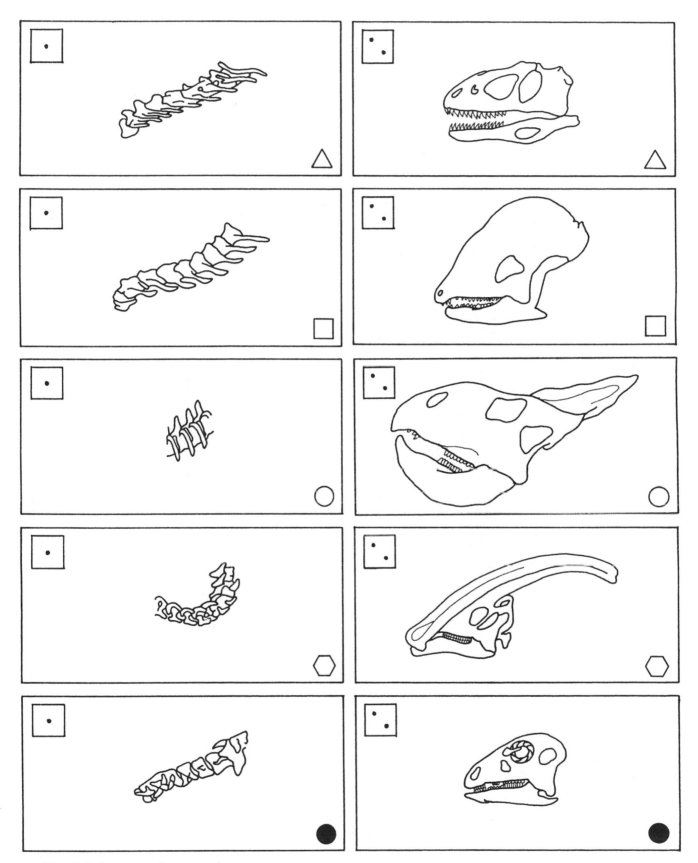

Fig. 3.5. Dinosaur bone cards.

From *Primary Dinosaur Investigations.* ©1995. Teacher Ideas Press. (800) 237-6124.

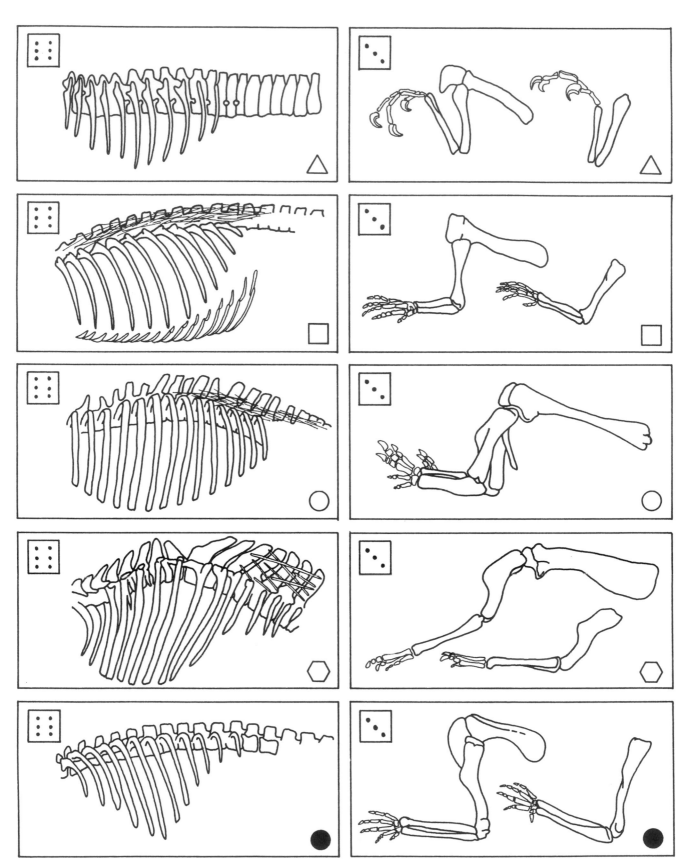

Fig. 3.6. Dinosaur bone cards.

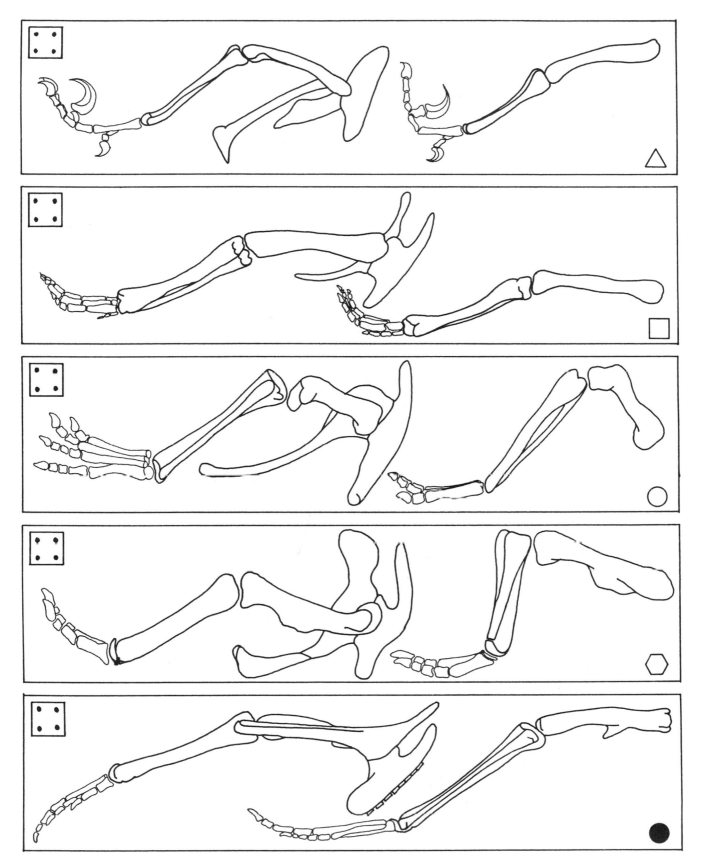

Fig. 3.7. Dinosaur bone cards.

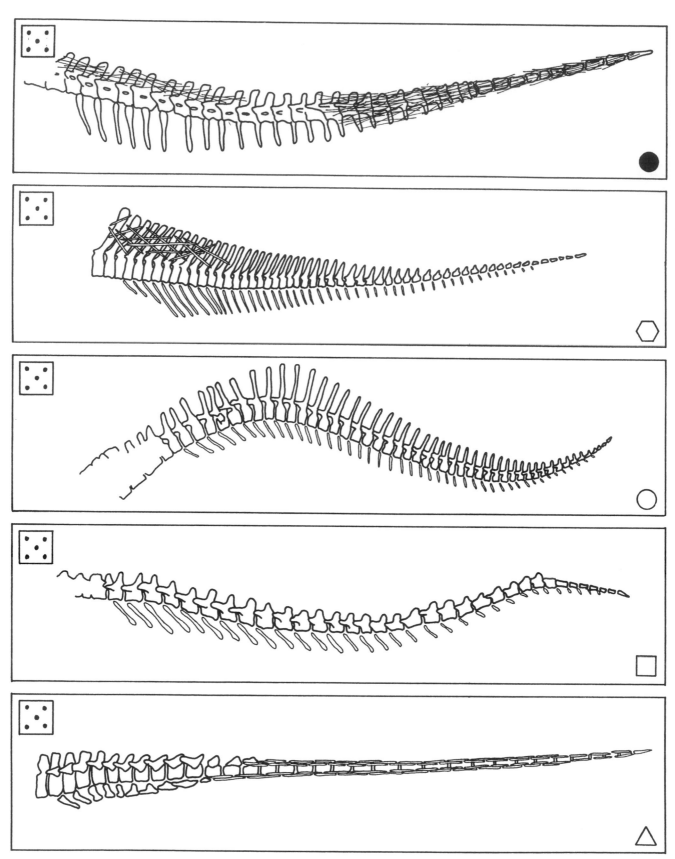

Fig. 3.8. Dinosaur bone cards.

DISCOVERY KEY

name	icon
Deinonychus	△
Stegoceras	□
Protoceratops	○
Parasaurolophus	⬡
Hypsilophodon	●

Neck vertebrae

Skull

Front legs

Hind legs

Tails

Ribs and torso

Fig. 3.9. Discovery Key.

Name _____

Discovery Sheet

Icon	What kind of bone?	New finds
1 □		
2 □		
3 □		
4 □		
5 □		
6 □		

Fig. 3.10. Discovery Sheet.

- For teacher demonstration:
    —Complete dinosaur skeleton with the following bones labeled:
        skull, torso and ribs, hind legs, front legs, tail, and neck (fig. 3.4)
    —Transparency of the Discovery Key (fig. 3.9)
    —Teacher demonstration die transparency (fig. 3.11, p. 62)
    —Transparency of the Discovery Sheet (fig. 3.10)
    —Brown paper grocery sack or a shirt box for the "museum collection"
    —Overhead projector

Grouping

Whole group for initial review and directions, then groups of four students to play the game (see appendix A for grouping suggestions)

DIRECTIONS

This game illustrates the components of the scientific method—asking, investigating, trying, recording, and evaluating—as they relate to a dinosaur bone excavation. Because it is not possible to create an authentic quarry in the classroom, we have designed this game to simulate the procedures that a group of scientists would follow from the discovery of dinosaur bones to the actual reconstruction of the skeletons for a museum exhibit. (Note: Read through the activity so you will know when to distribute materials to students.)

Explaining the Game

1. Tell students that during this activity they will be collecting drawings of dinosaur bones, sorting them and later assembling a dinosaur skeleton.

2. Gather the class together for a quick review of the sequence chain for *Digging Up Dinosaurs* (fig. 3.2).

3. Introduce the game Jumble, Jumble, Jumble. Project the Discovery Key (fig. 3.9) and explain that the die faces will tell them which bones they will be hunting for. Review the skeletal names on the Discovery Key: neck vertebrae, skull, front legs, hind legs, tails, ribs and torso.

4. Project the demonstration die face (fig. 3.11) and, referring to the Discovery Key, have children help you determine which of the skeletal parts has been discovered. Explain that much like scientists discovering bones in a quarry, they will be selecting bone cards that match the bone groups on the Discovery Key. (If there is concern about not knowing what dinosaur the bone belongs to, remind them that scientists don't know what dinosaur it is either until they have collected many bones.)

5. Introduce the Discovery Sheet (fig. 3.10). In the "Icon" column, students will record the icon that is located in the lower right corner of the bone card. In the empty boxes, they will record the die face, and under "What Kind of Bone?," they will make the appropriate identification (see, for example, fig. 3.12, p. 62).

6. Show the students one of the individual student envelopes. Tell them that each player will have six rolls of the die. Each student will collect six bone cards and put them in his or her personal envelope.

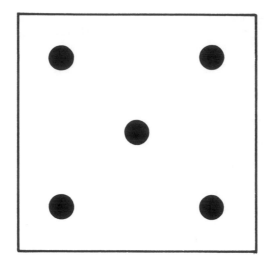

Fig. 3.11. Teacher demonstration die.

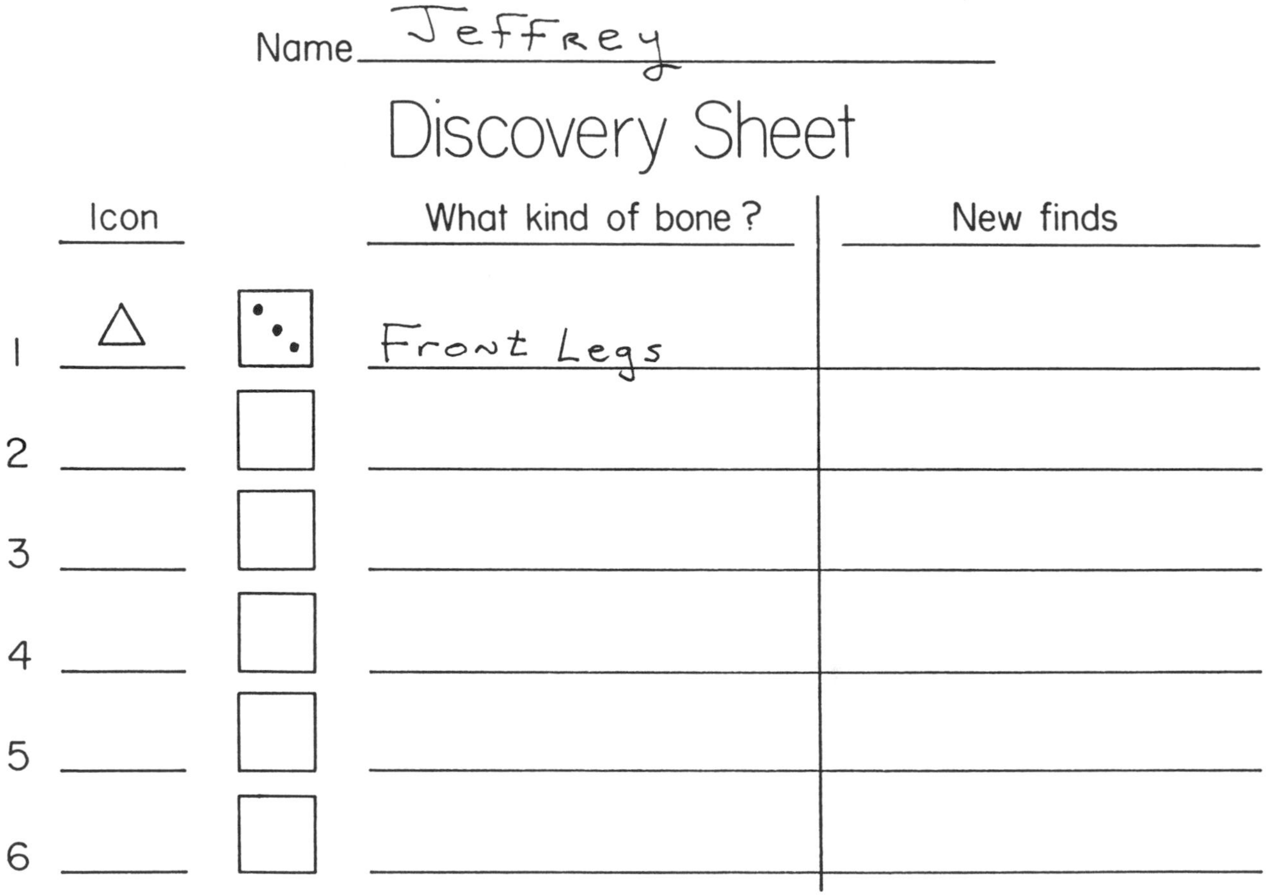

Name _Jeffrey_____

Discovery Sheet

Icon		What kind of bone ?	New finds
1 ___△___	⚄	Front Legs	
2 _____	☐		
3 _____	☐		
4 _____	☐		
5 _____	☐		
6 _____	☐		

Fig. 3.12. Partially completed Discovery Sheet.

7. All bones that are left at the end of the game will go into the museum collection. This is the shirt box or paper bag and is the teacher's responsibility.

8. Encourage students to ask questions to clarify the game procedure. Reassure them that some things will become clearer as they begin the game.

Playing the Game

1. Distribute the sets of dinosaur bone cards. Each group of four students has one complete set of dinosaur bone cards (30 cards in all).

2. Lay all five skull cards face down in a row on the floor (fig. 3.5, die face 2). Repeat this procedure for the vertebrae, tail, ribs and torso, front legs, and hind legs cards.

3. Have the first student in each group roll the die, match the die face with a bone category on the Discovery Key, and select a bone card from the appropriate row. If all the cards matching the die face rolled have been taken, have student roll again.

4. Have the student record the bone on his or her Discovery Sheet in the "What kind of Bone?" column and pass the die to the person to the right.

5. When each person in the group has six bones, have group members put the bones in the envelope with their name on it.

6. Have students raise their hands to signal that the group has completed its bone selection and is ready to continue.

7. After group members have completed their personal bone collections, go around to each group, collect the remaining bones, and place them in the museum collection (a shirt box or grocery sack). There should be six remaining bone cards in each group.

8. Collect all envelopes and save for Session 2.

9. Collect all Discovery Sheets and save for Session 2 (make sure students have filled in their names).

Closure

Gather students together again as a class. Encourage students to discuss the activity so far. What problems did they encounter? How was this activity similar to what a scientist might do while excavating dinosaur bones? What surprises did they experience?

Session 2

REQUIREMENTS

Time

One 45-minute session

Materials

- Discovery Sheets from Session 1

- Personal envelopes from Session 1

- Museum collection (extra bone cards collected from Session 1)
- One copy of each of the five complete dinosaur skeletons (figs. 3.13-3.17, pp. 65-69). (If you believe the icon groups [see "Directions" below] are too large to use one copy of the dinosaur skeleton as reference, it may be necessary to make additional copies. One copy is recommended for every four children.)

Grouping

Whole class for instructions. The icon groups will vary in size because the children will choose which of the bones they want to construct into a full skeleton.

DIRECTIONS

1. Gather students together.

2. Explain that using both the skeletal pieces they have collected and the pieces in the museum collection, they will be able to construct a dinosaur skeleton.

3. Have students look at their Discovery Sheets and decide which icon appears most frequently (for example, if a child has three triangles, one square, and two circles, the child should choose to construct the triangle animal).

4. Next, have groups reform according to the icon selected (for example, all students who have chosen the triangle icon will sit together).

5. When students are settled in their groups, have them discard the pieces they will not be working with (for example, the triangle group gives up all their squares, circles, and so on). These pieces now go into the museum collection.

6. Distribute the museum collection to the appropriate groups (for instance, the triangle group gets all the triangle pieces).

7. Have students in each of the icon groups work together to complete the skeletons. They will need to trade pieces and make sure that every person in their group has all six skeletal pieces needed to construct that animal.

8. Students will record their new finds in the "New Finds" column on the right side of their Discovery Sheets.

9. As students complete their Discovery Sheets and show you that they have all six pieces of the skeleton, collect the envelopes of bones and give each student the corresponding dinosaur skeleton sheet (figs. 3.13-3.17).

10. Have students put their names on the dinosaur skeleton sheet. Collect sheets for use in Session 3.

Closure

Gather students together as a class and discuss the activity. Why was the museum collection distributed? How was this activity similar to what a scientist might do? What discoveries did they make about the animal? Were there any bones that were confusing, such as necks and tails?

(Text continues on page 70.)

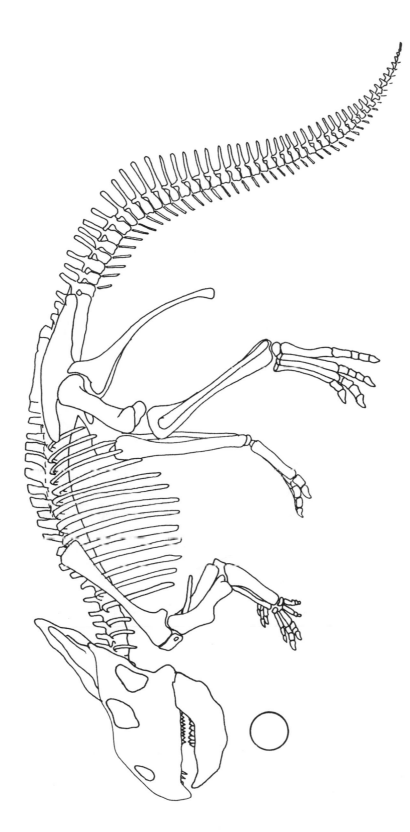

Fig. 3.13. Completed *Protoceratops* skeleton: circle icon.

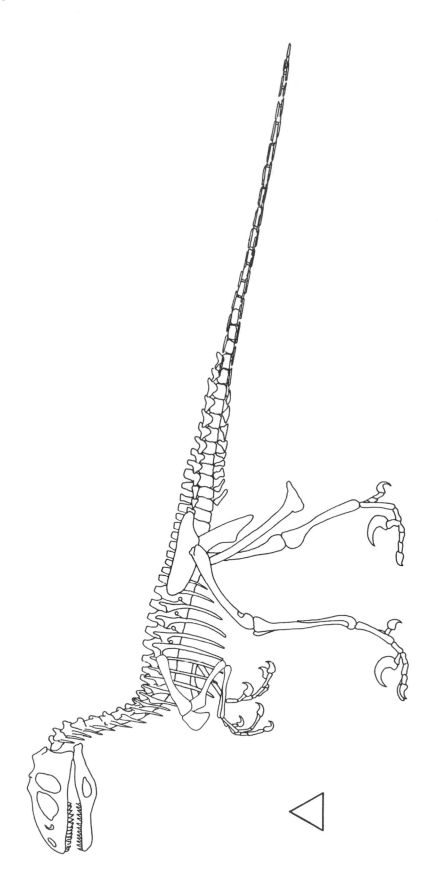

Fig. 3.14. Completed *Deinonychus* skeleton: triangle icon.

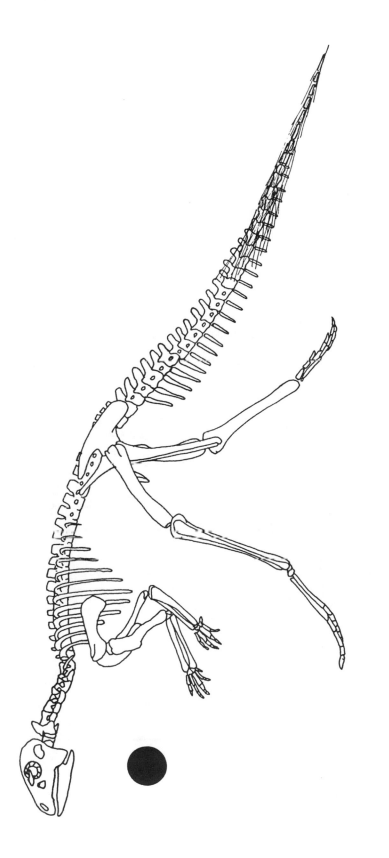

Fig. 3.15. Completed *Hypsilophodon* skeleton: black circle icon.

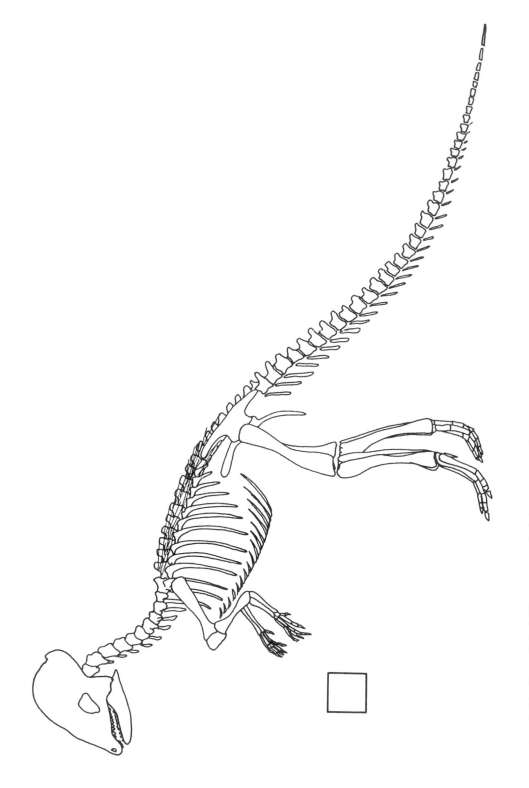

Fig. 3.16. Completed *Stegoceras* skeleton: square icon.

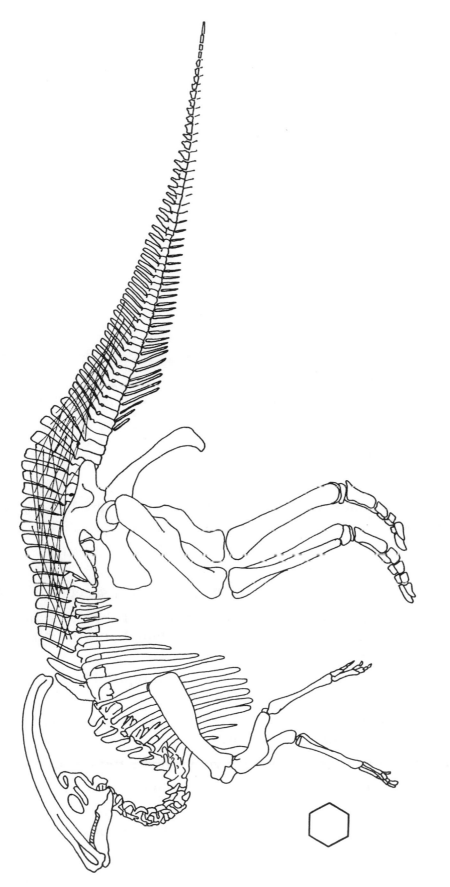

Fig. 3.17. Completed *Parasaurolophus* skeleton: hexagonal icon.

Session 3

REQUIREMENTS

Time

One 45-minute session

Materials

- Transparency of the front legs and hind legs of figure 3.18, page 72

- Articulated dinosaur skeleton sheets from Session 2 (figs 3.13–3.17)

- 8½-x-11-inch piece of black construction paper

- Scissors

- Glue

- One white or yellow crayon for each student

- A variety of dinosaur books (check with school library media specialist). Check them out for use in your classroom. Encourage students to bring books from home or the public library.

- Elephant and rhinoceros skeleton reference sheets (figs. 3.19-3.20, p. 73)

- Disarticulated dinosaur skeleton sheets (figs 3.21–3.25, pp. 74-78)

- Overhead projector

Grouping

Students may work independently or with their icon groups. Upper-grade helpers might be beneficial at this time (see appendix A).

DIRECTIONS

1. Students will be assembling a skeletal picture of a specific animal.

2. Using the transparency of figure 3.18, point out the difference between the bone structure of the front leg of an animal and the hind leg of an animal.

3. Encourage discussion of differences between bipedal (walks on two legs) and quadrupedal (walks on four legs) animals.

4. Ask students to make comparisons between their leg bones and their arm bones. Why are the bones different?

5. Encourage students to talk about size, number, and length of bones.

6. Distribute figures 3.21 through 3.25 according to students' icon groups.

7. Have students cut out their dinosaur skeletons (figures 3.21 through 3.25), assemble them on the black paper, and glue them in place. Advise students to lay out all the pieces before they start gluing. (This is a good time to make use of upper-grade helpers.)

8. Encourage students to look at the construction of a modern elephant or rhinoceros (figs. 3.19-3.20) as they assemble their dinosaur bones.

9. Once the dinosaur skeleton has been assembled, have students write their own names and the name of the animal they assembled on the black paper with the white or yellow crayon.

10. Show students the collection of dinosaur books that you have in the classroom. Recognize students who brought books in and encourage others to do the same. Tell them that the books are available for them to use after they complete the activity.

11. When the skeleton assembly is complete, direct students to the dinosaur books and suggest they try to locate their dinosaur in them.

Closure

Gather the class together and give students an opportunity to share their skeletons and the books in which they located their animal.

EXTENSIONS

Students may mount their assembled skeletons on a piece of poster board. Next to the assembled skeleton, have students write information about the dinosaur. Facts from their reading, such as name, food, enemies, habits, habitat, and size, should be included. These "reports" could be hung in the cafeteria or some other space that is frequented by many students. Students will create their own "dinosaur museum" to share with others.

Students may prefer to do a pictorial report. Drawings might illustrate the animal's habitat, showing its food sources, its predators, or its prey.

(Text continues on page 79.)

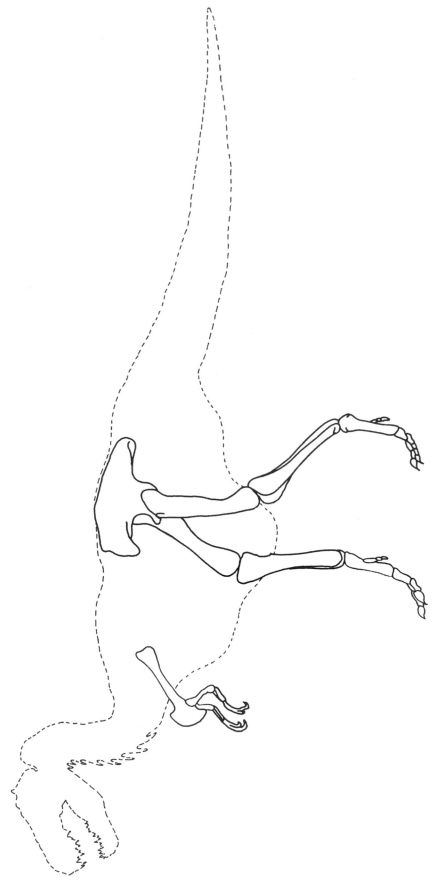

Fig. 3.18. Front and hind legs of a dinosaur skeleton.

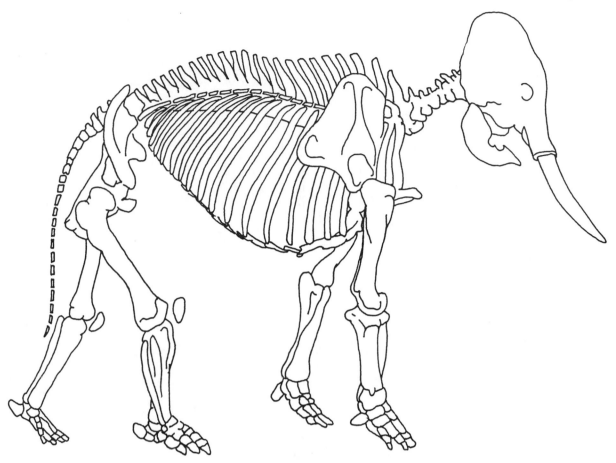

Fig. 3.19. Elephant skeleton.

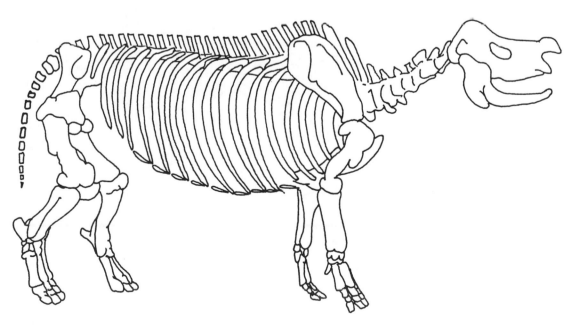

Fig. 3.20. Rhinoceros skeleton.

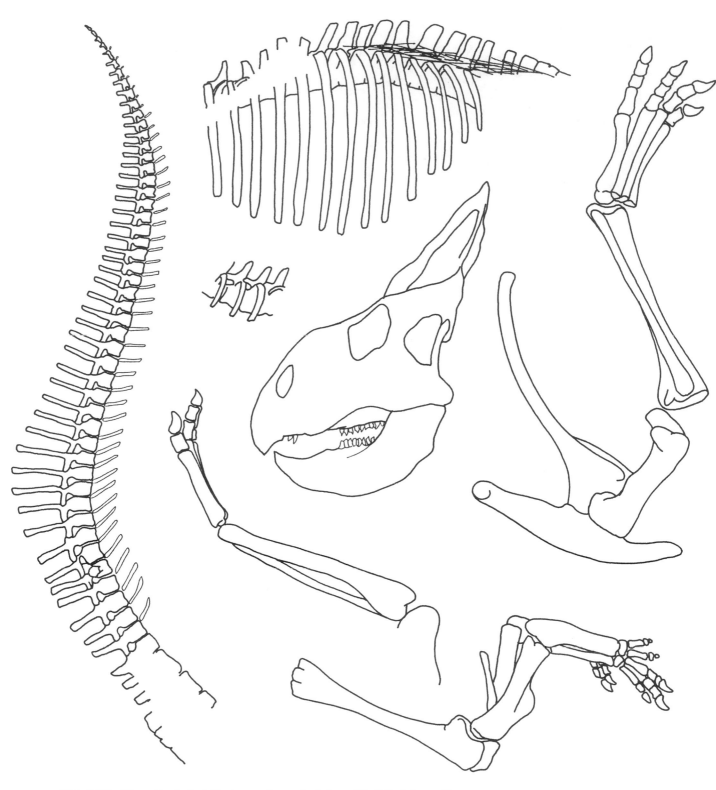

Fig. 3.21. Disarticulated *Protoceratops* skeleton. Modified from Norman.

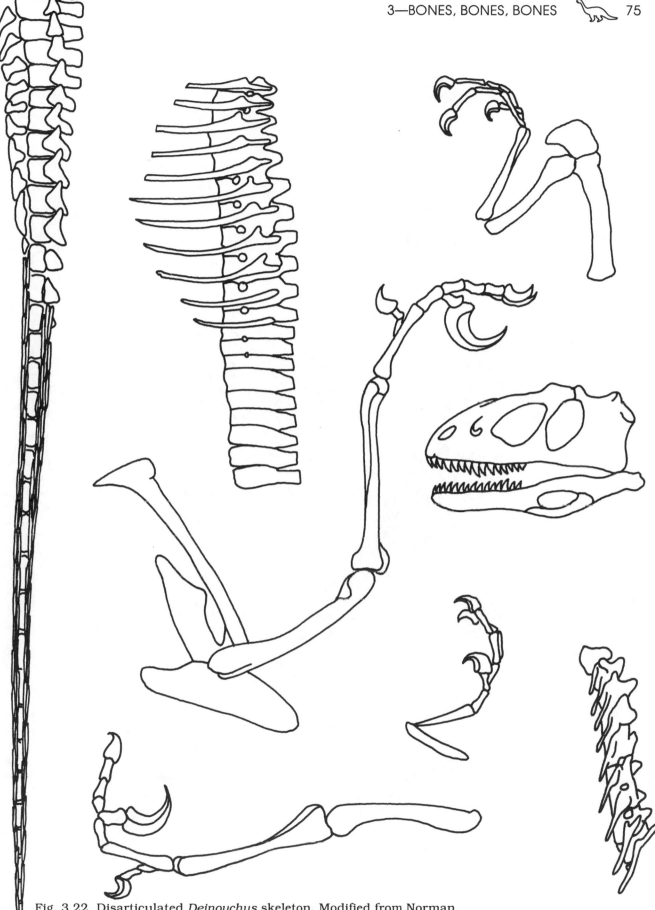

Fig. 3.22. Disarticulated *Deinoychus* skeleton. Modified from Norman.

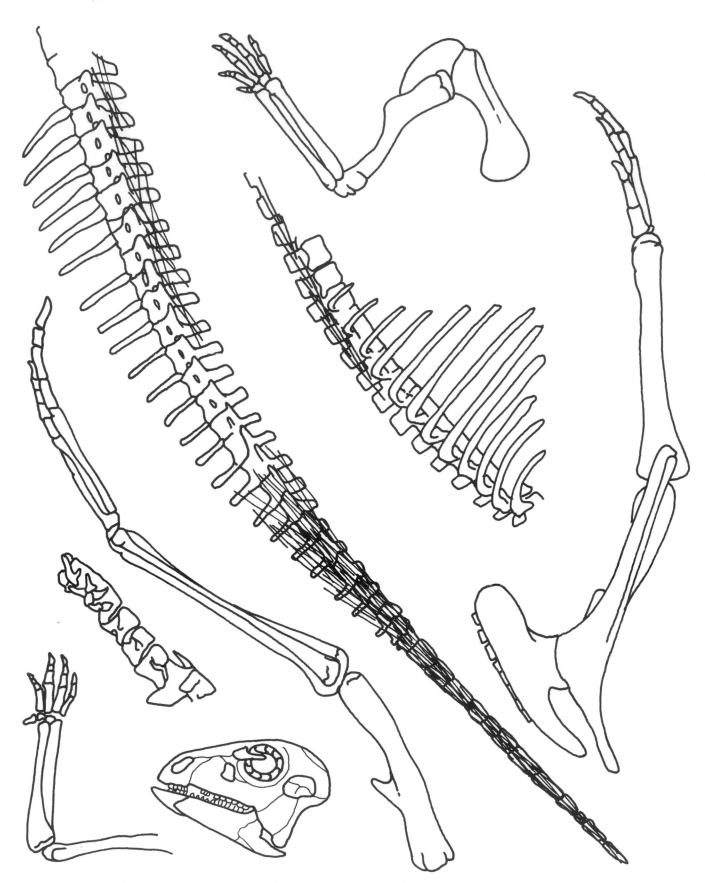

Fig. 3.23. Disarticulated *Hypsilophodon* skeleton. Modified from Norman.

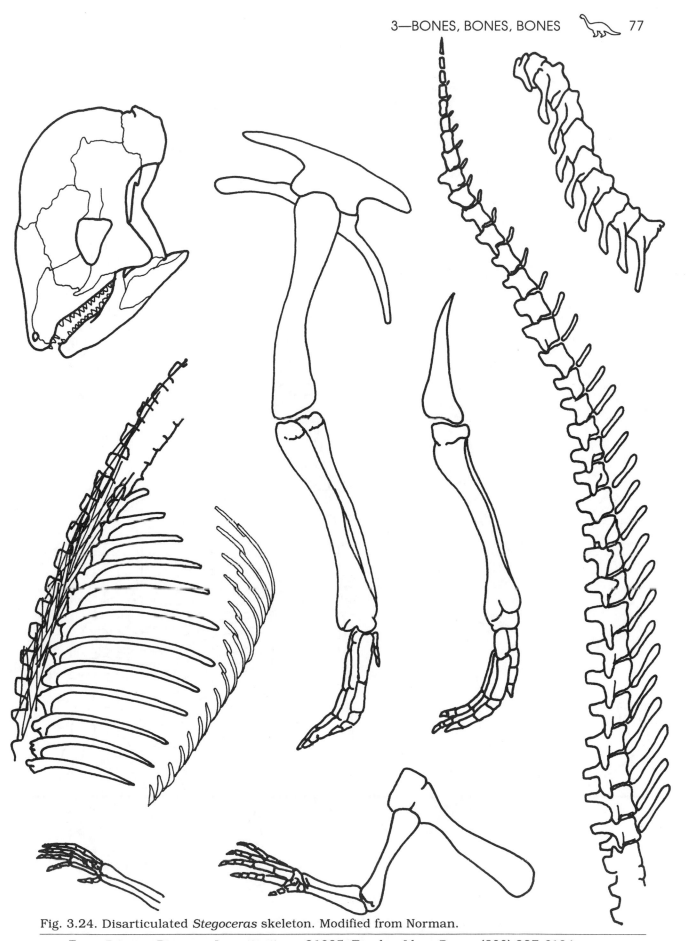

Fig. 3.24. Disarticulated *Stegoceras* skeleton. Modified from Norman.

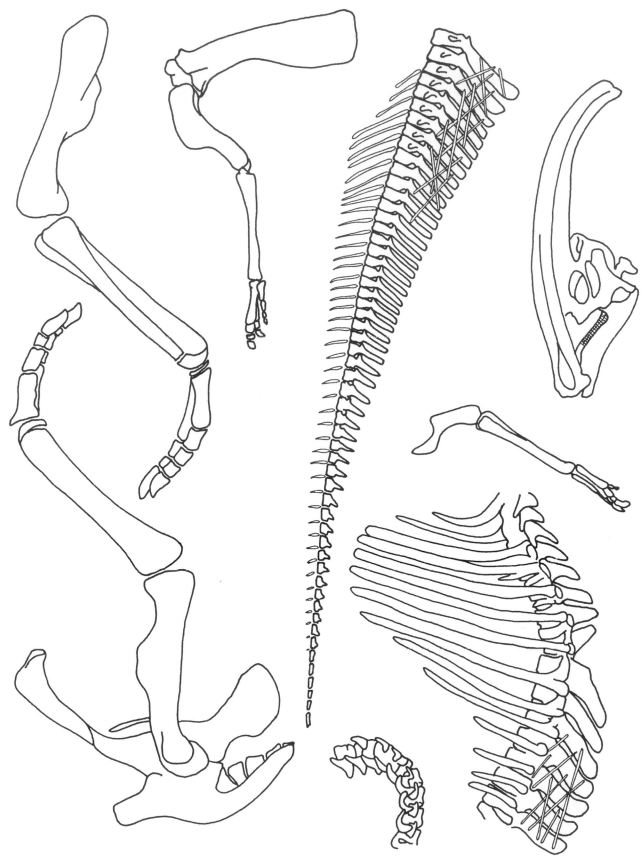

Fig. 3.25. Disarticulated *Parasaurolophus* skeleton. Modified from Norman.

REFERENCES

Aliki. 1988. *Digging Up Dinosaurs.* New York: HarperCollins.

Echoes, 1993-1994. *A Guide to Dinosaur National Monument.* Dinosaur, Colorado: The Dinosaur Nature Association.

Holmes, Arthur. 1965. *Principles of Physical Geology.* New York: Ronald Press.

Munsart, Craig A. 1993. *Investigating Science with Dinosaurs.* Englewood, Colorado: Teacher Ideas Press.

SUGGESTED READING

Czerkas, Sylvia J., and Stephen A. Czerkas. 1991. *Dinosaurs: A Global View.* New York: Mallard Press.

Dixon, Dougal. 1993. *Dougal Dixon's Dinosaurs.* Honesdale, Pennsylvania: Boyds Mills Press.

Norman, David. 1985. *The Illustrated Encyclopedia of Dinosaurs.* New York: Crown.

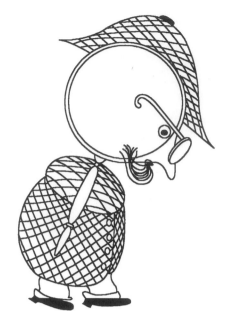

Full Size

INTRODUCTION

One of the physical attributes of dinosaurs that impresses students the most is size. When visiting museums, students stare up in awe at an *Apatosaurus* or *Tyrannosaurus* skeleton looming over them. In the classroom, however, such full-size resources are not available. Instead, students often study dinosaurs through posters, small models, or even smaller pictures in textbooks. Teaching about dinosaurs with a full-size drawing of a *Tyrannosaurus* head staring into the room (see fig. 4.1) provides students with an ongoing reminder of how intimidating many dinosaurs would have been. At the same time, full-size drawings of the smaller dinosaurs reinforce the fact that not all dinosaurs were large.

ACTIVITY: WOW, THEY CAN BE BIG!

The skill level of your students will largely determine which of the animal drawings can be completed successfully by your class. Another option would be to involve parents, an option we strongly believe in. Many of the full-size animals and skeletons can be completed by students and parents working together at home, with final assembly taking place at school conferences or a "Back to School" night. For the more complicated skeletons, completion might be more successful with the help of aides or parents working closely with students in the classroom.

The figures shown on the following pages may be enlarged to create full-size drawings of dinosaur bodies and skeletons. The final drawings are designed to fit on a typical classroom wall. It might be helpful for students to compare these dinosaur drawings to a full-size drawing of a large living animal; figure 4.2, page 82, may be used to create a life-size African Elephant and calf.

Fig. 4.1. Full-size wall mural of large dinosaur heads.

If the elephants and dinosaurs are shown together, students (and teachers) must be aware that these animals did not live on earth at the same time.

All of the figures are shown with a superimposed square grid. Each grid square represents a single, square piece of paper. Grid size may change from figure to figure (for example 6-x-6-inches, 12-x-12-inches, or 24-x-24-inches), but it is consistent within a figure. The choice of a square grid over the more readily available 8½-x-11-inch format was made because using regular letter-size paper would have required twice as many pieces of paper, and this would have complicated the drawing and assembling procedures for younger children. Large pieces of art, butcher, or newsprint paper should be easy enough to cut into square sheets.

REQUIREMENTS

Time

Minimum 45-60 minutes, maybe longer, depending on the project selected

Materials

- For the teacher:
  —Staples to attach drawings to wall (push pins or thumb tacks will also work, but these can fall to the floor, creating a hazard, and they are not recommended)
  —Clear cellophane tape to attach pieces to one another
  —Large wall (dimensions depending on the dinosaur selected)
  —Drawing selected from the figures that follow
  —Large envelope

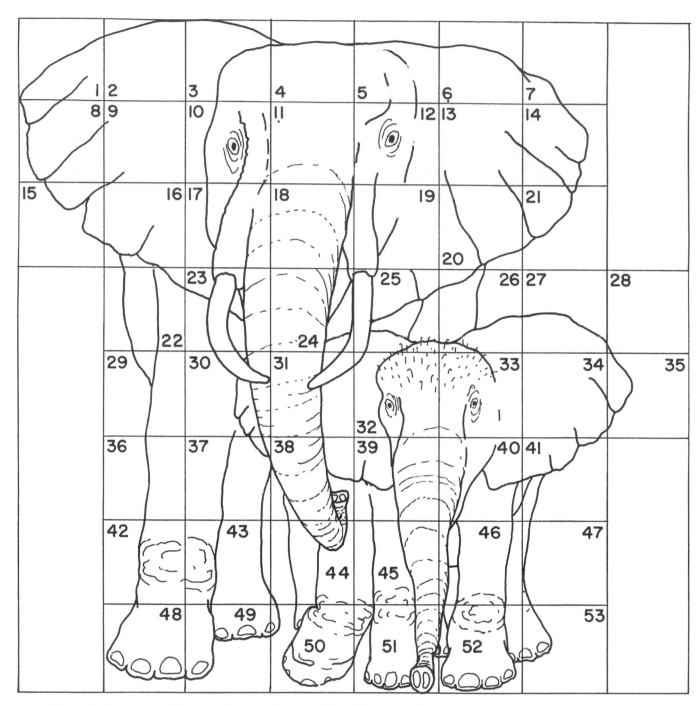

Fig. 4.2. Drawing of African Elephant and calf for life-size enlargement.

- For an indoor project, one of the following per student:
  —Pencil and eraser
  —Large square of newsprint, butcher, or art paper
      (size will depend on scale of animal chosen)
  —Wide black marker
  —Markers, paint, or other material to color the dinosaur skin

- For an outdoor project:
  —At least one large piece of chalk per student (have lots of extra chalk;
      some surfaces are very abrasive)
  —Precut 4-foot piece of string for establishing grid
  —Large paved area traffic-free during the activity
  —30-40-foot piece of rope or string

Grouping

Individuals, then whole class for animal assembly

Advance Preparation

Table 4.1 summarizes the information necessary to create full-size drawings of the animals presented in this activity. As you decide which ones might be appropriate for your class, remember that if animals are to be combined on a mural, only those animals that coexisted should be drawn together. For instance, it would be incorrect to show *Heterodontosaurus* being eaten by *Tyrannosaurus*: the former became extinct 120 million years before the latter appeared (see "Extensions"). In table 4.1 animals that coexisted have the same letter code.

Table 4.1. Summary of information needed to create full-size dinosaur drawings.

Summary Table

Dinosaur Name	Overall Size (Feet)	Number of Squares	Size of Square (inches)	Code
Brachiosaurus	28 x 68	48	48 x 48	B
Compsognathus	2 x 5	22	6 x 6	B
Heterodontosaurus	3 x 4	25	6 x 6	C
Hypsilophodon	3 x 8	19	12 x 12	A, B
Protoceratops	3 x 7	19	12 x 12	A
Stegosaurus	8 x 8	45	12 x 12	A, B
Triceratops head	9 x 6	50	12 x 12	A
Tyrannosaurus	14 x 32	51	24 x 24	A
Tyrannosaurus head	6 x 8	42	12 x 12	A
Velociraptor	3'9" x 8'3"	28	9 x 9	B

DIRECTIONS FOR INDOOR DINOSAUR DRAWINGS

1. Select a dinosaur from figures 4.3-4.7, pages 85-89, based upon wall space available and number of students.

2. Enlarge the chosen figure on a photocopier so each grid square measures 1½ to 2 inches, then cut the grid apart into individual numbered squares.

3. Give each student a grid square and a blank piece of paper that matches the scale of a grid square for the animal selected (refer to table 4.1).

4. For orientation purposes, have each student note the number that appears on the small grid square and mark it in the top right corner of the large piece of paper.

5. Instruct students to enlarge the drawing in their assigned grid square to fill the large piece of blank paper they have been given. Tell students the drawing must go all the way to the edge of the paper; they must not leave any margins.

6. Once students have enlarged the drawings on their small grid squares, have them place these squares in the envelope provided.

7. Make available a small drawing of the entire grid that shows the grid-square numbers but not the animal outline so that students can locate adjoining squares.

8. Have students check their own grid square with surrounding squares to make certain that all pencil lines connect.

9. Once all grid connections have been satisfactorily completed, instruct students to go over the pencil lines with black marker to improve visibility.

10. Assemble the enlarged grid squares and tape them to the preselected wall to complete the life-size dinosaur drawing. If you prefer, you may preassemble the squares on a large sheet of paper and then place the paper on the wall.

DIRECTIONS FOR OUTDOOR DINOSAUR DRAWINGS

1. Select either figure 4.8 or 4.9, page 90, and use the long string or rope to establish a baseline for the grid.

2. Give students chalk and guide them as they measure and draw the grid of the selected animal on the paved area, using the precut 4-foot string. All grid spaces should be identified with small numbers in the upper right-hand corner.

3. Give small grid squares to students as in Step 3 (indoor drawings) or have them select a square from a container.

4. Follow Steps 3-8 (indoor drawings).

5. Once the drawing is completed, have students identify the animal, using classroom resources.

(Text continues on page 91.)

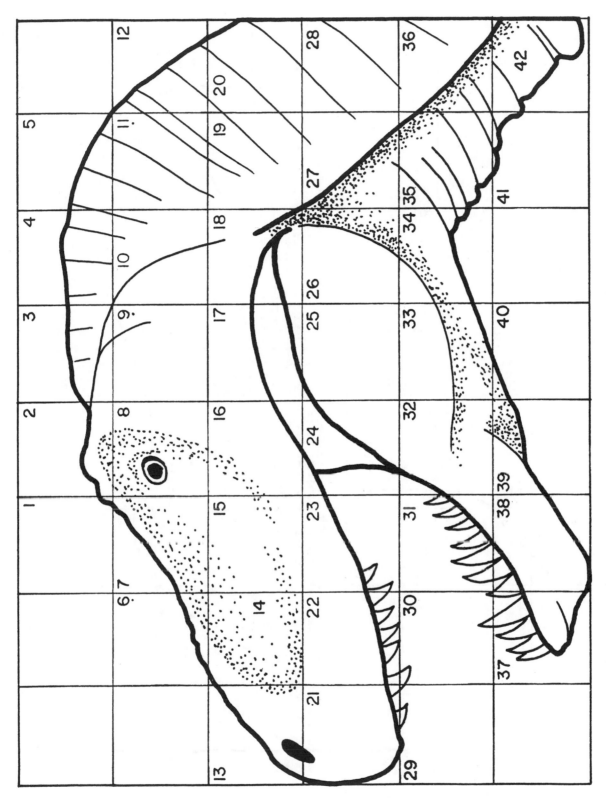

Fig. 4.3. *Tyrannosaurus* head. Modified from Lambert.

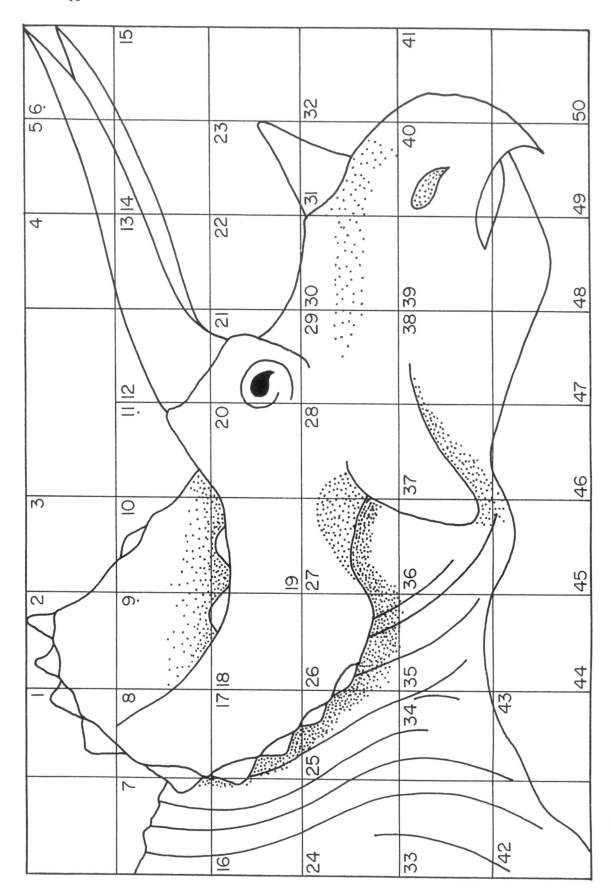

Fig. 4.4. *Triceratops* head. Modified from Lambert.

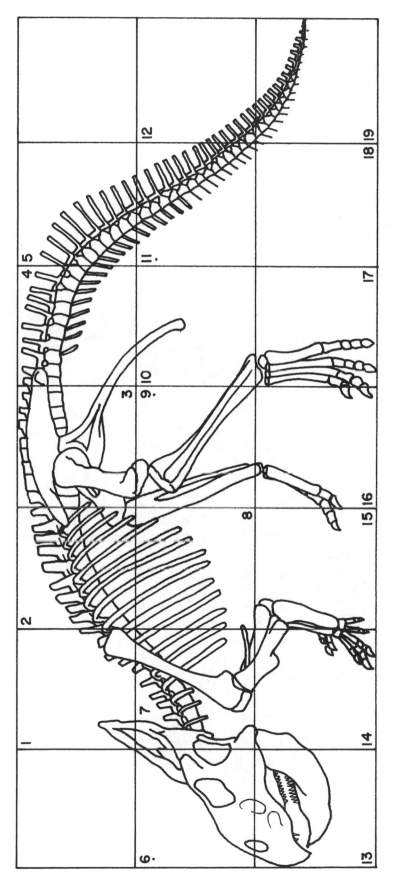

Fig. 4.5. *Protoceratops* head. Modified from Lambert.

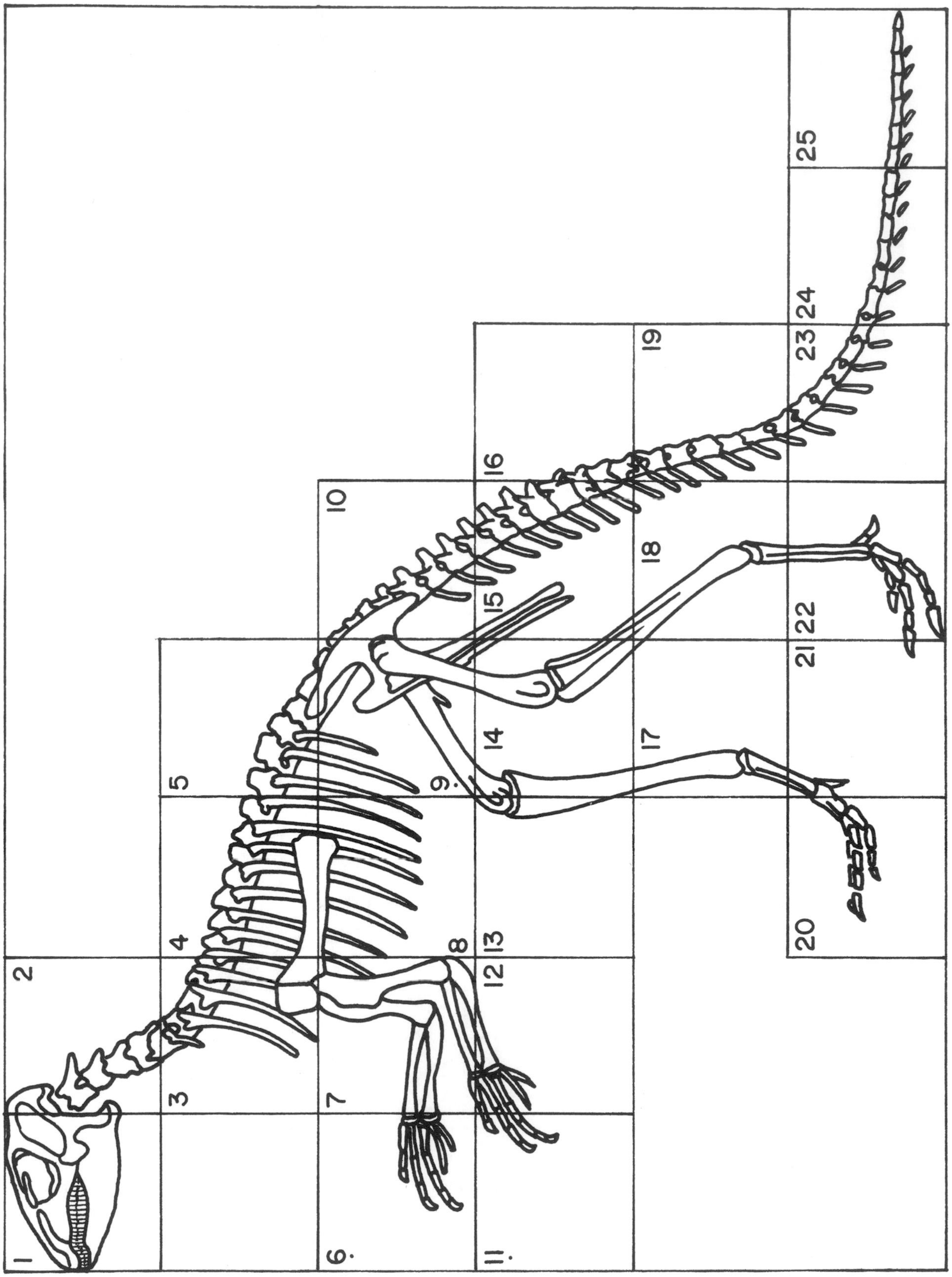

Fig. 4.6. *Heterodontosaurus* head. Modified from Lambert.

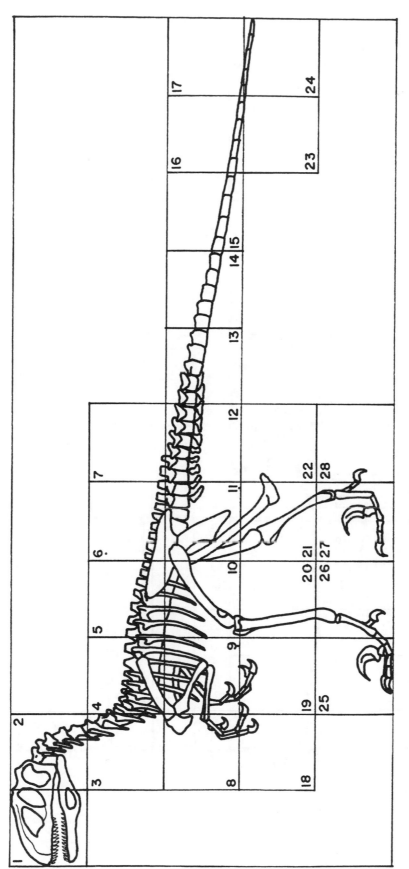

Fig. 4.7. *Velociraptor* head. Modified from Lambert.

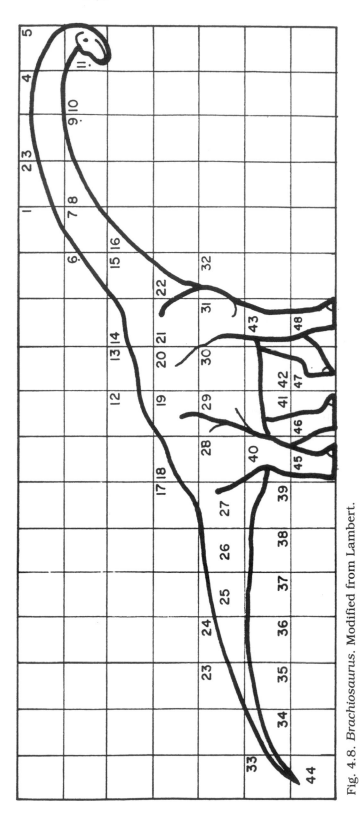

Fig. 4.8. *Brachiosaurus*. Modified from Lambert.

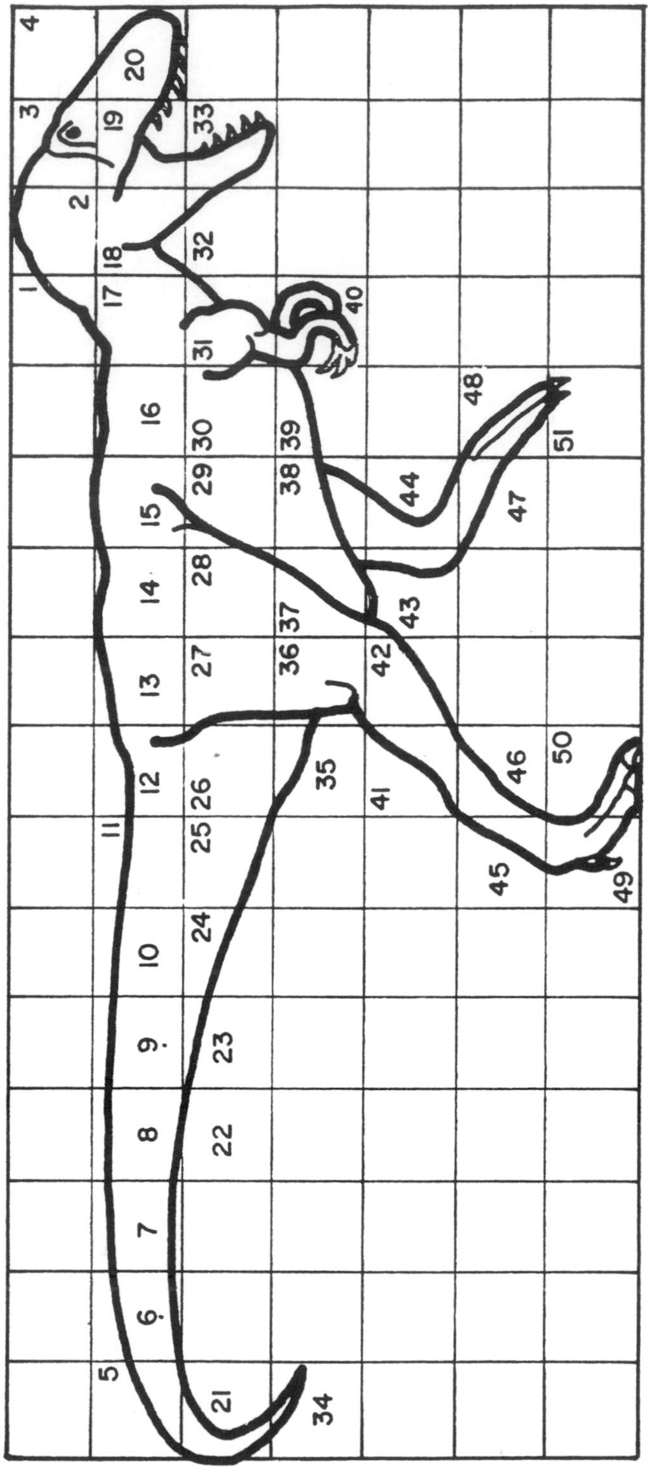

Fig. 4.9. *Tyrannosaurus*. Modified from Lambert.

EXTENSIONS

Mural drawing can be combined with library research on the selected animal to determine its habitat and other animals that coexisted with it. Wall murals can be enhanced by drawing appropriate plants. Students may be required to use library sources to document all elements of the mural for authenticity. Paleontologists might be invited to class as judges or advisors. A sense of depth can be created by drawing footprints on the floor of the classroom leading up to the wall or by constructing certain elements for the mural (a plant or an animal body part such as a tail) as three-dimensional models projecting from the wall. Similar procedures can be used to create a life-size classroom environment for studies in other subjects. Students could construct tipis for Native American studies or a small airplane or schoolbus for transportation studies.

ACTIVITY: BEAUTY IS NOT SKIN DEEP

Dinosaur bones and teeth are found as fossils, extracted from the rock in which they were preserved, carefully restored, then reassembled using clues from skeletons of modern animals. Dinosaur skin and other soft parts are rarely found. In reconstructing how the animal might have looked, scientists begin with the skeleton. Next, they calculate the placement of muscles, organs, tendons, and ligaments on the supporting skeletal structure and cover the assembly with the protective skin. Students will use figures 4.10a-4.12b, pages 92-95 to assemble a life-size skeletal drawing and cover it with skin, duplicating the process used by the paleontologist.

REQUIREMENTS

Time

   45-60 minutes for the skeleton preparation and assembly
   30-45 minutes for the skin covering

Materials

   • One skeleton/skin pair of figures (cut into individual squares) per class

   • Clear tape

   • One marker and pencil per student

   • Appropriately large surface on which to mount the completed assembly

Grouping

Individuals or pairs of students, then whole class

(Text continues on page 96.)

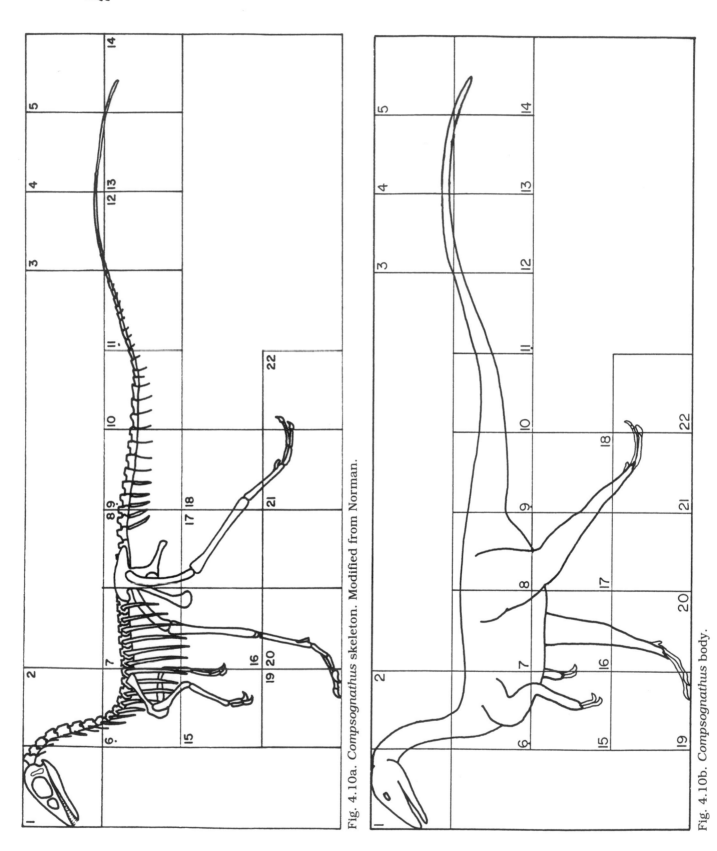

Fig. 4.10a. *Compsognathus* skeleton. Modified from Norman.

Fig. 4.10b. *Compsognathus* body.

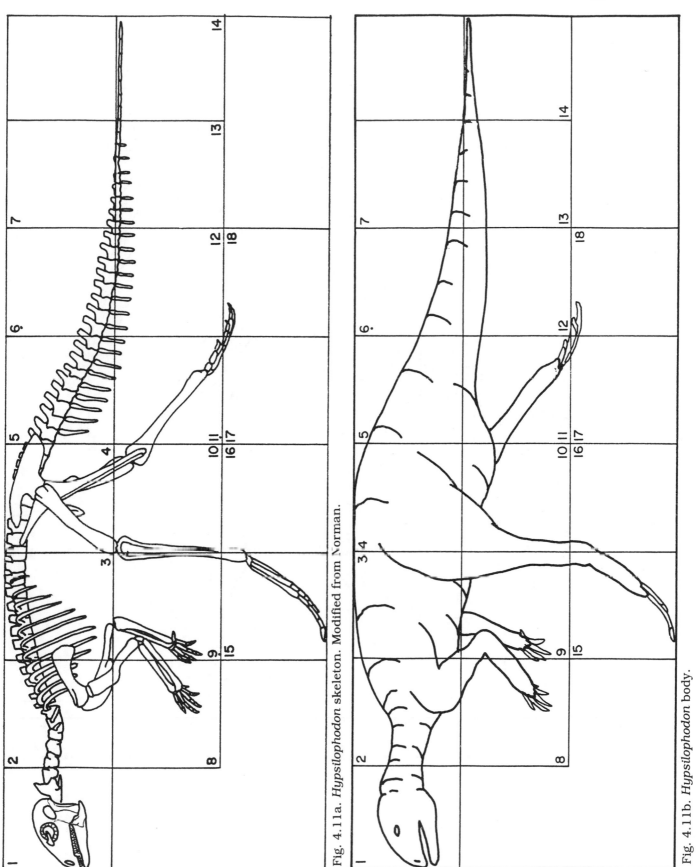

Fig. 4.11a. *Hypsilophodon* skeleton. Modified from Norman.

Fig. 4.11b. *Hypsilophodon* body.

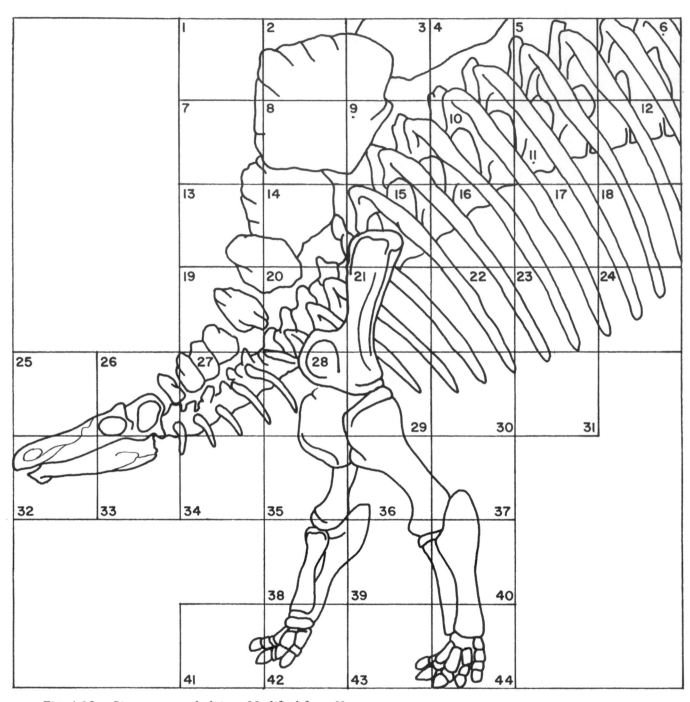

Fig. 4.12a. *Stegosaurus* skeleton. Modified from Norman.

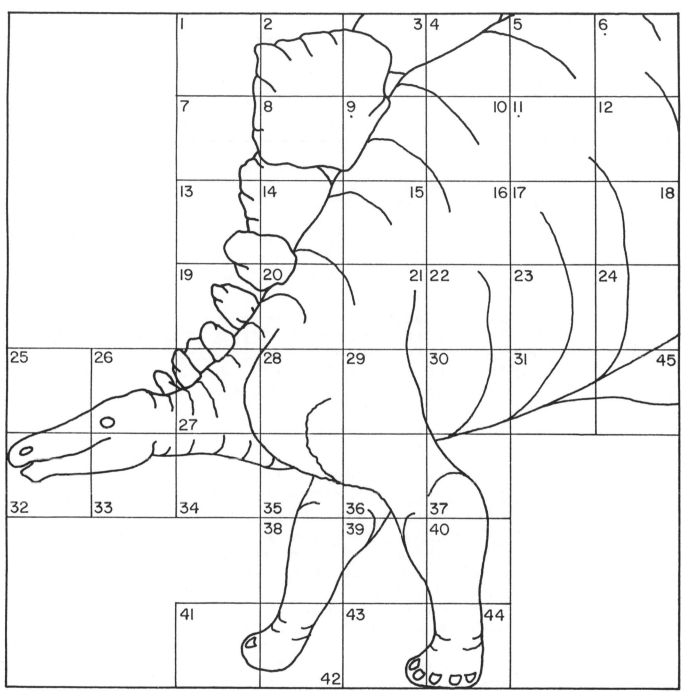

Fig. 4.12b. *Stegosaurus* body.

DIRECTIONS

1. Complete assembly of the skeleton as in the "Wow, They Can Be Big" activity in this chapter.

2. Mount the assembled skeleton in the predetermined location.

3. Complete grid-square drawing of the animal's skin, following the same directions. Do not mount the skin squares at this time.

4. As students complete their individual skin grid squares, have them color the square. You might decide to allow students to color squares individually or allow the class to decide on a single, grand scheme for the entire animal. For a discussion of dinosaur skin coloration, see chapter 9, "Color." Briefly, there is no wrong coloration. Skin color is not preserved, and ideas about dinosaur coloration come from animals alive today. Colors can vary from subtle earth tones that blend with natural surroundings to outlandish colors in bizarre patterns that allow the animal to be conspicuous for mating rituals.

5. Tape a skin grid square over the corresponding skeleton square by attaching it with clear tape along the top edge like a hinge. This way, skin grids can be lifted to reveal the skeletal structure beneath. Because skin grids are attached individually, they must be aligned carefully atop the skeleton sections beneath; otherwise the outer skin may appear ragged and mismatched.

EXTENSIONS

1. X-rays of limbs illustrate the idea of bones beneath skin. X-rays may be available from the discards of medical offices or veterinarians. Broken bones may be of particular interest to students.

2. Figure 4.13 is a drawing of a human skeleton. Bone arrangements of humans and dinosaurs are quite similar. The most obvious differences are the absence of tails and long necks on humans. In both humans and dinosaurs, paired bones exist in the lower arms and legs. As in bipedal dinosaurs, the lower limbs of humans have evolved to support the entire body weight. By coloring similar bones similar colors, students will be made more aware of the similarities in skeletal systems. Comparisons can be made with other animal skeletons as well. Romer (1945) is an excellent source of drawings of animal skeletons.

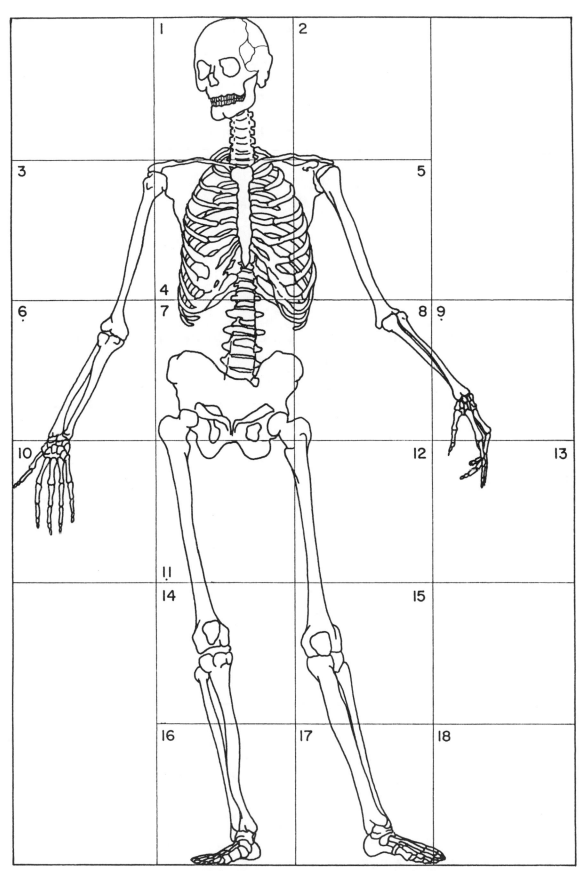

Fig. 4.13. Grid pattern for creating a full-size human skeleton drawing.

REFERENCES

Lambert, David. 1990. *The Dinosaur Data Book.* New York: Avon.

Norman, David. 1985. *The Illustrated Encyclopedia of Dinosaurs.* New York: Crown.

Romer, Alfred Sherwood. 1945. *Vertebrate Paleontology.* Chicago: University of Chicago Press.

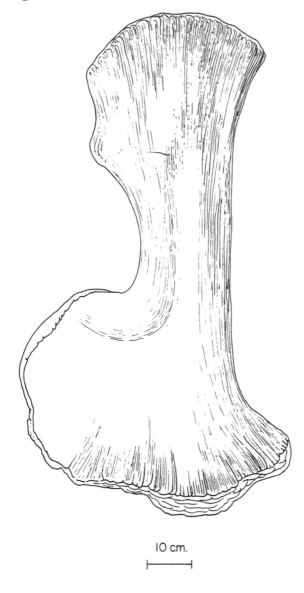

Camarasaurus grandis

scapula
(shoulder blade)

10 cm.

"have taken up the Femur. it is a beauty, but so heavy that I canot pack it on a horse. one end is all three of us can cary. shall get it down to the R.R. and Bring it in on the hand car."

March 20, 1880

"that Femur is a poser we tried today to get the head down to the RR got it part way and had to leave it will get it down to morrow."

March 24, 1880

5

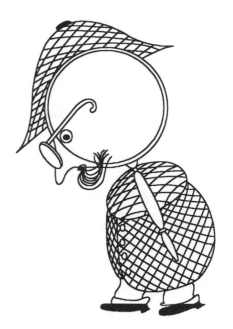

Eyes

INTRODUCTION

Animals have a wide array of senses: in addition to sight, sound, smell, touch, and feel, some species have also developed magnetic, electrical, and heat-sensitive sensory systems. Of all these systems, the eyes are perhaps the most important. They not only advise an animal that objects are present but also may tell the animal the color, size, quantity, speed, and distance of these objects. They can also provide important information for the paleontologist. If the animal's eye sockets are in the front of its head, much like human eyes, then the animal could focus on distant objects and pursue prey and therefore was probably a carnivore. If, on the other hand, the eye sockets of the dinosaur are on the sides of the head, like a horse, the dinosaur was more concerned with its immediate environment and was probably a herbivore.

An excellent experiment that will help students understand how the human eye works can be found in *175 Science Experiments to Amuse and Amaze Your Friends* by Brenda Walpole (1988, 147).

ACTIVITY: FOR YOUR EYES ONLY?

Eyes are among an animal's most recognizable features. In this activity, you will show students pictures of animals' eyes only, and they will try to guess which animals the eyes belong to.

REQUIREMENTS

Time

Approximately 30-45 minutes

Materials

- Figure 5.1 for each student
- Figure 5.1 as an overhead transparency
- Figure 5.2, page 102, as an overhead transparency
- 3 sheets of blank opaque paper
- Overhead projector

Grouping

Individuals or pairs

DIRECTIONS

1. Discuss with students how eyes differ from animal to animal and talk about how you might identify an animal by looking at its eyes.

2. Figure 5.1 shows a collection of animal eyes. Distribute one copy to each student or pair of students. Have students try to identify the animals from the eyes. The shape of the bones around the eyes can provide some clues. Encourage an open discussion among the class about each animal's identity.

3. After an allotted time period, show the correct answers on the overhead in the following manner:

   a. Place the transparency of figure 5.1 on the overhead projector.

   b. Ask the students for their animal identifications and record them by letter on a board for the class to see.

   c. *With the projector off,* place the transparency of figure 5.2 over the transparency for figure 5.1, making sure to align them carefully. Arrange the opaque pieces of paper so that only animal A is revealed. Give the students one more opportunity to guess the animal. Build the suspense, then turn on the projector to reveal the animal's identity.

   d. Repeat the procedure with animals B through G.

   e. As a closure, encourage discussion about other choices students made as they attempted to identify the animals.

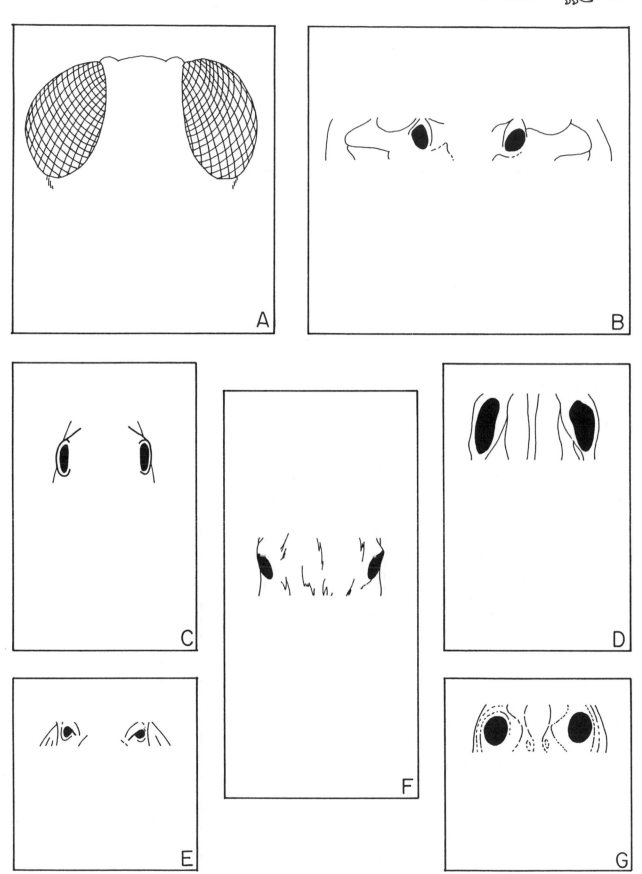

Fig. 5.1. The eyes of various animals.

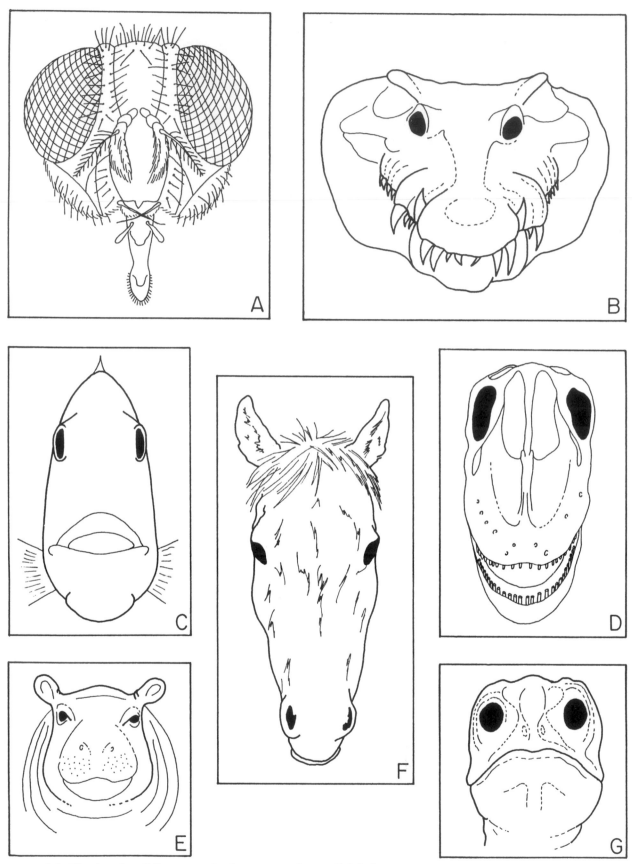

Fig. 5.2. The heads of the animals the eyes in figure 5.1 belong to.

ACTIVITY: COMPARE TO MODERN ANIMALS

Show students pictures of modern animals. Pictures of heads are particularly useful. See whether the principles introduced in "For Your Eyes Only?" apply. Large cats (lions, leopards, cheetah) all have eyes in the front of their heads, but so do monkeys. Which features do the animals share? Which features are unique? Students will be using a Venn diagram (fig. 5.3, p. 104) to illustrate similarities and differences.

Animal eyes can provide clues to what an animal eats. The eyes of carnivores are set in the front of the head, providing binocular vision that yields good depth perception and helps the animal target prey. Eyes of herbivores are usually set more to the sides of the head, giving the animal a wide field of vision that alerts them to the presence of predators. Omnivores (sharing characteristics of both carnivores and herbivores) may have either eye type. By observing eyes of animals that exist today, students can determine these relationships for themselves. This activity can be completed in school or as part of a zoo or aquarium visit. An accommodating pet store might also allow a small class to visit.

REQUIREMENTS

Time

Variable; depends on whether the activity is structured for the classroom, library, or field trip

Materials

- Transparency of figure 5.4, page 104

- Transparency of figure 5.5, page 105

- Copy of figure 5.5 for each student or pair of students

- Overhead projector

- Two large animal pictures or posters, one with eyes in front and one with eyes to the sides

- If done as a classroom activity, picture books, magazines (such as *Ranger Rick* or *National Geographic*), or videos of animals

- If part of a zoo trip, a surface for students to use to support their response sheets (fig. 5.5), plus lapboards or magazines

- Large sheet of butcher paper

- Red and blue markers

- Transparency of figure 5.6, page 106

- Vis-à-Vis pen

- Overhead projector

(Text continues on page 107.)

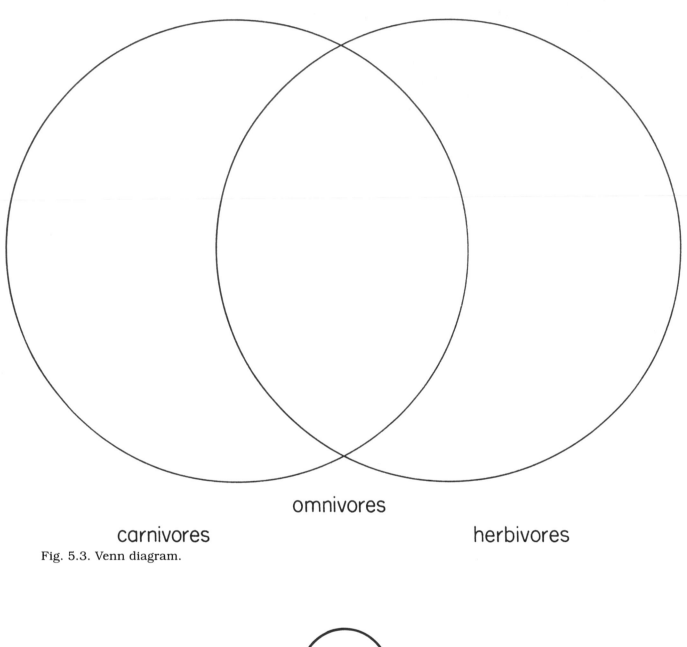

omnivores

carnivores   herbivores

Fig. 5.3. Venn diagram.

lion   meat

Parrot   fruit, seeds

Fig. 5.4. Completed entries for eyes/diet chart.

YOUR NAMES_____,_____

animal name	where eyes are (front view of head)	what it eats
_____	◯	_____
_____	◯	_____
_____	◯	_____
_____	◯	_____
_____	◯	_____
_____	◯	_____
_____	◯	_____
_____	◯	_____
_____	◯	_____
_____	◯	_____

Fig. 5.5. Blank eyes/diet chart.

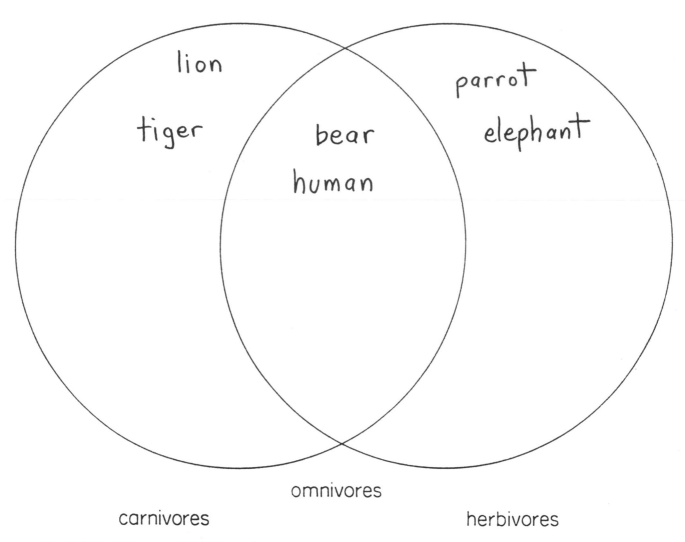

Fig. 5.6. Partially completed Venn diagram.

Grouping

Pairs or individuals, then whole class

DIRECTIONS

1. Show students posters or pictures of the two animals. Ask them to pay particular attention to the eyes.

2. Have an open class discussion of the differences between the eyes. Students may observe differences in size, color, shape, and, hopefully, position.

3. Ask students the following questions: Are the eyes located in the front of the head or to the sides of the head? What are the advantages of each position?

4. Figures 5.4 and 5.5 will give students an opportunity to record what they see. Explain to students that they will be receiving a chart (fig. 5.5) that will help them understand the relationship between what an animal eats and where its eyes are positioned in its head. As you explain how to fill the charts in, refer to figure 5.4, which shows completed chart entries for a lion and a parrot. Students should be able to fill in the name of the animal in the left-hand column. The circle in the center represents a front view of the animal's head. The student should draw two circles representing the approximate position of the eyes in the head. Point out how the eyes are drawn in on figure 5.4 for the lion and parrot. The right-hand column is for the animal's diet. In some cases students will have to guess based on other information, such as the kind of teeth it has. On a zoo trip, information cards at the exhibits often provide such information.

5. Project the transparency of figure 5.5 and, with student input, fill in the blanks for the two animals represented on the posters or pictures. Pay particular attention to marking eye position on the circle representing the head to be certain students understand how it is to be done.

6. If the activity is to be completed in the library or classroom, distribute copies of figure 5.5 to the students at this time and ask students to write their names at the top. Instruct students to complete figure 5.5 after finding pictures of 10 animals. If the activity is to be completed as part of a zoo or aquarium visit, distribute figure 5.5 to students on the bus or at the facility. Before the trip remind students to bring some kind of writing surface or provide one for them.

7. To review and share ideas, reproduce figure 5.3 (the Venn diagram) on the large sheet of butcher paper so it will be visible to the entire class. Project the transparency of figure 5.6, which shows the partially completed Venn diagram. The circle on the left contains the names of animals that are carnivores (eat other animals); the circle on the right contains the animals that are herbivores (eat only plant materials). The area where the circles intersect contains the names of omnivores (animals that eat both meat and plants). Using student data, you will be filling in animal names in the appropriate place on the butcher paper diagram. If an animal has eyes in

the front of its head, write the name using the red marker; if the eyes are on the sides of its head, use the blue marker.

8. Ask students to draw conclusions based upon the color distribution of the names. For example, carnivores will have eyes in the front of the head, so animal names in the left circle should be written in red. Conversely, herbivores generally have eyes on the sides of the head, so the right circle should have names written with the blue marker. Omnivores will share characteristics of the other two groups, and the middle section should contain names written in both red and blue.

EXTENSIONS

Skulls and stuffed animals are excellent classroom study resources. Contact local taxidermists or university biology departments to arrange a short loan of such material. Skulls are often fragile, and teeth might still be sharp, so student handling should be kept to a minimum.

ACTIVITY: TWO ARE BETTER THAN ONE!

In this two-part activity students will learn that each eye sees a slightly different image and that the brain combines the two separate two-dimensional pictures into a three-dimensional image that allows depth perception. In some animals, such as fish (Ommanney, 1963, 41), the image from the right eye is processed only in the left side of the brain and the image from the left eye only in the right side. Humans process the image from each eye in both sides of the brain simultaneously, providing a much better picture than most animals see (Ommanney, 1963, 42).

Part 1

REQUIREMENTS

Time

5-15 minutes

Materials

- Overhead projector
- Transparencies of figures 5.7 and 5.8

Grouping

Teams of two students

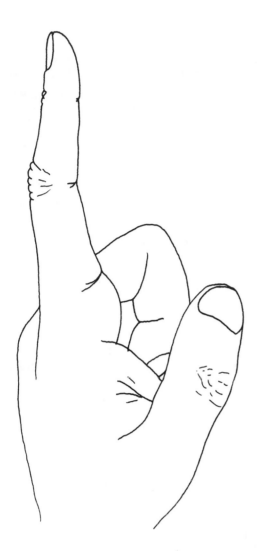

left hand

Fig. 5.7. Left hand with index finger extended.

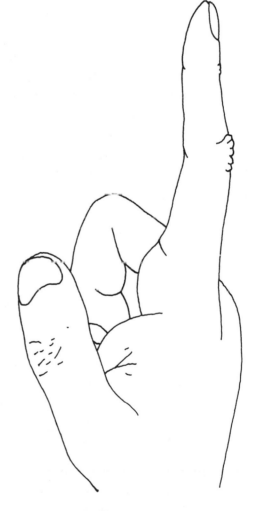

right hand

Fig. 5.8. Right hand with index finger extended.

DIRECTIONS

1. Make certain students know which finger is their index finger. Show the transparency of figure 5.7. Have each student hold up the index finger of his or her left hand as shown in figure 5.7. Explain to students that with one eye closed, they will hold up the index fingers of both hands (at this point, add the transparency of figure 5.8 to the projector) in front of their open eye until the fingers appear to line up and one disappears behind the other. Demonstrate what will be happening by lining up the two overhead transparencies so that the index finger of the right hand covers the index finger of the left hand. It might be helpful to color the two transparency fingers different colors.

2. Have two students sit on opposite sides of a desk facing each other.

3. Student A should hold up the index fingers of both hands (one behind the other) approximately 3 inches in front of student B's face. With the right eye closed, student B should tell student A how to position the two fingers so that one seems to disappear behind the other.

4. Student A, with the right eye also closed, should then move so the two fingers also line up from his or her point of view. At that point the fingers should appear one behind the other to both students.

5. *Without moving their fingers or their heads,* both students should close their right eye and open only the left eye. Students should closely observe the positions of the fingers. Are they still one behind the other, or do they appear to have moved?

6. Discuss with students what they observed and why this was so.

Students are now aware that each eye sees a slightly different image. This may seem confusing at first, but as the signals from the eye are combined by the brain, it produces a picture that is better than either one of the two original images; the combined picture allows the brain to perceive depth much more clearly.

Why is depth perception important to animals? People going down stairs must know where each step is to avoid falling as they descend; a tiger running through the jungle must be able to determine the distance to trees before turns are made; a monkey or squirrel must be able to determine exactly how far away a branch is before it jumps; and a pack of *Velociraptors* chasing prey must obtain targeting information such as direction and speed to complete a successful attack.

Imagine a hawk diving from high in the sky, attempting to snare a mouse as it flees across a field. The hawk is moving toward the ground at 50-60 miles per hour. The mouse is running for its life to avoid becoming lunch. Without excellent depth perception, not only would the hawk miss its meal, but it might also be killed if it misjudged the distance and crashed to the ground. A similar need for depth perception exists for virtually every animal that actively pursues moving objects as a food source. Even less active pursuits (for example, a hummingbird obtaining nectar from a flower) require excellent depth perception. The second part of this activity will show students that using both eyes together affords better depth perception than using one eye alone.

Part 2

REQUIREMENTS

Time

15-20 minutes

Materials

- One pencil per team
- One copy of figure 5.9, page 112, per team
- Overhead transparency of figure 5.9
- Overhead projector

Grouping

Teams of two students

DIRECTIONS

1. Discuss vision with students. Remind them of the first part of this activity when they learned about how each eye sees a different image. Now they will learn why seeing different images is important.

2. Have students sit in pairs on opposite sides of a desk so they face each other.

3. Show the overhead transparency of figure 5.9. Explain that student A must close one eye and place the pencil point in the circle his or her partner, student B, designates. Each time it is done correctly, student A gets one point. The two students will take turns.

4. Demonstrate the game on the overhead. Select a student from the class and give the student a sharp pencil. Have the student stand so the overhead transparency of figure 5.9 is at eye level. Ask the student (with both eyes open and holding the pencil horizontally) to point the pencil to circle 6 on the transparency. The student should be able to do so easily. Now ask for a volunteer to repeat the experiment. This time ask the student to do so with only one eye open. The second student should be less successful. Ask the second student to describe to the class what seemed to be the problem.

5. Give each pair of students one pencil and a copy of figure 5.9.

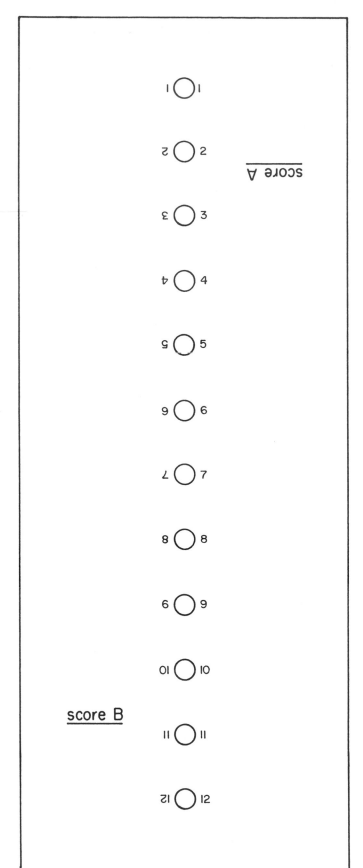

Fig. 5.9. Binocular vision activity score card.

6. Ask students to duplicate the student demonstration. Place figure 5.9 on the desk, with circle 1 closest to student A. Student B should select a circle by number and ask student A to use the pencil to point to that circle with one eye closed. If student A places the pencil on the correct circle, he or she receives one point.

7. Continue the process, reversing the roles of students A and B after each attempt.

8. Have the students keep score. After five attempts per student, the one with the most correct points wins.

9. Have students repeat the entire process with both eyes open. Scores from this round should convince students that depth perception is much more reliable with both eyes open. Discuss results with the class. Information from one eye provides basic information about what can be seen. Images from both eyes are necessary to provide a complete picture, including accurate depth perception.

ACTIVITY: IS A WHOLE BUNCH BETTER THAN TWO?

This activity introduces students to the unique way some animals see. Some specialized equipment will be necessary so that students can duplicate multiple-image visual systems. Many animals have what is known as a compound eye. A housefly needs to worry more about something catching it than it does about obtaining its food. Its visual system must detect changes in light caused by objects moving around it, such as a person's hand. In this instance, many small eyes are better than one large eye on each side. Flies have thousands of small eyes, each individually providing the brain with only a small picture but together seeing a very broad area. Each small eye is called a *facet*, and these facets are clustered into two large areas on either side of the head called the *compound eyes*. Flies are not the only creatures with multiple visual systems: dragonflies have 28,000 facets in their eyes (Tinbergen, 53, 1965), and the common scallop has 32 blue eyes (Engel, 128, 1961).

REQUIREMENTS

Time

One 45-minute period

Materials

- Not required but recommended for better student visualization and "WOW, this is neat" is a multiple-image fresnel lens (one source is Edmund Scientific Company, Barrington, New Jersey, 1-609-573-6270, at a cost of $7.75 in March 1994).

- Kaleidoscope

- One of the following per student:
  - —Sheet of blank paper
  - —Ruler
  - —Pencil and eraser
  - —Colored pencils, crayons, or markers

Grouping

Individuals

DIRECTIONS

1. Ask students to look through the fresnel lens and kaleidoscope so that they become familiar with the concept of seeing multiple images.

2. Discuss how animals with compound eyes might have an advantage (they have a wider field of vision to see enemies coming).

3. Tell students they will be drawing a picture of what an object looks like when seen through a compound eye. Distribute the drawing materials, ruler, and paper to the students.

4. Ask students to draw a grid on the sheet of paper. It should be 4 spaces across and 4 spaces up: a total of 16 spaces. Have students make each grid space 2-x-2 inches.

5. Ask students to select an object in the classroom to draw. They will draw the same object in each of the 16 spaces. After all the drawings are completed, the students should color them. Discuss with students how they should be colored: all the same color or different colors? Through a compound eye, multiple images are all the same; the images should therefore all be the same color.

6. Display student work around the room and have students share thoughts behind the drawing. This will reinforce the concepts of the compound eye and multiple images.

EXTENSIONS

An experiment from *101 Science Tricks: Fun Experiments with Everyday Materials* by Roy Richards (1991, 11) shows students how to construct their own kaleidoscopes. Kaleidoscopes are a good way to experience the multiple images of a compound eye.

Animal masks are usually simple, flat masks that cover the faces of the children wearing them. They may look cute, but unfortunately, they do not accurately portray the visual system of the animal they represent; animals do not always see forward from their faces the way humans do. Carnivores—whether reptiles, mammals, or birds—are usually predators and have eyes facing forward. Their overlapping, binocular vision provides the excellent depth perception that hunting animals require to target their next meal, whether that meal is fleeing through the jungle ahead of a tiger or zigzagging across a field below a diving hawk.

Herbivores are prey animals. It might seem, at first, that acute sight is unnecessary for prey animals. After all, they do not require a sophisticated visual system to "target" blades of grass or leaves of trees. Prey animals, however, are not worried about finding a next meal; they are worried about being a next meal. The animal is less concerned with what is directly ahead of it than what might be lurking off to the side or behind it. Because prey animals have eyes located on the sides of the head, they can better survey the immediate environment for potential predators. As the head moves from side to side, the eyes can detect even minimal movement, and the animal can react accordingly, sprinting to safety or assuming a defensive posture.

ACTIVITY: SEE LIKE A DINOSAUR

In this activity students will be duplicating predator and prey visual systems using large paper bags. The intent is not to create a realistic dinosaur head but to model the appropriate visual system. Headpieces can be colored and decorated, but the intent is not to create a detailed *Triceratops* head.

REQUIREMENTS

Time

45-90 minutes; possibly time at home or in an art class

Materials (for each student)

- One large paper supermarket bag
- Scissors
- Colored pencils, markers, paint, or crayons to decorate bag
- Books about dinosaurs and modern animals
- Large student-safe indoor or outdoor area
- Overhead projector
- Transparency of figure 5.10, page 116

Grouping

Individuals and whole class

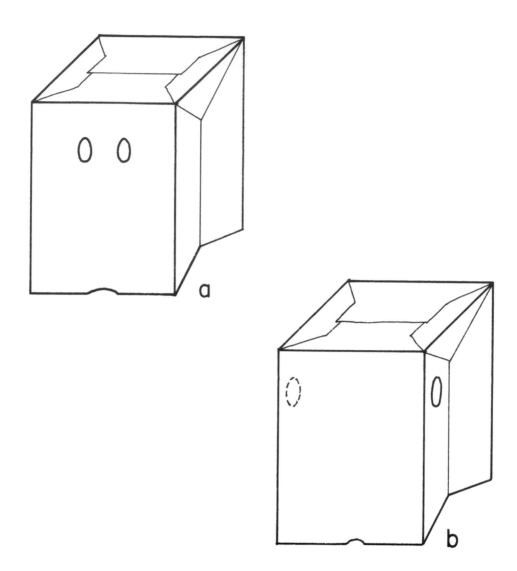

Fig. 5.10. Predator and prey headpieces, with eyehole placements. Figure 5.10a shows a predator headpiece, and figure 5.10b shows a prey animal headpiece.

DIRECTIONS

1. Discuss animal eye placement with students. Talk about what kinds of things a particular animal needs to see. Does it need merely to be aware of another animal's movements, or does it need to have more definitive information for targeting?

2. Distribute materials to students. The paper bags will be used to make predator and prey headpieces as shown in figure 5.10.

3. Explain that predator headpieces will have eyeholes cut in the front. This gives predators a narrower field of view but also permits better depth perception. To see its surroundings, a predator must turn its head.

4. Explain that prey headpieces will have eyeholes cut toward the front of the sides of the bag, expanding the field of view but sacrificing depth perception. To look forward or backward, the prey must turn its head.

5. Have at least one sample of each headpiece style already cut out. These will serve as models that students can try on to fine-tune the placement of the eyeholes on their own headpieces (the eyeholes may need to be closer together on some predator headpieces and more toward the front on some prey headpieces).

6. Once the students have cut out the eyeholes, they can decorate their headpieces to resemble their favorite dinosaur predator or prey (living animals may also be represented).

7. Once all the headpieces are completed, take the class to the predetermined play area. Here students will experience the virtues of the two types of visual systems.

8. Scatter easily findable objects around the area you have selected. Provide enough objects so that each student will have some success. Explain to students that the items they are looking for are food and they must try to recover as much as possible. Then turn them loose. See how many items can be retrieved in a predetermined time (approximately two to four minutes, depending upon the size of the area and number of students). Predators, with superior forward vision and depth perception, should be able to recover far more than prey. Prey might be able to see more objects at a distance, but they will have a harder time actually retrieving the items. Have students switch roles so they can each experience both visual systems. Make a contest out of it and see who finds the most objects in the shortest time.

9. Let students play "Dinotag." Have predator animals try to sneak up on prey animals. Have students playing both roles pay close attention to how they see the other animals. Once again, have students switch roles to encourage appreciation of the respective visual systems.

10. When Steps 8 and 9 are completed, ask students to write a short paragraph about whether they would rather be predator or prey, and why.

EXTENSIONS

This activity can be done in connection with an art class, where elaborate papier-mâché masks can be made. The only constraint is that eye placement must be correct for the animal being modeled.

REFERENCES

Engel, Leonard. 1961. *The Sea.* New York: Time-Life Books.

Ommanney, F. D. 1963. *The Fishes.* New York: Time-Life Books.

Richards, Roy. 1991. *101 Science Tricks: Fun Experiments with Everyday Materials.* New York: Sterling.

Tinbergen, Niko. 1965. *Animal Behavior.* New York: Time-Life Books.

Walpole, Brenda. 1988. *175 Science Experiments to Amuse and Amaze Your Friends.* New York: Random House.

6

Tails, Legs, Feet, Arms, and Hands

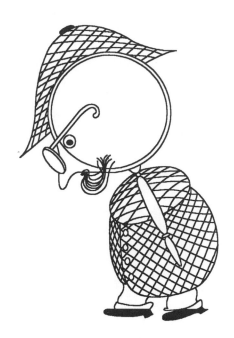

INTRODUCTION

What most helped dinosaurs achieve dominance of the planet was their structure, not their size. The most important aspect of their structure was the relationship between the legs and the rest of the body. Another important structural element was the tail, which provided balance and support and in some cases could be used as a weapon.

Early interpretations of dinosaurs show animals so cumbersome that they are barely able to support themselves. Large dinosaurs like apatosaurs and brachiosaurs were depicted wading in deep water, which provided the necessary buoyancy to help the animal support its own weight. Dinosaurs are classified as reptiles, and because of this, early representations structure dinosaur legs and tails in a reptilian stance: the legs stick out to the side, and the tails drag along the ground behind, much like a lizard. However, as investigators like Jack Horner and Robert Bakker challenged the early anatomical and behavioral interpretations and new evidence from trackways was interpreted by paleontologists like Martin Lockley, a new picture of dinosaurs emerged.

Based upon skeletal information only, some early European interpretations of dinosaur structure generated bizarre-looking animals with unlikely walking postures (see fig. 6.1, p. 120).

Figure 6.1a shows an early European interpretation of *Diplodocus*; figure 6.1b shows a modern American interpretation modified from Desmond. Studies of trackways combined with skeletal data revealed that interpretations such as that shown in figure 6.1a were unlikely. If such an assembly were correct, the animal's footprints would be far apart and its tail would leave drag marks on the ground.

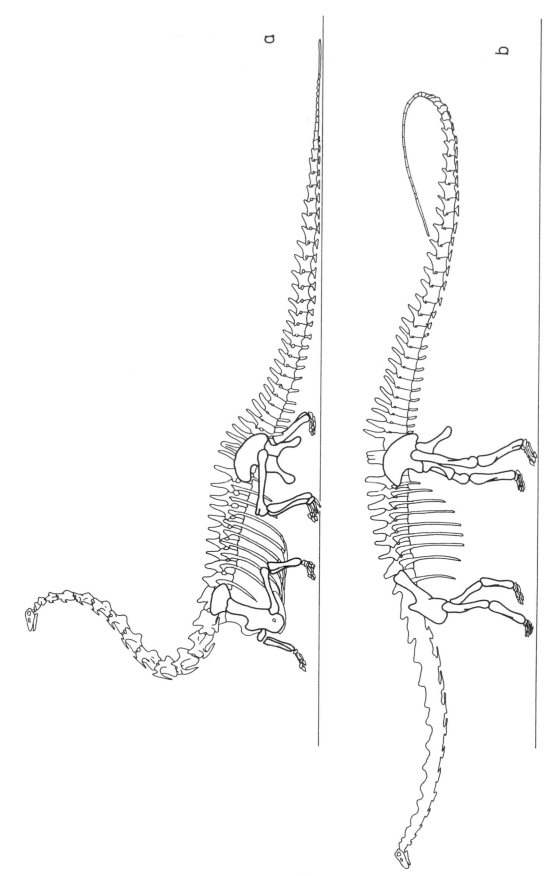

a

b

Fig. 6.1. A set of dinosaur bones reassembled into two different skeletal configurations (shown with hips and shoulders aligned).

Trackways reveal that neither is the case. Figure 6.1b is an American interpretation of the same set of bones, based on both body- and trace-fossil data. Although scientists generally agree that dinosaurs benefited from having legs directly beneath their bodies, Sylvia J. Czerkas and Stephen A. Czerkas (1991, 212) believe they were probably both bow-legged and pigeon-toed.

Recent interpretations (not unanimously agreed upon within the scientific community) show active, agile dinosaurs, often moving large distances at reasonable speeds, standing on hind legs to reach up into higher trees (with additional support provided by the tail), and moving in large groups (much like modern elephant herds).

ACTIVITY: WHICH IS EASIER?

In this activity, students will duplicate the walking posture of both dinosaurs and nondinosaurian reptiles such as lizards. On the day preceding the activity, you might want to suggest to students that they wear jeans or something other than their best clothing.

This is a fun activity to do outdoors in a grassy area. The whole class can race, lizard-style or dinosaur-style. Students with light-colored pants might be warned about grass stains.

REQUIREMENTS

Time

5-10 minutes

Materials

- Transparency of figure 6.2, page 122

- Overhead projector

Grouping

Whole class

DIRECTIONS

1. Show students transparency of figure 6.2. Explain the following significant differences between the walking posture of a dinosaur and that of a nondinosaurian reptile such as a lizard:

   a. The legs of dinosaurs are positioned under their bodies *not* out to the sides.

   b. As dinosaurs walked, their legs were able to swing freely from front to back, much like human legs; lizards must swing their bodies from side to side to walk.

   c. Dinosaurs walked up on their fingertips and toes; lizards walk with their hands and feet flat on the ground.

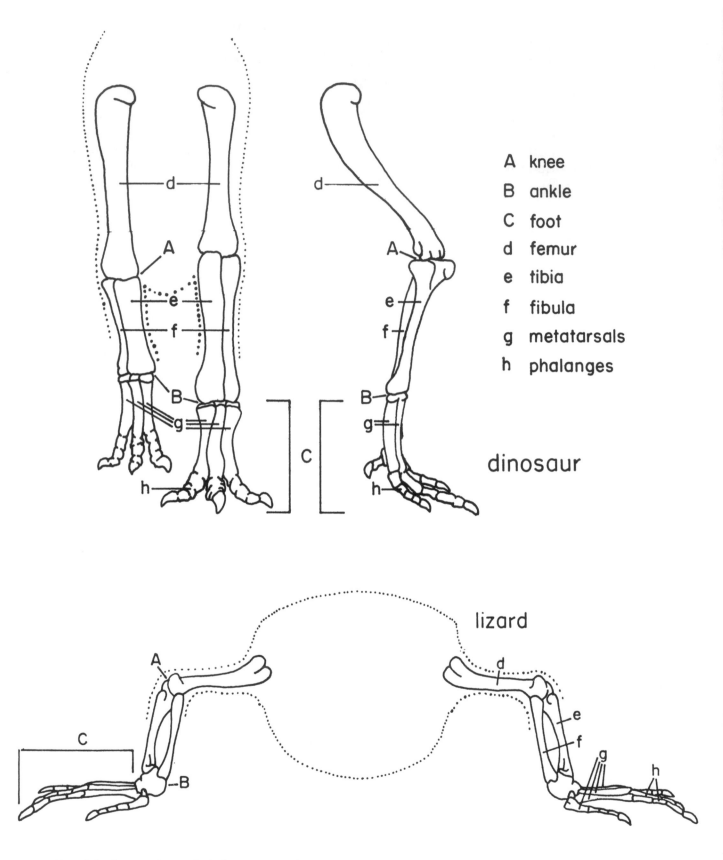

A knee
B ankle
C foot
d femur
e tibia
f fibula
g metatarsals
h phalanges

dinosaur

lizard

Fig. 6.2. Comparison of skeleton and posture of dinosaurs (top) and nondinosaurian reptiles such as lizards (bottom).

2. Tell students they will be duplicating the walking posture of both animals and deciding which is more efficient. Ask them to remember how each gait feels, because afterward they will be writing about it.

3. Ask students to get on the floor in a crawling position.

4. Once students have assumed the crawling position, have them bend their elbows so that their upper arms are parallel to the floor (they will be duplicating the position of the nondinosaurian reptile in fig. 6.2). Their hands should be slightly farther from their bodies than their elbows are, with palms flat on the floor and fingers pointed away from their bodies. They will probably have to lower their torso to accomplish this. Explain to students that they are now in a lizardlike, reptilian posture.

5. Ask students to walk forward. They should notice that it is uncomfortable and awkward and that they move slowly and must swing their bodies from side to side to walk.

6. Have students return to their original crawling position. Arms should be directly below their shoulders and extended fully (as in the dinosaurian posture in figure 6.2). They should stretch out their fingers so that their weight is supported on their fingertips.

7. Ask students to walk forward. As they walk in this position, they should be aware of how much more quickly they can move and how much more comfortable it is.

8. Ask students to return to their seats and describe the differences in a paragraph. Several students might want to read their paragraphs aloud to the class. You might also ask them to draw a picture of each posture.

EXTENSIONS

To simulate the walking posture of a bipedal dinosaur, students should stand on the balls of their feet with their legs slightly bent. As they walk in this manner, they are duplicating the way *Tyrannosaurus* walked.

TAKE A LOOK AT TAILS

Apparently, all dinosaurs had tails. A 60-foot *Diplodocus* could have had a tail more than 20 feet long. Surprisingly, however, tail marks are never found with dinosaur tracks. Lizard and turtle tracks, for example, consist of two parallel sets of footprints with a tail drag mark between them (see fig. 6.3, p. 124); dinosaur tracks show footprints only, no tail marks. As Martin Lockley (1991, 174) observes, "energetically speaking, it is difficult to drag a tail, and tough on the tail as well." Dinosaurs are not alone. The tails of many large African cats, such as the lion and cheetah, are long enough to trail along the ground as the animal walks, yet they do not.

If all dinosaurs had tails, what, then, did they use them for? Depending on the dinosaur, the tail had a variety of uses, among them counterbalance (tyrannosaurs and *Deinonychus*), defense (stegosaurs, ankylosaurs, and sauropods used the whiplike motion of their tails to club enemies), and support while the animal reared up on hind legs to feed in trees (stegosaurs and sauropods).

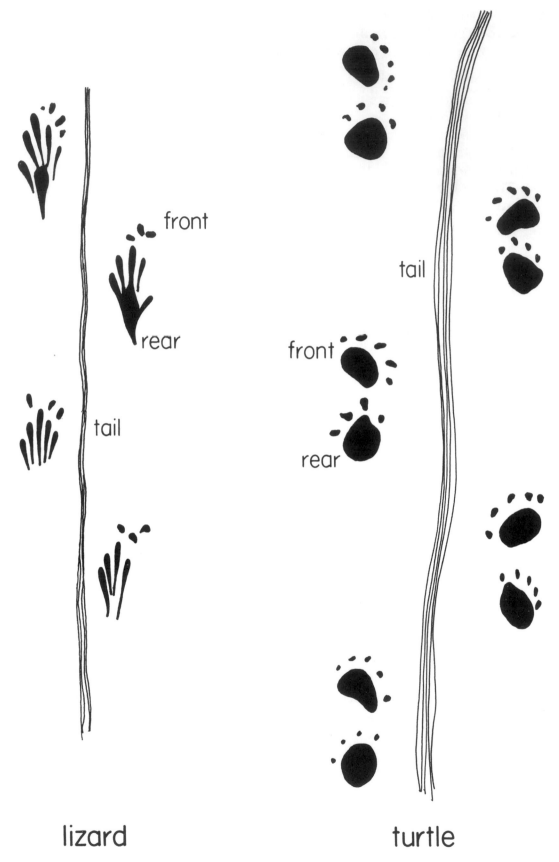

lizard

turtle

Fig. 6.3. Lizard and turtle tracks with tail drag marks.

ACTIVITY: TALL TAIL TALES

Like dinosaurs, animals that exist today use their tails in a variety of ways:

Kangaroos, big cats—tails provide balance as the animals run.

Kangaroos—tails provide balance as the animals sit up on hind legs.

Alligators, crocodiles, whales, fish—tails help propel the animals through the water.

Birds—tails help the animals slow down when landing and provide a flight control surface; they are used as part of ritual or mating displays.

Gila monsters—tails provide storage space for food.

Squirrels (some)—tails help shade their bodies from the sun.

Cattle, horse, zebra—tails help keep insects away.

Beavers—tails are used to sound alarm by smacking on water's surface.

Monkeys—long tails help monkeys swing through trees (New World only).

Electric eels—tails produce electrical charges to stun prey.

Anteaters—tails help provide warmth when wrapped around the body.

Tree-dwelling boas—tails anchor body to tree while animal attacks prey.

Note: students will be interested to know that humans have a vestigial tail (the coccyx, or tailbone) at the base of the spine.

A zoo or library visit focusing on tails will clearly demonstrate the many different ways animals use their tails. Students will consider whether the dinosaurs might have used their tails in similar ways.

REQUIREMENTS

Time

One library, aquarium, or zoo visit, or a short time each week if you choose to make this a multiweek unit

Materials

• Pencil and paper for notes in the library or on field trip

Grouping

Individuals

DIRECTIONS

1. Once students have been introduced to the many ways animals use their tails, take them on a field trip to a zoo or aquarium. If a field trip is impractical, substitute a visit to the library.

2. Ask students to select an animal, observe how it uses its tail under different circumstances (walking, running, sitting), then draw a picture of the tail during one or more of these activities and write an essay describing how the tail was used by the animal. Age and skill level of the students will dictate the length of the essay.

3. Prior to the trip, prepare a table to be completed during the zoo visit. Column headings might include Animal Name, Number of Legs, Tail Length (Short or Long), Habitat, Tail Uses.

4. For closure, draw conclusions as a class about different groups of animals (for example, do animals that live in trees tend to have long tails?).

EXTENSIONS

This activity can also be tied to student pets.

ACTIVITY: SIMPLE TAIL MODEL

This activity can be done as a quick classroom demonstration or whole-group activity and can give students an idea of how the shape of the vertebrae that constitute the tail can provide clues as to how the tail was used.

REQUIREMENTS

Time

15-30 minutes (depends on whether this is done as a demonstration or whole-group activity)

Materials

- Transparency of figure 6.4
- Overhead projector
- One piece of cardboard (approximately the size of a 12" ruler) per student
- One thin marker or colored pencil per student (if done as whole-group activity)

Grouping

If demonstration, whole class; if whole-group activity, individuals

DIRECTIONS

1. Discuss with the class how an animal might move its tail, particularly if it has a long tail like *Diplodocus*. It might move its tail from side to side (like alligators and fish do) or up and down (like beavers or whales do). Ask how the tail shapes of these various animals differ.

2. Distribute the cut pieces of cardboard to each student. Tell students the cardboard is like the tail of an animal.

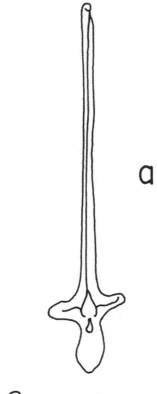

Ouranosaurus

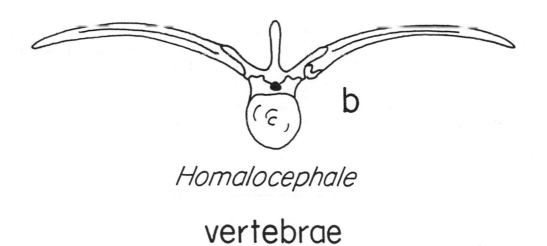

Homalocephale

vertebrae

Fig. 6.4. Two different types of caudal vertebrae.

3. Have students hold one short end of the cardboard strip so that the cardboard strip is vertical and pointing away from the boy. It is now similar to a tail with vertebrae as shown in figure 6.4a. Ask students whether the cardboard can bend up and down (the answer should be no). Have them try it. Next, ask them whether the strip will bend from side to side. It should do this easily. In this position, the strip is like the tail of a fish, an alligator, or *Ouranosuarus*.

4. Now have the students hold the short end of the strip so it is horizontal or flat and still pointing away from the body. The vertebrae would now be similar to figure 6.4b. Can it bend side to side now? The answer should be no. Now ask them to make it bend up and down. It should do so easily. It is now moving like the tail of a whale, beaver, or *Homalocephale*.

JUST LOOK AT THOSE HANDS AND LEGS!

The reasons people can congratulate each other with "high fives" are that (1) our arms can stretch upward and (2) we have five fingers on each hand. As Robert Bakker is fond of demonstrating, a *Tyrannosaurus rex* could only offer a "low two": its arms could not stretch above its head, and it only had two fingers on each hand. Is there anything special about having five digits? Do we always use all five? Do other animals also have five digits? The following activity will explore the structure of arms and hands.

ACTIVITY: APPENDAGES, HOW DO THEY COMPARE?

To understand arms and hands, we need a frame of reference. Two distinct animal arms are readily available for study. The first is conveniently attached to our shoulders; the second is less readily accessible but tastes considerably better. Once upon a time, in Buffalo, New York, a restaurant owner was looking for a quick snack to serve with drinks. A large bag of frozen *Gallus* (common chicken) wings was defrosted, sautéed with butter and hot pepper, and the spicy chicken wing was born.

Chicken wings and human arms have much in common:

1. Both have two major joints: the elbow and wrist.
2. Both have one bone in the upper arm.
3. Both have two bones in the lower arm.
4. Both have fingers.

REQUIREMENTS

Time

30-45 minutes

Materials

- One cooked chicken wing per student. KEEP ALL THREE PIECES OF THE WING INTACT! DO NOT SEPARATE THEM. Chicken wings are readily available, and a "classroom set" should be inexpensive. They can be cooked ahead of time, cooked in class, or purchased cooked; they can be prepared hot and spicy, or breaded and deep-fried. Because of the mess, barbecue sauce is not recommended.

- Plenty of paper towels

- Paper plate for each student

- Pencil and paper for each student

- Transparency of figure 6.5, page 130

- Overhead projector

Grouping

Individuals

DIRECTIONS

1. Explain to students that they will be comparing the arms of two different animals: one is cooked and the other is raw—in fact, still living! Students will be eating the cooked arm, drawing a picture of the bones inside, and then comparing it to the "raw" arm.

2. Distribute one paper towel and one paper plate to each student.

3. Tell students (you might want to put the sequence on the board or overhead) that when they get the cooked arm, they are to do the following:

   a. look carefully to see how the parts are arranged,

   b. remove the meat from the bones by eating or pulling it off,

   c. arrange the bones on the plate in their original configuration, and

   d. clean their hands, get pencil and paper, and then draw a picture of the bones.

4. Have extra paper towels handy.

5. Show figure 6.5 on the overhead. Explain to students that the figure shows the arm bones of a dinosaur (top) and a pigeon (bottom). Point out the similarities to the chicken wing:

   a. All have two major joints, the wrist and the elbow.

   b. All have one bone (the humerus) in the upper arm.

   c. All have two bones (the radius and the ulna) in the lower arm.

   d. All have three fingers—the thumb (I), the first finger (II), and the second finger (III). In the pigeon, fingers II and III have fused. (Bakker, 1994)

6. Ask students to compare figure 6.5 to their chicken wing drawings and label the similar parts they find.

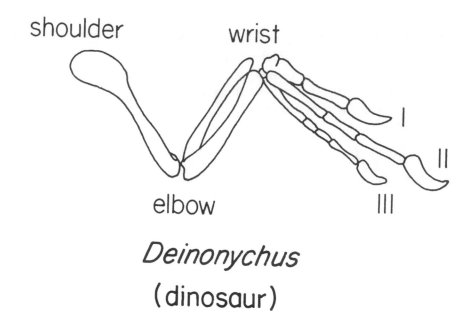

shoulder   wrist

I

II

III

elbow

Deinonychus

(dinosaur)

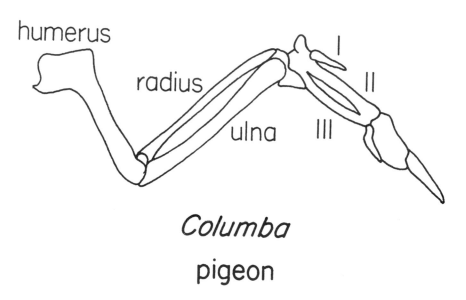

humerus

I

radius

II

ulna

III

Columba

pigeon

Fig. 6.5. Comparison between the arm bones of a dinosaur and a pigeon.

7. Ask students to look at their own arms and hands. How do they compare with those of the chicken? (People have five fingers; otherwise, they are the same.)

EXTENSIONS

As part of a zoo or museum visit, have students focus on arms, legs, and hands of other animals. Both legs and arms have one bone in the upper section (in the leg, it is the femur) and two bones in the lower section (in the leg, they are the tibia and fibula). "Hands" often have fewer than five digits. Ask students to sketch the hands and feet of different animals and label the fingers or toes. The thumb is I, and fingers are numbered II, III, IV, and V as they move away from the thumb. This might be a good time to introduce students to Roman numerals if they are unfamiliar with them.

ACTIVITY: LET'S BUILDASAUR

Constructing a simplified model of a dinosaur helps students to better understand the structural relationships between different types of legs and the body. Students will assemble dinosaur bodies with lizard legs and dinosaur legs. Models are designed to be generic but can be enhanced to represent a student's favorite animal. A week or so prior to the activity, students should be reminded to bring materials (especially the cardboard tube) to class.

REQUIREMENTS

Time

45-60 minutes; longer if artwork is included (activity can be done in two sessions)

Materials

- For each student:
  —Cardboard tube (from aluminum foil, plastic wrap, paper towel, or toilet paper)
  —White glue
  —Tape
  —Scissors
  —Old newspapers
  —Figures 6.6 and 6.7, pages 133 and 134, preferably copied onto card stock
  —Two sheets of blank 8½-x-11-inch paper
  —Markers, crayons, paints, or colored pencils

- For the teacher:
  —Overhead projector
  —Transparencies of figures 6.6-6.8, pages 133-135

Grouping

Individuals

DIRECTIONS

1. Show students overhead transparencies of figures 6.6 and 6.7. Remind them of the structural differences between lizards and dinosaurs: lizard legs stick out to the side, whereas dinosaur legs are positioned beneath the body; lizards walk with feet flat on the ground and feet angled sideways, whereas dinosaurs walk on their toes with feet pointed straight ahead; lizards' bodies are closer to the ground.

2. Ask students to spread newspapers on each desk to make cleanup easier (this is particularly important if they will be using glue and paints).

3. Distribute scissors, glue, tape, coloring materials, and figure 6.6 to each student.

4. Ask students to write their names on each item to be assembled. Have students select a color scheme and color the legs and body tube now. (No one knows what color skin dinosaurs had, so students should be free to use their imaginations. Color schemes of animals alive today can be used as models.)

5. Have students cut out two pairs of lizard legs (fig. 6.6).

6. Have students assemble the two pairs of legs, using the following directions: cut along the solid lines and fold along the dotted lines. Put glue or tape on tab A and attach to back of the outer leg. Tape shoulder tabs down as appropriate. (Note: tape is more convenient and cleaner; glue is more permanent but messier and requires waiting time for it to dry.)

7. Once the pairs of legs are assembled, have students place their tube in the semicircular depressions at the top. Place (do not glue) one leg assembly approximately one inch (2.5 centimeters) from each end of the tube (see fig. 6.8). Students should note the position of the body: low to the ground, legs to the side, and feet flat on the ground. Tell students they have built a body with lizardlike legs.

8. Give each student the two pieces of blank paper. Have students roll sheets into cones to make a neck and tail. Cones can be rolled into different lengths and placed (do not glue) inside the body tube (see fig. 6.8 for approximate angles). Bend down the tip of the neck to make a head. Color the two cones to match the body. Because this is a lizardlike model, the tail should touch the ground.

9. Distribute figure 6.7 and repeat Steps 5-8. Dinosaur tails should not drag on the ground.

10. Review the completed models with students and ask them to describe the differences.

11. Save the models for the next activity.

(Text continues on page 136.)

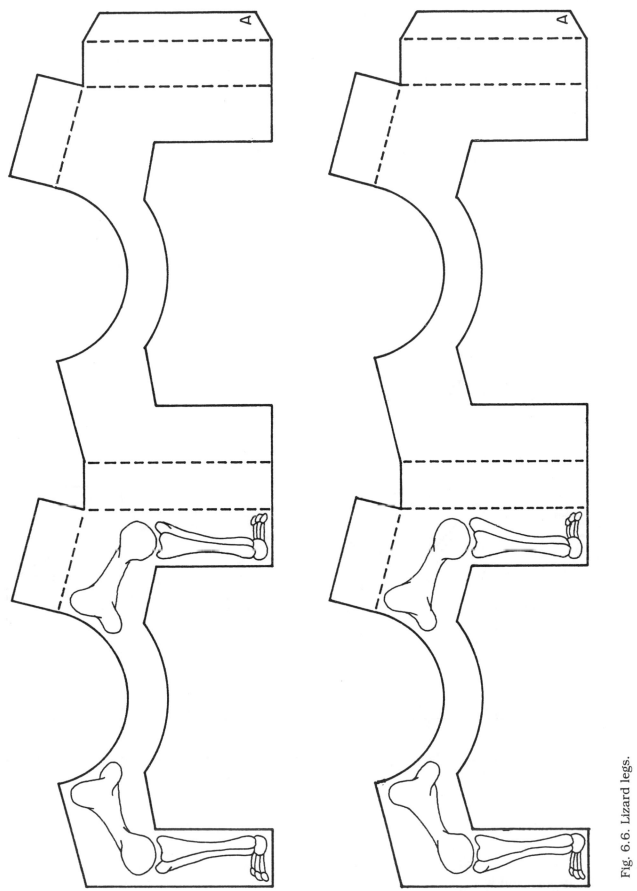

Fig. 6.6. Lizard legs.

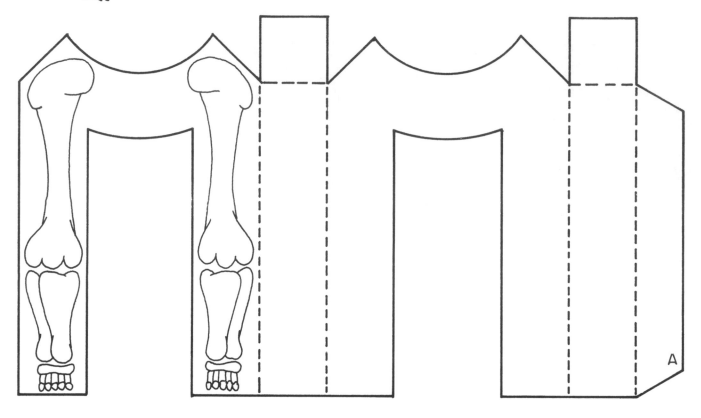

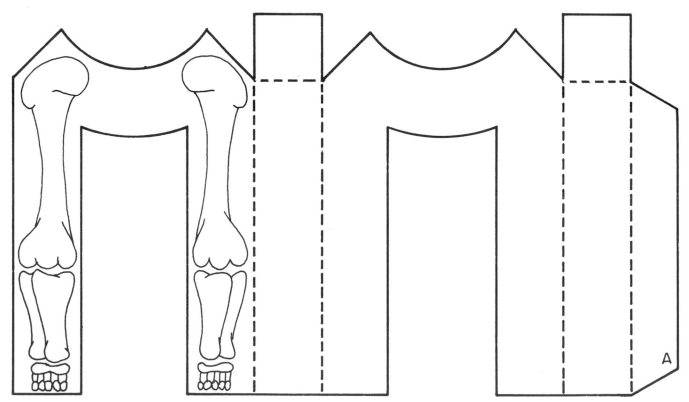

Fig. 6.7. Long dinosaur legs.

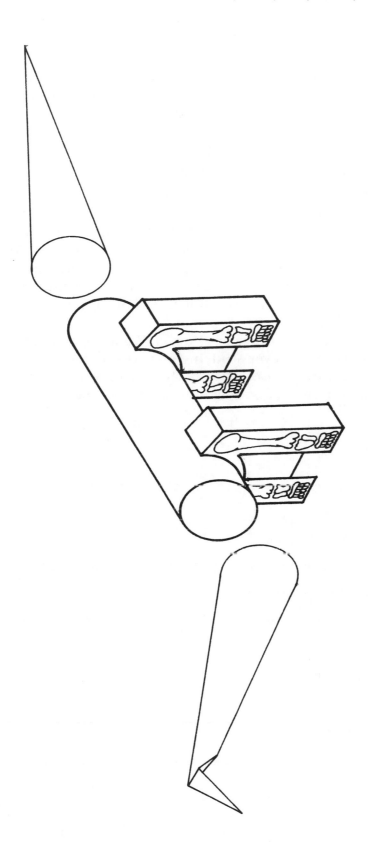

Fig. 6.8. Assembly diagram for dinosaur models.

ACTIVITY: LEGS COME IN PAIRS

Observation is a critical skill that students must develop. As students examine dinosaurs, they should become aware that legs of quadrupedal dinosaurs are not always the same. There are three possible combinations:

1. front and rear legs of the same height (apatosaurs),
2. front legs shorter than rear legs (stegosaurs),
3. front legs taller than rear legs (brachiosaurs).

Each of these arrangements provides certain advantages. Two pairs of legs of the same height allow the animal to move easily with a uniform gait. Animals with short front legs (like stegosaurs) may have had the ability to stand up on their larger rear legs, allowing them to reach higher into trees for food. Animals with longer front legs (the brachiosaurs) could also reach food supplies that were inaccessible to other animals.

This activity can be done in a library or at a zoo. We feel that studying animals in a zoo offers obvious advantages over studying pictures on a page. It is important for students to see live animals. Appreciation of their size, beauty, and motion may ultimately determine the survival of both captive and wild species.

REQUIREMENTS

Time

Continuous with other activities or individual library visits

Materials

- Supplies from "Let's Buildasaur" activity
- Dinosaur books and articles from library or student sources
- Paper and pencil for each student
- Copies of figures 6.9 and 6.10, pages 138 and 139, for each student
- Overhead projector
- Transparencies of figures 6.9 and 6.10

Grouping

Individuals or small groups

DIRECTIONS

1. Introduce students to different kinds of dinosaur leg arrangements by showing figure 6.10. Discuss the fact that both dinosaurs and animals alive today have legs that allow them to do different things. For instance, if people had legs of a different size or configuration, it might not be possible to do ballet or play baseball. Animal legs allow them to do certain special things as well.

2. Distribute figure 6.9 to students and have them color and assemble it the same way as in steps 5-8 of "Let's Buildasaur."

3. While showing the transparency of figure 6.10, have students assemble and disassemble various dinosaur models using combinations of the short and long pairs of legs to match the overhead.

4. Discuss the advantages or disadvantages of different leg heights for various animals.

5. As an introduction to the library or zoo visit, ask students to think about what different kinds of legs can do: they can help animals run fast, dig in the ground, reach food, or jump.

6. Ask students to look though library books or look carefully at the zoo animals to see how the legs help the animals do special things. For instance, kangaroo legs help the animals jump; giraffe legs allow the animal to reach food on high branches; cheetah legs allow the animal to run fast.

7. Distribute figure 6.11, page 140, to students. Have students complete the table during the field trip to the zoo or during the library research. Under the column headings "Front" and "Back" the students should fill in "S" for short and "T" for tall. If leg heights are the same, students should place a check under "Same."

8. After returning from the library or zoo, have the class share observations and ideas by listing animals and observations about their legs on the board.

(Text continues on page 141.)

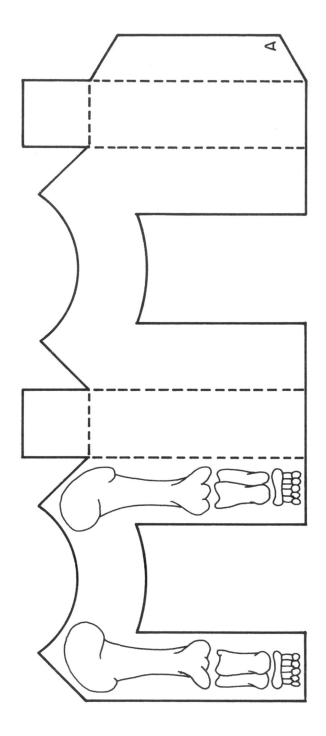

Fig. 6.9. Short dinosaur legs.

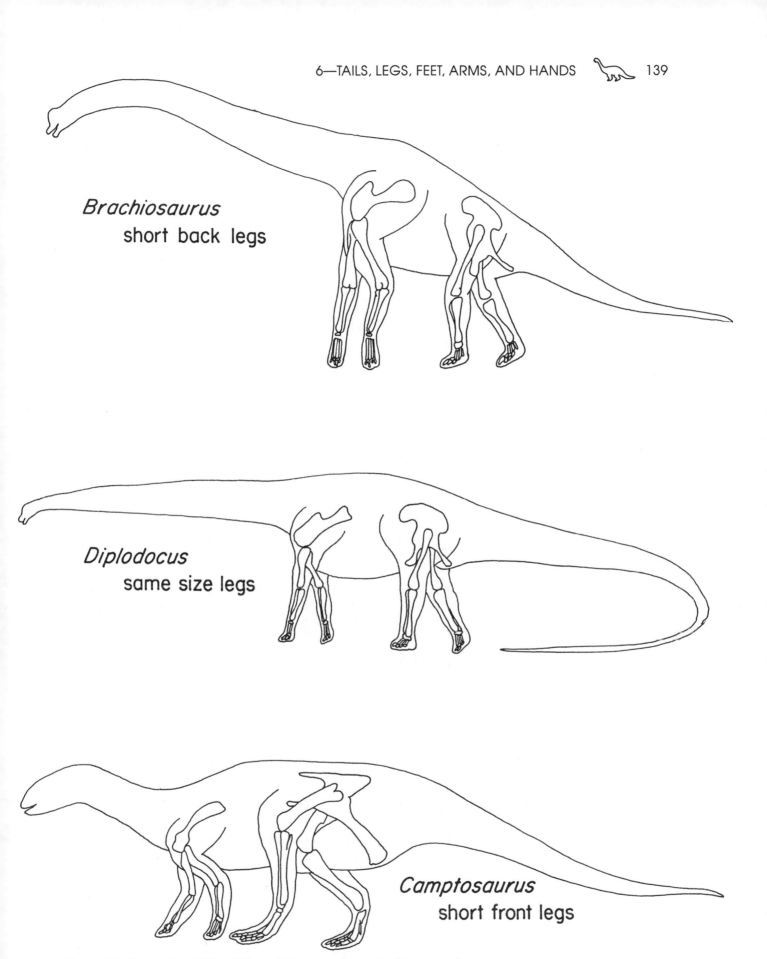

Brachiosaurus
short back legs

Diplodocus
same size legs

Camptosaurus
short front legs

Fig. 6.10. Examples of the different leg arrangements dinosaurs have.

Animal Name	Front Short	Back Short	Same	What Animal Can Do

Name _____

Fig. 6.11. Zoo or research table.

REFERENCES

Bakker, Robert T. 1994. *Dr. Bob's Guide to Teaching Dino Science.* Chicago: World Book.

Czerkas, Sylvia J., and Stephen A. Czerkas. 1991. *Dinosaurs: A Global View.* New York: Mallard Press.

Desmond, Adrian J. 1976. *Hot Blooded Dinosaurs.* New York: Dial Press.

Lockley, Martin. 1991. *Tracking Dinosaurs.* Cambridge: Cambridge University Press.

SUGGESTED READING

Benton, Michael J. 1989. *On the Trail of the Dinosaurs*, New York: Crescent Books.

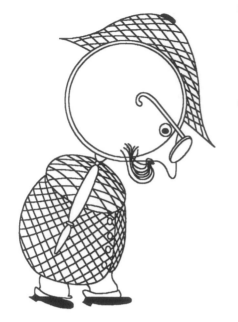

Tracks: They Make a Great Impression

INTRODUCTION

Each dinosaur left only one skeleton to become a fossil. If paleontologists are really lucky, they can recover most of it. By contrast, that same animal made millions of footprints during its lifetime. Skeletons provide clues about the weight and height of an animal, whether it was two- or four-legged, and whether it was a herbivore or a carnivore. More recent dinosaur investigations have focused on fossils created by animals while they were alive: footprints and trackways. Footprints and trackways are trace fossils that provide valuable information that skeletons cannot. They can help scientists answer questions such as the following: Did dinosaurs move across the earth as individuals or in herds? Did the animals migrate? How did the young behave during the migration? How fast did the animals move? Did dinosaurs drag their tails across the ground?

One of the most common questions that footprints and trackways can help answer is, How fast did dinosaurs move? By combining evidence such as hip heights and foot size from skeletons, distance between footprints at tracksites and observations of living animals (such as emus), paleontologists have been able to make educated guesses about dinosaur speeds. It is likely that most tracks represent dinosaurs as they walked (very large animals moved slightly slower than a human walks [one to three miles per hour, or approximately one meter per second]). Only rarely does a track seem to represent an animal as it ran. Based upon trackway evidence, R. McNeil Alexander (1989, 40-41) describes a running speed of 27 miles per hour (12 meters per second) for a two-legged dinosaur from Texas (of course, it wasn't Texas at the time). Such a speed is fast; it is faster than a human runs during the 100-yard or 100-meter dash. Based upon anatomical information, Robert T. Bakker (1986, 218) speculates that a *Tyrannosaurus* could have run at speeds of 45 miles per hour (20 meters per second). Some scientists believe Bakker's estimate is high.

ACTIVITY: WHAT WENT ON HERE?

While living in New Mexico in the late 1800s, Ernest Thompson studied animal tracks. Each night, he would sweep the dirt around his cabin smooth so any animals that passed by would leave a clear set of tracks that could be seen in the morning. Figure 7.1, page 144, is a copy of his drawing of the animal tracks he found one morning after a sleepless night of smelling skunk. He called it *The Skunk and the Unwise Bobcat*.

This activity will introduce students to the concept of interpreting trackways to tell a story, based upon knowledge about how two animals behave. Introduce the activity by describing what Thompson did outside his cabin and discuss with the class what bobcats and skunks are like (the former is a large, aggressive, and formidable hunter larger than a housecat; the latter is a small black mammal with white stripes down its back whose defense mechanism is a foul-smelling and blinding spray). Also explain that the bobcat is larger than the skunk.

During the initial discussions of trackway interpretation, it is important to let students know that as long as their interpretation does not violate what is known about the animal or what the tracks clearly indicate, it is valid. No one saw what actually happened, so there could be many possible explanations. However, in the skunk and bobcat scenario, it would, for example, be incorrect to say the skunk flew away.

REQUIREMENTS

Time

15-30 minutes (varies according to student response)

Materials

- Transparency of figure 7.1
- Writing materials for each student
- Overhead projector

Grouping

Pairs

DIRECTIONS

1. Project figure 7.1 and introduce the activity.

2. Explain to students that they will be interpreting the tracks of the skunk and the bobcat. They may discuss with their partners what the tracks represent, but they will each have to write down their own interpretation.

3. Pass out sheets of paper and have students write down their names. On the left side of the paper, instruct them to make a list, skipping lines, lettered A through K.

4. Have students interpret the tracks in figure 7.1, paying particular attention to what they think might have happened at each of the letter-designated sites on the transparency.

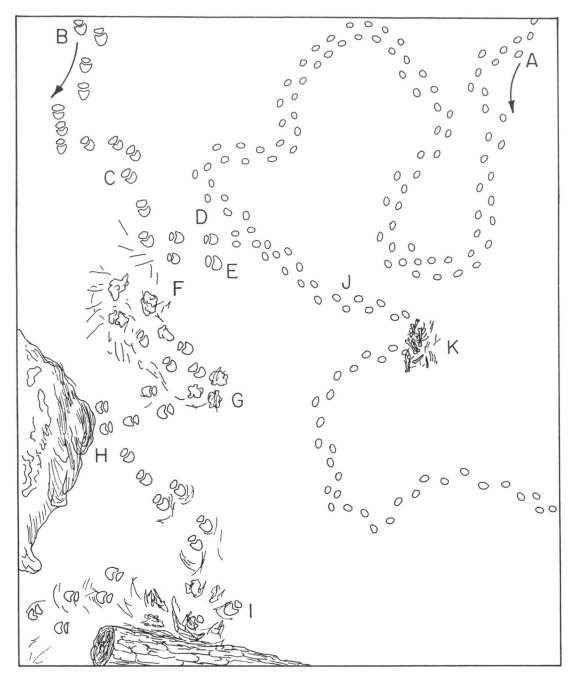

Fig. 7.1. Tracks from *The Skunk and the Unwise Bobcat.*

Fig. 7.1a. Skunk footprint of *The Skunk and the Unwise Bobcat.*

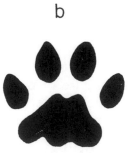

Fig. 7.1b. Bobcat footprint of *The Skunk and the Unwise Bobcat.*

5. Have students write a short description of the events next to the corresponding letter on their answer sheets.

6. At the conclusion of the writing activity, ask students to pass their work to the front of the class for collection.

7. Choose one of the interpretations to share with the class. Without reading the student's name, read and discuss the interpretation with students. Freely discuss what is valid and invalid about it. Discuss as many interpretations as you consider appropriate.

For your information, Thompson's interpretation follows. Remember, it's only his *interpretation*. He didn't see it either.

A. The skunk appears.

B. The bobcat appears.

C. The bobcat sees the skunk.

D. The bobcat chases the skunk, and the skunk says, "You'd better let me alone."

E. The skunk defends itself by spraying the bobcat.

F/G. The bobcat is rushing around, confused and hurting.

H. The cat bumps into a rock.

I. The cat bumps into a log and finally bounds away.

J. Meanwhile, the skunk walks away, thinking, "I told you so!"

K. The skunk finds some chicken remains, has a feast, then leaves the area.

EXTENSIONS

Ask each student to select two animals and create their trackways. Several sources are listed in references and additional reading at the end of this chapter. Each student should then exchange trackways with another student. Once trackways have been exchanged, students should interpret the trackways they received and guess the identity of the two animals that made them.

ACTIVITY: TIPTOE THROUGH THE CYCADS

In this activity students will duplicate the tracks of two dinosaurs: a bipedal, ostrichlike carnivore ("a" in all the figures) and a quadrupedal herbivore, probably a hadrosaur, also known as a duck-billed dinosaur ("b" in all the figures). Figures 7.2a and 7.2b, pages 146 and 147, show drawings of two dinosaur skeletons and the footprints these bipedal and quadrupedal animals make. These footprints were traced from the Cretaceous Dakota Sandstone on Dinosaur Ridge, approximately 17 miles west of downtown Denver. Figures 7.3a and 7.3b, page 148, show the same footprints, this time presented in a measured trackway.

(Text continues on page 149.)

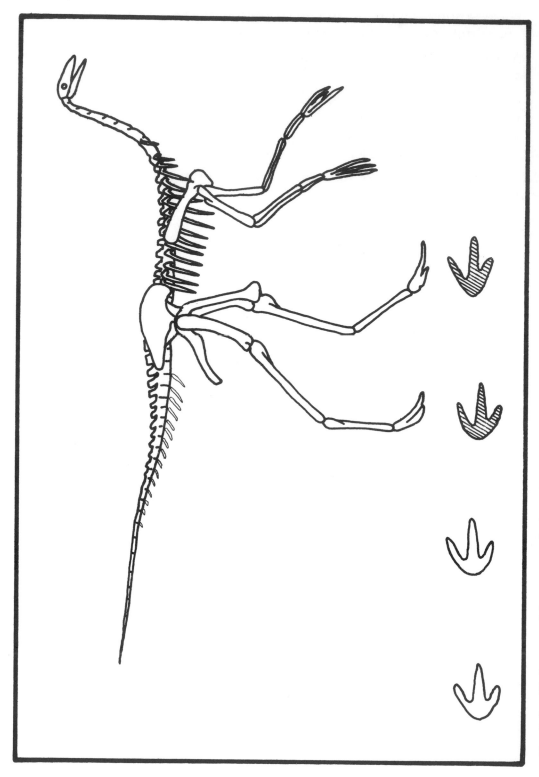

Fig. 7.2a. Skeleton and footprints of a bipedal, carnivorous dinosaur.

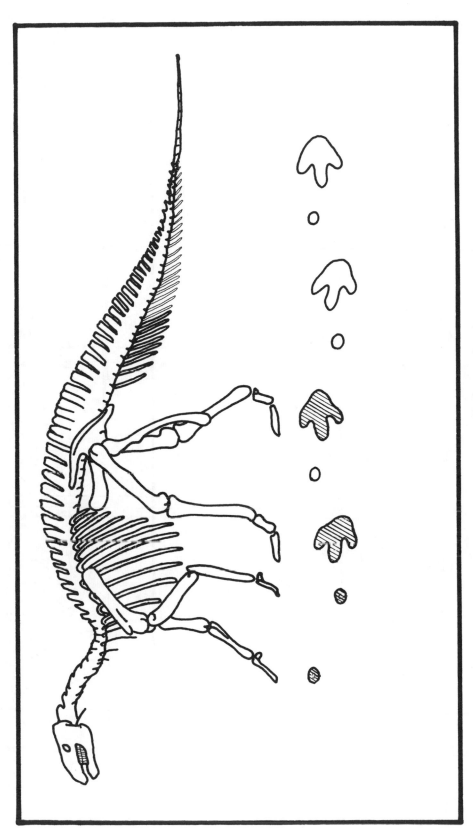

Fig. 7.2b. Skeleton and footprints of a quadrupedal, herbivorous dinosaur.

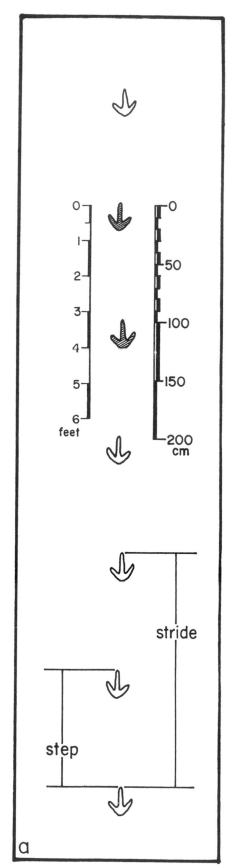

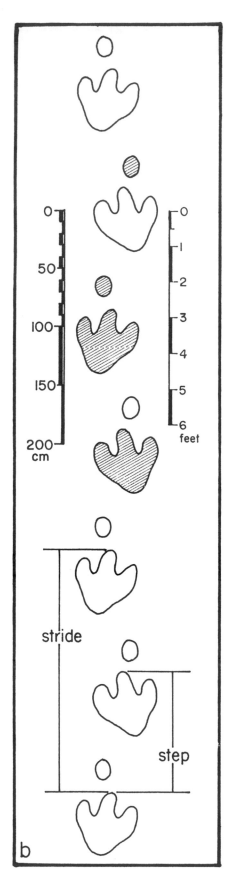

Fig. 7.3a. Measured trackway of
the carnivorous dinosaur.

Fig. 7.3b. Measured trackway of
the herbivorous dinosaur.

REQUIREMENTS

Time

Variable, depending upon how large a track is needed

Materials

- Stiff paper or cardboard patterns made from figures 7.4a and 7.4b, pages 150 and 151

- Pencils and erasers

- Scissors

- Paper from which to cut footprints

- Double-sided tape

- Transparencies of figures 7.2a, 7.2b, 7.3a, and 7.3b

Grouping

Individuals in an assembly-line format to make footprints, then two large groups to measure and create the tracks

DIRECTIONS

1. Before beginning the classroom activity, enlarge figures 7.4a and 7.4b to the sizes indicated (either mechanically or manually). To make footprint patterns, transfer them to stiff paper or cardboard and cut them out. As drawn, the figures will make a right bipedal foot and left quadrupedal foot. To make the left bipedal foot and right quadrupedal foot, simply flip the pattern over. Mark the appropriate sides with L or R for students. You might want to make several patterns to speed the process along or have spares in case of damage.

2. Early on, you will need to decide where the tracks will go, how long they will be, and how many footprints will be required. Use figures 7.3a and 7.3b to ensure that footprints are spaced appropriately (measurements are given both in feet and meters).

3. Organize students into two groups: carnivores and herbivores. Within each group there will be tracers tracing the patterns, cutters cutting the footprints, and assemblers measuring and building the tracks (this is the most complex of the three jobs and the one that will require most of your direct supervision). As the project continues, all students will eventually become assemblers.

4. Tracks can be attached to the floor, walls, or ceiling(!) with double-sided tape or staples. Dinosaur tracks have been found in the roofs of underground coal mines (Lockley 1991, 179-180), so stapling them to the acoustical ceiling is not as absurd as it might at first sound. For a more permanent trackway, you might choose to "laminate" the footprints to a tiled floor with clear contact film; if you are considering this option, be sure to check with the custodial staff or school secretary first.

(Text continues on page 152.)

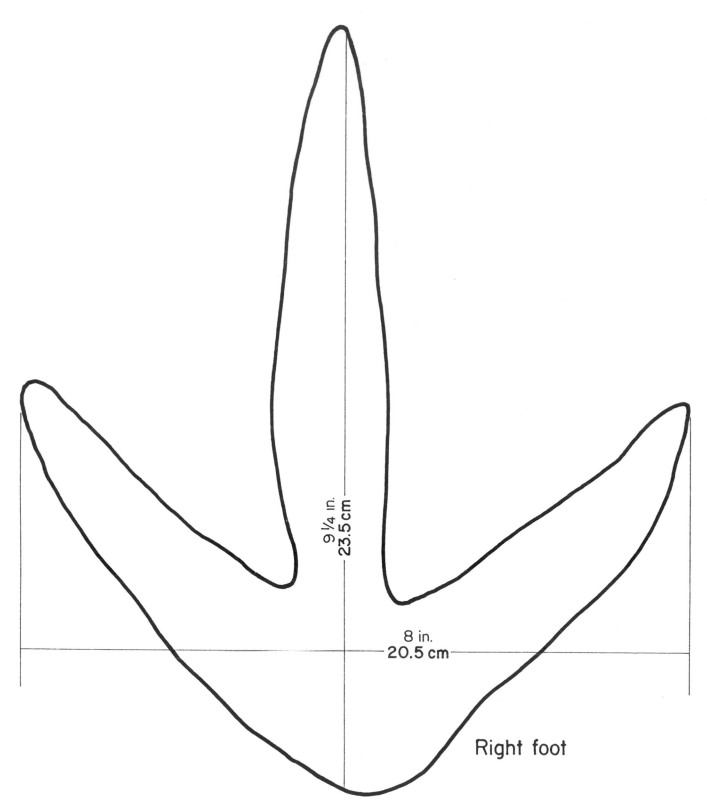

9¼ in.
23.5 cm

8 in.
20.5 cm

Right foot

7.4a. Pattern for footprint of the carnivorous dinosaur.

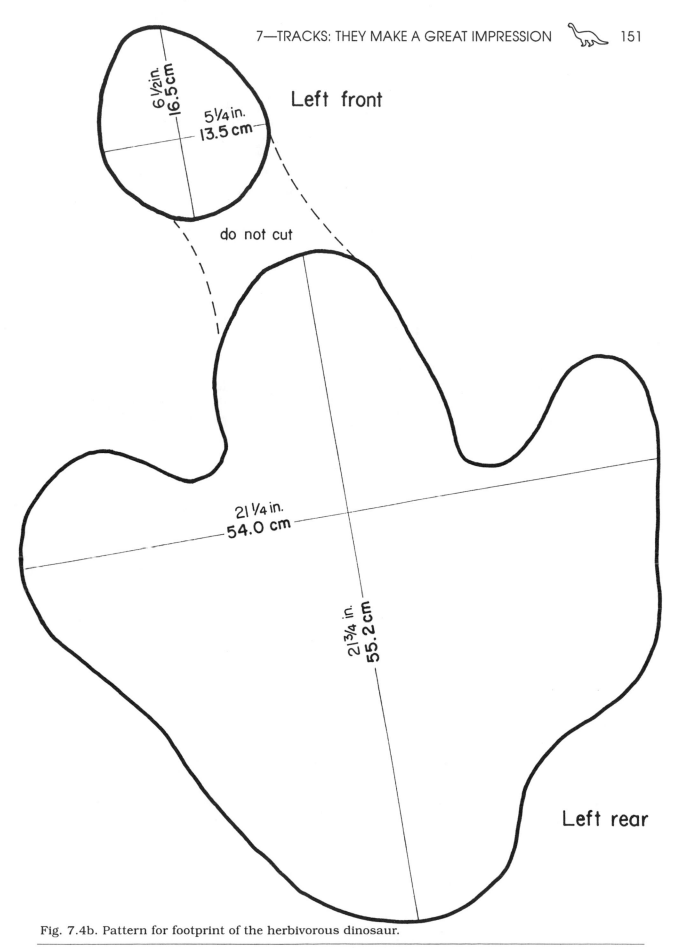

Left front

6 ½ in.
16.5 cm

5 ¼ in.
13.5 cm

do not cut

21 ¼ in.
54.0 cm

21 ¾ in.
55.2 cm

Left rear

Fig. 7.4b. Pattern for footprint of the herbivorous dinosaur.

EXTENSIONS

1. Interpreting trackways allows students to apply their imaginations and interpretive skills to understanding animal behavior. Figure 7.5, page 153, shows examples of tracks illustrating behavior of single dinosaurs. Figure 7.5a is a set of tracks made by carnivores from Cactus Park, Colorado; figure 7.5b is an example of the behavior of a group of dinosaurs from Texas traveling in the same direction; figure 7.5c was made by an *Apatosaurus* in Utah; and 7.5d was made by a carnivorous dinosaur in Canada. In small groups, students can write an interpretation of these actual tracksites.

2. For a "Back to School" night, tracks attached to the floor can serve as guides to your room (see chapter 14).

3. Students should be encouraged to look for different types of tracks in their environment: a muddy dog coming into the house, footprints on a damp lawn, contrails of a high-flying jet, the wake of a boat moving through the water, the trail of a wet bicycle tire on a sidewalk, or tire tracks on a snowy street. Even a short trip around the school building when the ground is soft should provide many examples. David Webster (1968) and Olaus J. Murie (1974) are excellent resources for track identification.

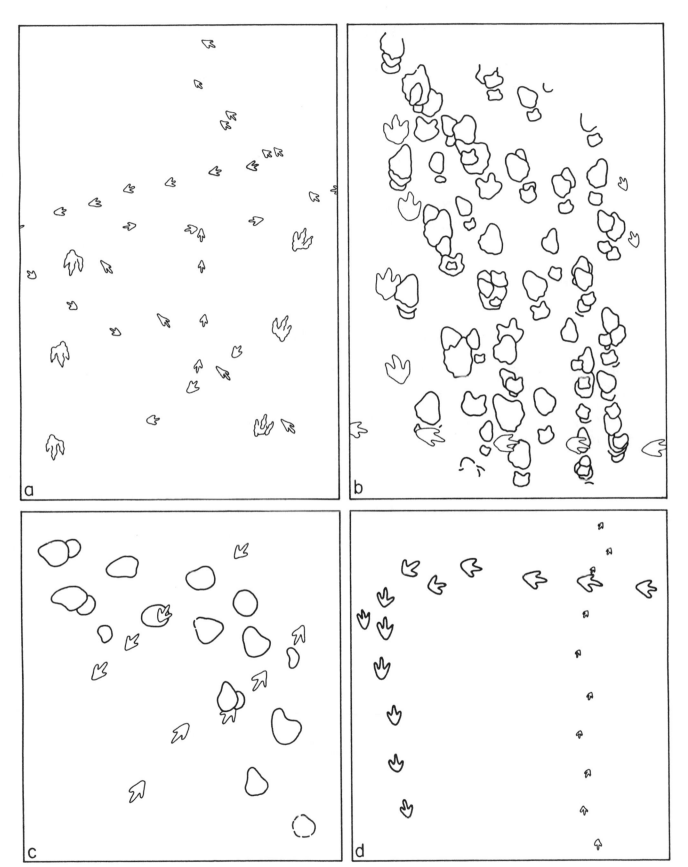

Fig 7.5. Examples of dinosaur trackways.

REFERENCES

Alexander, R. McNeil. 1989. *Dynamics of Dinosaurs and Other Extinct Giants.* New York: Columbia University Press.

Bakker, Robert T. 1986. *The Dinosaur Heresies.* New York: William Morrow.

Lockley, Martin. 1991. *Tracking Dinosaurs.* Cambridge: Cambridge University Press.

Murie, Olaus J. 1974. *A Field Guide to Animal Tracks.* The Peterson Field Guide Series. Boston: Houghton Mifflin.

Webster, David. 1968. *Track Picture Book.* Newton, Massachusetts: Education Development Center.

SUGGESTED READING

Seton, Ernest Thompson. 1958. *Animal Tracks and Hunter Signs.* Garden City, New York: Doubleday.

Stall, Chris. *Animal Tracks of the Rocky Mountains.* Seattle, Washington: The Mountaineers.

8

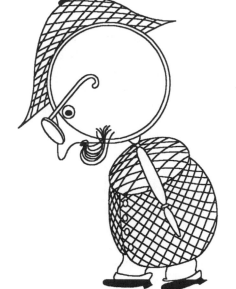

Names

INTRODUCTION

Many longer everyday words are made up of smaller pieces of words by combining forms (prefixes, roots, and suffixes). These often come from other languages like Greek or Latin and when combined, form common English words. For instance, the four following combining forms

tele-	(Greek, meaning far)
micro-	(Greek, meaning small)
scope	(Greek, meaning to watch or see)
phone	(Greek, meaning sound)

yield several common words:

telephone	(allows far away sound to be heard)
telescope	(allows far away objects to be seen)
microphone	(allows small sounds to be heard)
microscope	(allows small objects to be seen)

The names of dinosaurs are formed the same way. Although they often seem specifically designed to be difficult to pronounce, dinosaur names are composed of combining forms that always describe something about the animal. For example, combining the following three forms

tri-	(Latin, meaning three)
cerat-	(Greek, meaning horn)
-ops	(Greek, meaning face)

yields the name *Triceratops,* a dinosaur with three horns on its face. Another difficult-sounding dinosaur name is *Pachycephalosaurus.* Broken down into its combining forms

pachy-	(Greek, meaning thick)
cephalo-	(Greek, meaning head)
-saurus	(Greek, meaning lizard)

it means "thick-headed lizard." This is not a comment on the animal's intelligence; it is a description of an animal with a projection on the upper part of its skull that makes the head look thicker than normal.

Dinosaur names can also describe where the animal was first discovered: *Albertosaurus* was discovered in the province of Alberta, Canada, and *Bactrosaurus* was discovered in Bactria, Mongolia. Other dinosaur names honor the person who was instrumental in the animal's discovery: *Lambeosaurus* was named for Lawrence Lambe, a paleontologist with the Geological Survey of Canada, and *Diplodocus carnegii* was named for Andrew Carnegie, who financed the expedition on which it was discovered.

ACTIVITY: THE NAME GAME

The combining forms that comprise dinosaur names come from Greek and Latin. Not coincidentally, many of the same forms are found in everyday English words: corrugated cardboard (L, corrugat- = to wrinkle), dinner plate (G, platy- = flat).

In this activity students will add multiple combining forms to the suffix *-saurus* (Greek for lizard) to create the name of a "dinosaur," which they will then draw.

REQUIREMENTS

Time

Approximately 60 minutes

Materials

- Six opaque containers (plastic buckets or envelopes)
- Six small (business-size) cards in each of six different colors
- Drawing paper for each student
- Colored pencils, crayons, or markers for each student

Grouping

Six groups

DIRECTIONS

1. *Before class,* write each of the 36 combining forms and meanings from table 8.1 on a separate card (you may want to laminate these cards for durability). Use a different color card for each group. Put each group of cards into a separate container centrally located so it is readily accessible to all students.

Table 8.1

Colors	Size
black - (L) atri-, nigri-; (G) melano-	dwarf - (L) pumili-; (G) nano-
blue - (L) cerule-; (G) cyano-	gigantic - (L) ingenti-; (G) colosso-
green - (L) viridi-; (G) chloro-	large - (L) grandi-; (G) macro-, mega-
white - (L) albi-; (G) leuco-	short - (L) brevi-; (G) brachy-
yellow - (L) flav-; (G) xantho-	tall - (L) proceri-, alti-; (G) aepy-
Shape	**Texture**
curved - (G) cyrto-, gampso-	bare - (L) nudi-; (G) gymno-
egg-shaped - (L) ovat-	bearded - (L) criniti-; (G) pogono-
flat - (L) plani-; (G) platy-	hairy - (L) hirsut-; (G) lasio-, trichodo-
hollow - (L) cavi-; (G) coelo-	rough - (L) asper-; (G) trachy-
horned - (L) cornut-; (G) cerato-	spiny - (L) spini-; (G) acantho-, echino-
round - (L) circuli-; (G) cyclo-, gyro-	wrinkled - (L) corrugat-; (G) rugos-
Numbers	**Animal Parts**
one - (L) mono-; (G) uni-	beak - (L) rostr-; (G) rhyncho-
two - (L) bi-, duo; (G) di-	claw - (L) ungui-; (G) chelo-, onycho-
three - (L) tri-; (G) tria-	foot - (L) pedi-; (G) podo-
four - (L) quadri-; (G) tetra-	head - (L) capit-; (G) cephalo-
seven - (L) septem-; (G) hepta-	tail - (L) caud-; (G) cerco-
ten - (L) decim-; (G) deca-	tooth - (L) denti-; (G) odonto-

(G) indicates a combining form from Greek and (L) indicates a combining form from Latin.

2. Divide the class into six groups and arrange the groups so they form a circle around the six centrally located containers.

3. Explain that each container holds words that may be used to describe an animal. To demonstrate the activity, ask one member of each group to select a card from each container and read the cards to the class. For example, one selected card combination might yield *albi-, grandi-, plani-, lasio-, duo-, ungui-.* These descriptors would be combined with the word *-saurus* to form *albigrandiplanilasioduounguisaurus,* or a white, large, flat, hairy, two-clawed lizard. Explain that students will be drawing a picture of the dinosaur described by the cards they select. Students should be encouraged to rearrange the six descriptors any way they like. Have remaining students choose cards.

4. Distribute drawing materials to each student.

5. Each member of the group should then draw a picture of the animal described by the six combining forms and write the combining forms across the bottom of the drawing.

6. At the end of the allotted time, have each group present all of its drawings to the class.

EXTENSIONS

1. The drawing exercise can be combined with a writing activity in which students write a paragraph describing their animal. This activity may be used instead of or in addition to Step 6.

2. Encourage students to look through the dictionary for words that contain the combining forms they selected for their dinosaurs (you could award peanuts or extra credit, or you could arrange a competition among student groups).

3. Table 8.2 is a list of combining forms that commonly appear in dinosaur names. As students study dinosaurs in class, they could use this as a reference list to decipher the meaning of dinosaur names. The table could be enlarged to make a wall chart that could be added to as new combining forms are found or new discoveries announced in the media.

Table 8.2. Greek and Latin Descriptors

a, ar, an	no, not	**mimus**	mimic
acro	top	**mono**	single
allo	strange	**morpho**	shaped
alti	tall, high	**mucro**	pointed
angusti	sharp	**nano**	dwarf
apato	deceptive	**nodo**	lumpy
baro	heavy, pressure	**nycho**	clawed
bi	two	**ornitho**	bird
brachio	arm	**pachy**	thick
brachy	short	**ped, pod, pes**	foot
bronto	thunder	**penta**	five
canthus	spiked, spined	**phalangia**	toes
cera	horned	**phobo**	fearsome
coelo	hollow	**placo, plateo**	flat
compso	pretty	**pola, poly**	many
datyl	finger	**preno**	sloping
deino	terrible	**ptero**	winged
derm	skin	**quadri**	four
di	two	**raptor**	thief
don, den	tooth	**rex**	king
dromaeo	running	**rhino**	nose
drypto	wounding	**saurus**	reptile, lizard
echino	spiked	**segno**	slow
elasmo	plated	**stego**	roofed
elmi	foot	**steneo**	narrow
gnathus	jaw	**stenotes**	finger
hetero	mixed	**stereo**	twin
lana	wooly	**struthio**	ostrich
lepto	slender	**tarbo**	alarming
lestes	robber	**tetra**	four
lopho	ridged	**thero**	beast
luro	tail	**top**	head, face
macro	large	**tri**	three
maia	good mother	**tyranno**	tyrant
mega	huge	**velox, veloci**	speedy, fast
metro	measured		

REFERENCES

Munsart, Craig A. 1993. *Investigating Science with Dinosaurs*. Englewood, Colorado: Teacher Ideas Press.

SUGGESTED READING

Borror, Donald J. 1960. *Dictionary of Word Roots and Combining Forms*. Palo Alto, California: Mayfield.

Norman, David. 1985. *The Illustrated Encyclopedia of Dinosaurs*. New York: Crown.

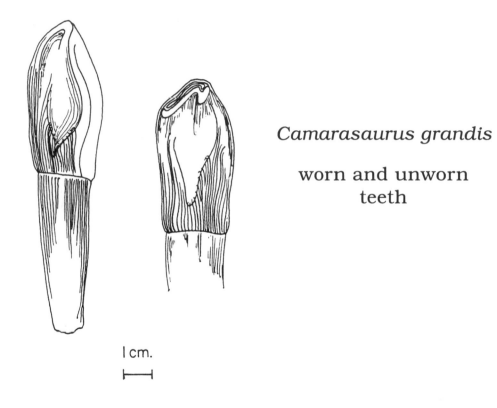

Camarasaurus grandis

worn and unworn
teeth

I cm.

"All these bones have been got out with considerable difficulty owing to the spring bursting out and covering them with a lot of water. I had to bale with one hand and dig out bones as I got a glimpse of it with the other, sitting at the time in a frog pond more like fishing for eels than digging for bones meanwhile snowing and freezing hard so what with water mud and slush it is no wonder if some small pieces are missing."

March, 1880

9

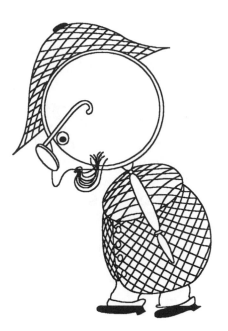

Color

INTRODUCTION

In animals, coloration is determined by need. Coloration can function as a defense mechanism by providing camouflage. By blending in with its surroundings, an animal (for instance a fawn) can become invisible to predators. Other color patterns provide the opposite effect. Animals "dress to impress" just like humans do; conspicuous coloration is often used to attract a mate (peacocks are a particularly good example). Coloration can also serve as a warning to potential predators that the animal may be poisonous or inedible (for example, a Monarch butterfly). Some animals try to trick predators into thinking they are poisonous or dangerous by emulating the coloration of animals who truly are (Viceroy butterflies copy Monarchs; milk snakes emulate coral snakes).

During the fossilization of dinosaur remains, color, unfortunately, is lost. Any discussion of color is therefore speculative, based on coloration in modern animals and conjecture about dinosaur behavior. We know that modern animals use several different methods of camouflage for survival. The complex classifications of camouflage have been explored by many scientists. One researcher (Powzyk 1990, 7) has provided a list that works well for the age group of children targeted in this book. Camouflage, including *concealing coloration* (coloring that helps the animal blend in with its environment) and *disruptive coloration* (coloring that disrupts the animal's outline and makes it hard to distinguish), will be explored in the following activities.

ACTIVITY: ANIMAL DESCRIPTIONS

In this activity students will provide detailed descriptions of familiar contemporary animals. The descriptions should be so complete that other students will be able to guess the animal being described. The students should be encouraged to include color, size, diet, habitat, and so on in their descriptions.

REQUIREMENTS

Time

45-60 minutes

Materials (for each student)

- Small paper lunch bag
- 3-x-5-inch index card
- Markers, crayons, or colored pencils

Grouping

Individuals, then groups or whole class

DIRECTIONS

1. Read through the directions and prepare a sample card and bag to show the class.
2. Each student chooses an animal.
3. Instruct students to draw and color the animal on the index card.
4. Students place their card inside the bag and close the bag.
5. Students write words, phrases, or sentences on the bag that describe the animal picture within.
6. In collaborative groups or as a whole class, have students read their descriptions and allow others to guess what is in the bag.
7. Share pictures after several guesses.

ACTIVITY: IF AT FIRST YOU DO NOT SEE

A shared reading lesson using the book *If at First You Do Not See* by Ruth Brown (1982) will help children understand that our eyes often do not see things as they really are. Check with the librarian to locate similar titles.

REQUIREMENTS

Time

20-30 minutes

Materials

- *If at First You Do Not See* by Ruth Brown
- One piece of 3-x-3-foot butcher or chart paper
- One marker for the teacher

DIRECTIONS

1. Open discussion by asking students what they already know about camouflage.

2. Introduce the book *If at First You Do Not See.*

3. As you read the book to students, show the illustrations to them from several different angles.

4. Referring to the illustrations, discuss the use of color and shapes in camouflage.

5. After the reading, brainstorm about things that are camouflaged in nature and list them on the chart paper.

6. Post the brainstorming list on a wall or board for future discussions.

ACTIVITY: COMMUNITY CAMOUFLAGE EXPERTS

This activity provides an excellent opportunity for you to involve community members by inviting them to speak about camouflage. Hunters and military personnel are an excellent resource. These people practice many techniques to fool animals or other human beings.

REQUIREMENTS

Time

30-45 minutes, depending on the age of the students

Materials

- Honor any speaker requests for materials

Grouping

Whole class

1. Select a date and time for the presentation. Send a copy of the sample Camouflage Volunteer Letter (fig. 9.1, p. 164) to parents or interested community members.

2. Before your speaker comes in, review with the students what they know about camouflage. You may also want to have students brainstorm some questions about hunting or military camouflage. Planning the question/answer session will avoid discussions centering around weapons and all the stories about "When my dad went hunting . . ."

CAMOUFLAGE VOLUNTEER LETTER

(date)_____

Dear (volunteer name),

Students in my class are studying the importance and effects of camouflage in the predator-prey relationship. I would like to invite all of you who are interested in hunting or have military camouflage experience to come in and share your expertise with the class. This will involve speaking to a group of (#)_____ students.

Please keep in mind that the students are studying camouflage. Please focus on camouflage and avoid weaponry.

PROJECT DATE:_____

PROJECT TIME:_____

Sincerely,

(teacher name)

- -

RSVP

I am interested in helping with this project. Please contact me at (volunteer phone #)_____ to confirm the date and time of the project.

(volunteer signature)_____

Fig. 9.1. Sample Camouflage Volunteer Letter.

ACTIVITY: WHAT DID YOU FIND?

Students will go on a nature walk and look specifically for insects and small animals that live near the school. They will record their findings on the Nature Walk Record Sheet (fig. 9.2, p. 166).

REQUIREMENTS

Time

60-75 minutes

Materials

- One Nature Walk Record Sheet (fig. 9.2) for each pair of students

- A well-defined outdoor area near the school yard

- Optional—parent helpers: one adult for six children (use the sample Nature Walk Volunteer Letter [fig. 9.3, p. 167])

- One pencil per student

- Onc plastic hand lens per student

Grouping

Pairs

DIRECTIONS

1. Some advance planning will help this activity progress smoothly. If you are having parents help with this activity, arrange a meeting to explain the activity and a short tour of the designated area.

2. Decide where you can safely allow the children to explore for insects and animals in their natural habitat.

3. Discuss with children the importance of respecting the insect and animal habitats. (This is an opportunity to observe wildlife, not harass it.)

4. Discuss any safety rules you deem necessary for this activity.

5. Review the Nature Walk Record Sheet (fig. 9.2) with students. Tell students they will be completing this while making their observations outdoors.

6. Begin the nature walk.

7. Following the nature walk, have students share their findings with one another or the entire class.

8. Add any new information to the camouflage brainstorming sheet from the activity "If at First You Do Not See."

(Text continues on page 168.)

NATURE WALK RECORD SHEET

Names of Group Members

_____

_____

_____

_____

_____

_____

Describe some observations about animals or insects that your group members discover in the area where you are searching. Include the creature's color, size, and habitat.

_____

_____

_____

_____

What are some questions that your group has about the creatures that have been observed in the search area?

_____

_____

_____

_____

_____

Fig. 9.2. Nature Walk Record Sheet.

NATURE WALK VOLUNTEER LETTER

(date)_____

Dear (volunteer name),

    Students in my class are studying the importance and effects of camouflage in animal habitats.

    The children will need some assistance with a nature walk project. If you are interested in helping with a small group of children, please detach and return the lower portion of this note.

PROJECT DESCRIPTION: An adult volunteer will assist a small group of students to research the importance of camouflage in a natural animal habitat. The students will be searching for animals and insects in a designated area near the school and recording their findings.

PROJECT DATE:_____

PROJECT TIME:_____

Sincerely,

(teacher name)

- -

    I am interested in helping with this research project. Please contact me at (volunteer phone #) _____ to confirm the date and time of the project.

(volunteer signature)_____

Fig. 9.3. Sample Nature Walk Volunteer Letter.

ACTIVITY: "MY MOTHER'S MAGIC EYES INVENT HORSES"

The poem "My Mother's Magic Eyes Invent Horses" tells of a mother and her child and the enjoyment they derive from imagining figures in the bushes. In a sense, camouflage is nature's magic: it helps animals achieve safety, identify a mate, and serve as a warning to other animals.

REQUIREMENTS

Time

20-30 minutes

Materials

- For the teacher:
    —*To Ride a Butterfly* by a collection of 52 distinguished authors and illustrators; the poem "My Mother's Magic Eyes Invent Horses"
- For each student:
    —One sheet of 8½-x-11-inch drawing paper
    —Crayons or markers

Grouping

Individuals

DIRECTIONS

1. Share the poem "My Mother's Magic Eyes Invent Horses" by Nancy Willard.
2. Share the picture accompanying the poem and encourage students to find the hidden images.
3. Instruct children to look at what they are wearing and decide in what type of environment they might be able to camouflage themselves.
4. Ask students to use their imagination and draw themselves in a habitat that would camouflage them in the clothing they are presently wearing.
5. Bind the students' artwork to create a class camouflage book.
6. Optional: students may enjoy sharing the book with another grade level or with study partners from another class.

ACTIVITY: ANIMAL HIDE AND SEEK

Students will be exploring concealing coloration and disruptive coloration. *Concealing coloration* is the most familiar form of camouflage, in which the body colors of an animal match or blend well with its immediate surroundings. *Disruptive coloration* is the type of camouflage in which stripes, spots, or patches disrupt the visible outline of an animal, making the animal hard to spot or identify.

REQUIREMENTS

Time

One 30-40 minute session

Materials

- A variety of nature magazines to be cut apart (ask the school library media specialist for help locating these but make sure he or she knows that the magazines will be defaced)

- A copy of the National Geographic Society's *How Animals Hide*

- Two pieces of 4-x-4-foot butcher or chart paper

- Marker

- Glue or masking tape

- Stapler

Grouping

Groups of four

DIRECTIONS

1. At the top of one piece of butcher paper, write *Concealing Coloration*. This will become chart 1.

2. At the top of the second piece of butcher paper, write *Disruptive Coloration*. This will become chart 2.

3. Display the two charts by taping or stapling them side by side to a board or wall in a location where students can reach them.

4. Gather students together as if for storytime. Share several examples of concealing coloration and disruptive coloration with them from the book *How Animals Hide* or another camouflage resource.

5. Discuss the two types of coloration and ask students to brainstorm several examples of animals that would fit each category.

6. List some of these examples on the charts to serve as guides and reminders.

7. Distribute the nature magazines to students.

8. Instruct children to cut out animal pictures from the nature magazines that illustrate one of the patterns of coloration.

9. As students find pictures, they should glue them to chart 1 or chart 2, depending on the type of coloration they best exemplify.

10. At the end of the session, gather students together and make some observations about the selections they have chosen for each of the two charts. Allow students to move their choices from one chart to the other, if appropriate. (It is a good idea to do this follow-up while the glue is still wet or use tape for easier removal.)

EXTENSIONS

It is thought that the conspicuous stripes on a zebra (see fig. 9.4) are designed less for concealment purposes than to disrupt its outline, making it difficult to see. If it is difficult to tell which way the zebra is facing or moving, the zebra is less likely to become a lion's dinner.

Fig. 9.4. The stripes on a zebra make it difficult to distinguish the animal or tell which way it is facing or moving.

Similar coloration was used on ships during World War II (see fig. 9.5). The strange patterns and color scheme of the camouflage made it difficult for enemy submarines to determine the ship's type or heading, making it a more difficult torpedo target.

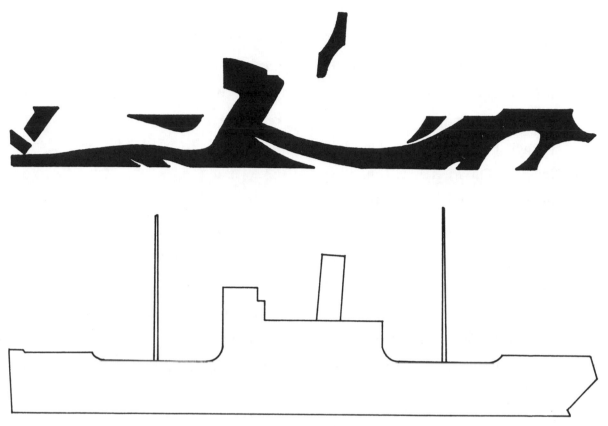

Fig. 9.5. World War II ship (bottom) and the coloration pattern (top) used to make it a difficult target.

ACTIVITY: DINNER OR DINER?

This activity will increase students' understanding of predator, prey, herbivore, and carnivore. Students will gain an appreciation for the importance of camouflage in the world of both prey and the predatory animals.

REQUIREMENTS

Time

45-60 minutes (activity may also be broken into two 30-minute sessions as indicated)

Materials

- Masking tape

- A variety of dinosaur books from the school library, the teacher's personal collection, the public library, and students' collections. The following titles on page 172 would be extremely helpful for this activity; however, do not limit your collection to these titles.

Aliki. 1995. *Dinosaurs Are Different.*

Dixon, Dougal. 1993. *Dougal Dixon's Dinosaurs.*

Fornari, Giuliano. 1991. *The Great Dinosaur Atlas.*

Horner, John R., and James Gorman. 1989. *Maia: A Dinosaur Grows Up.*

Lauber, Patricia. 1987. *Dinosaurs Walked Here and Other Stories Fossils Tell.*

Lauber, Patricia. 1991. *Living with Dinosaurs.*

Norman, David. 1991. *Dinosaur!*

Riehecky, Janet. 1988. *Apatosaurus.*

Schlein, Miriam. 1991. *Discovering Dinosaur Babies.*

Selsam, Millicent. 1987. *Strange Creatures That Really Lived.*

Simon, Seymour. 1986. *The Largest Dinosaurs.*

Simon, Seymour. 1990. *New Questions and Answers About Dinosaurs.*

- Two pieces of 4-x-4-foot butcher or chart paper
- One Compare and Contrast graphic organizer (fig. 9.6) made into an enlarged chart or a transparency
- Kitchen minute timer
- For each group:
  —One Compare and Contrast graphic organizer
  —Pencil for each student
  —Twelve 3-x-5-inch index cards

Grouping

Groups of four

DIRECTIONS

Session 1

1. Gather students together.

2. If your class did the "Animal Hide and Seek" activity, direct students' attention back to the two charts on coloration. (If your class did not work on this activity, take some time to discuss the two different types of coloration discussed in the "Animal Hide and Seek" activity before beginning this lesson.)

3. Direct students' attention to the two terms *Prey* and *Predator* on the graphic organizer. Solicit two or three definitions for them from the class; add the phrases or words that the children suggest to the graphic organizer as shown in figure 9.7, page 174. Tell students that for the next five minutes they will be adding information to their group Compare and Contrast graphic organizer in the same way.

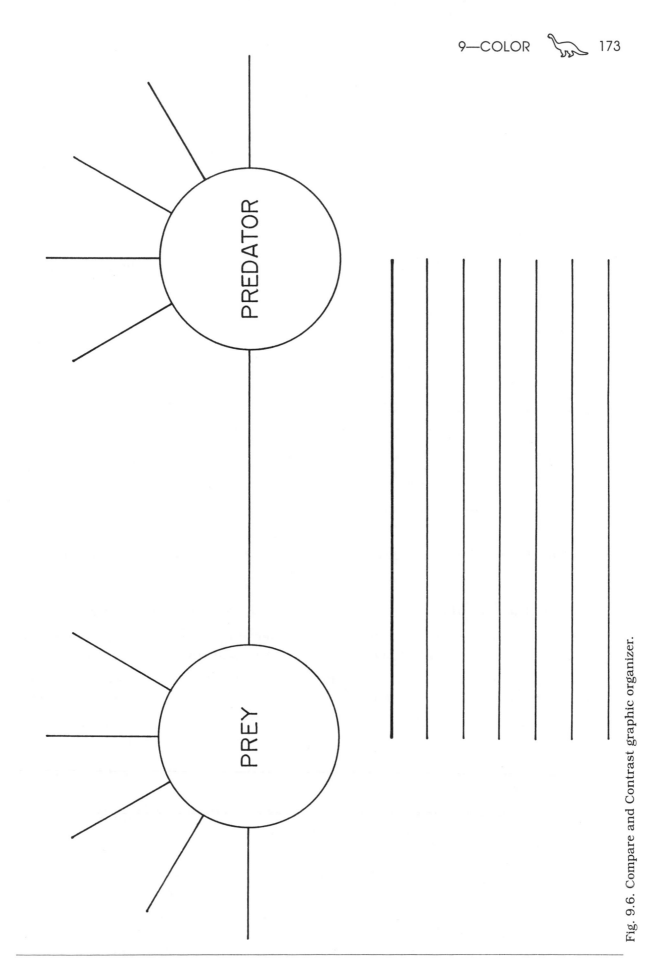

COMPARE AND CONTRAST

PREDATOR

PREY

Fig. 9.6. Compare and Contrast graphic organizer.

COMPARE AND CONTRAST

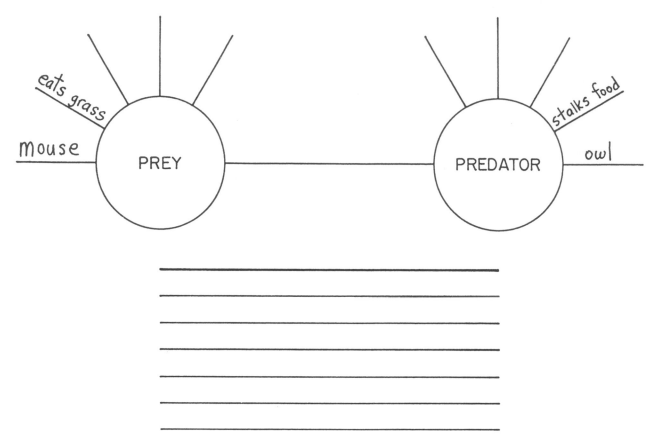

Fig. 9.7. Partially completed graphic organizer showing student definitions of predators and prey.

4. Set the timer for five minutes and monitor individual group progress.

5. When the five minutes are up, ask students to put their pencils down and discuss some of their additions to the group graphic organizers.

6. Next, ask some leading questions to generate discussion of camouflage and its role in the predator/prey relationship. Here are some examples:

   a. How is concealing coloration advantageous to a prey animal?

   b. How is concealing coloration advantageous to a predatory animal?

   c. Why would disruptive coloration serve prey animals differently at different times of day?

7. In the center space of the class Compare and Contrast graphic organizer, write the word *camouflage* (see fig. 9.8). Instruct students to do the same on the group graphic organizer.

8. Tell students that for the next five minutes, they will be listing reasons that camouflage is important to all animals—both prey and predator.

9. Set timer for five minutes and monitor group progress.

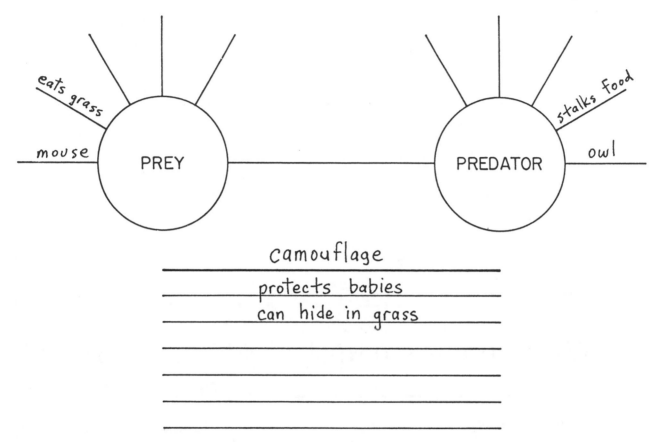

COMPARE AND CONTRAST

eats grass

mouse

PREY

camouflage

protects babies

can hide in grass

stalks food

owl

PREDATOR

Fig. 9.8. Partially completed graphic organizer showing how to fill in information on camouflage.

10. At the end of five minutes, instruct students to stop writing and discuss some of the ideas they have developed about camouflage.

Session 2

1. Title one of the pieces of butcher or chart paper *Concealing Coloration*, and title the remaining piece *Disruptive Coloration.*

2. Tell students they will be working as "camouflage experts" in groups of four. The job of the "camouflage experts" is to determine which dinosaurs were most likely to have exhibited concealing colors and which may have had disruptive coloration.

3. Remind students that dinosaurs were animals and filled the same predator/prey niches during their lives as modern animals do. Although there is little evidence about dinosaur coloration, scientists assume that they were colored similarly to modern animals because their survival needs were the same.

4. Explain to students that each group will be using the 12 index cards to record its findings.

5. Students will refer to the dinosaur books and look at the illustrators' ideas about the possible coloration of the animals.

6. Students will record the information indicated in figure 9.9 on each card, providing the dinosaur's name, whether it was a predator or a prey animal, and what type of coloration it probably displayed.

a. This animal's name was

_____.

b. This animal was a

_____.

c. We believe this animal would have displayed
_____ coloration
because_____

_____.

Fig. 9.9. Information to be included on each index card.

7. As students complete their cards, have them post them by taping them on the appropriate chart (concealing coloration cards on the concealing coloration chart and disruptive coloration cards on the disruptive coloration chart).

Closure

Gather students together and discuss their findings. Some dinosaurs may appear on both charts. This is not a problem, because no one knows for sure what colors the animals were. Accept the choices students made in posting the cards but encourage students to justify their choices.

Save the index cards and use them for the next activity.

ACTIVITY: MESOZOIC MURALS

Keeping in mind that the Mesozoic Era included the Triassic, Jurassic, and Cretaceous periods and that the dinosaurs lived and died within these three periods, students will also recognize that other environmental changes occurred. Not least among the changes were those in plant life. Because animals often take on coloring that blends with the environment, it is worthwhile spending time exploring the flora changes that occurred during the Mesozoic Era. Robert Bakker (1986, 185) has described a coevolution between dinosaurs and plants. He has identified three periods:

1. The Age of Anchisaurs (*Anchisaurus*). During the late Triassic and earliest Jurassic, there were long-necked, rudimentary plant eaters. They had iguana-like teeth that were suitable for soft leaves only, and their digestive systems were very simple. Plants of this period were the gymnosperms including cycads and ancient conifers.

2. The Age of the High Feeders (the stegosaurs and brontosaurs). During the Mid- and Late Jurassic, the stegosaurs coexisted with the gigantic sauropods such as apatosaurs and brachiosaurs. More effective teeth and fermenting chambers in the digestive systems allowed these animals to eat plants more effectively. Plants of this period included cycads and more modern conifers.

3. The Age of the Low Feeders (ceratopsians and hadrosaurs). The Cretaceous was dominated by big-beaked dinosaurs that fed close to the ground. Plants of this period were the angiosperms, or flowering plants.

In this activity, students will be asked to identify which period the dinosaurs lived in and design a mural depicting the animals in their appropriate habitat.

REQUIREMENTS

Time

Two 30-minute sessions

Materials

-   Collection of dinosaur books from the school library, public library, teacher's personal collection, and students' collections

-   Transparency of Mesozoic flora and the animals of the era (fig. 9.10, p. 178)

-   Overhead projector

-   For each group:
    —One sheet of 8½-x-11-inch drawing paper
    —One 6-foot sheet of butcher paper
    —Crayons and/or markers
    —Copy of figure 9.10

Fig. 9.10. Mesozoic flora, with animals of the era. Modified from Bakker.

Grouping

Six groups

DIRECTIONS

Session 1

1. Project transparency of Mesozoic flora and animals of the era (fig. 9.10).

2. Point out the three different periods (figs. 9.10 a, b, c), noting that the plants—and the animals that coevolved with them—were different for each.

3. Emphasize that during the late Triassic and Jurassic—the periods of anchisaurs and high feeders—the plants and trees were green.

4. Explain that it wasn't until the Cretaceous—the period of the low feeders—that the angiosperms, or flowering plants, came into being. These flowering plants were similar to those we see today.

5. Divide the class into six groups, two for each of the three periods: Triassic, Jurassic, and Cretaceous.

6. Give each group a piece of 8½-x-11-inch planning paper.

7. Give each group a copy of figure 9.10a, 9.10b, or 9.10c (whichever is appropriate to their period) to refer to for mural planning.

8. Instruct the students to plan their mural and draw the *plants* that would have existed during that time period.

9. At the end of the drawing session, collect the papers and save them for use in Session 2. Check them for accuracy. Be sure that only those groups that will be creating murals of the Cretaceous have included flowering plants.

Session 2

1. Set out the collection of dinosaur books.

2. Randomly distribute the index cards from the "Dinner or Diner" activity to students.

3. Each group will be responsible for looking through the dinosaur books and discovering during which period the dinosaur on each card lived.

4. Students will add that information to each card. They will identify dinosaurs as either Triassic, Jurassic, or Cretaceous. The students now have a collection of dinosaur cards showing the animal's name, prey/predator status, coloration, and period of existence.

5. Collect the dinosaur cards and redistribute them to the appropriate mural groups (the Triassic group will have all of the Triassic dinosaurs; the Jurassic group will have all of the Jurassic dinosaurs; and the Cretaceous group will have all of the Cretaceous dinosaurs).

6. Return the plant life drawings from Session 1 to the appropriate groups.

7. Give each group a 6-foot piece of butcher paper.

8. Have students incorporate the appropriate dinosaurs and plants to create an accurate mural of the period they are representing.

9. Remind students to keep the colors of the surroundings in mind as they color the animals in their environment.

10. Hang the completed murals for the class to enjoy and compare.

ACTIVITY: IT WAS HERE A MINUTE AGO

Students will color two dinosaur silhouettes differently, one as a prey animal, one as a predator (see figs. 9.11 and 9.12, p. 182).

Each student will then switch silhouettes with another student in the class. The second student will prepare a colored background that matches the coloration of the prey. The student will then place the prey and predator against the background so it appears that the predator is chasing the prey. Because the prey matches its background, it will seem to disappear (see fig. 9.13, p. 183), pointing out to students the importance of camouflage.

REQUIREMENTS

Time

45-90 minutes (25-45 minutes to cut and color silhouettes; 30-45 minutes to color a background and place dinosaurs on it)

Materials

- Transparencies of figures 9.11, 9.12, 9.13

- Overhead projector

- For each student:
  —Pair of dinosaur silhouettes (one predator and one prey; figs. 9.14-9.18, pp. 184-188).
  —Several students will have the same animal pairs.
  —One sheet of 8½-x-11-inch paper for background
  —Colored pencils or markers (several per student)
  —Scissors
  —Stapler (preferably one with a deep throat)

Grouping

Individuals and pairs

DIRECTIONS

1. Discuss dinosaur color with students. For what purposes do modern animals use color? What kinds of patterns do animals exhibit (stripes, dots, color patches, solid natural colors)? Would dinosaurs have used color for the same reasons modern animals use color?

2. Show students transparencies of figures 9.11 and 9.12. Explain that they will be receiving prey/predator pairs of dinosaurs to cut out and color. They will then be trading pairs with another student, preparing a background to match the prey, and placing the prey and predator silhouettes against the background (show students transparency of figure 9.13 to make sure they understand). Explain that relative sizes are shown.

3. Distribute dinosaur pairs, scissors, and colored pencils to each student.

4. Ask students to color the predator and prey with different colors and patterns, making sure to stay within the outline. Make sure students do not leave any border but color in the outline all the way to the edge.

5. After both dinosaurs are colored, ask students to carefully cut out each of the outlines and write their names on the back.

6. Have students switch dinosaurs with those of the student next to them (this way the colors used for the dinosaurs will be easily accessible to both students for coloring the backgrounds).

7. Give each student a piece of unlined 8½-x-11-inch paper.

8. Have students staple the colored prey dinosaur outline to the right side of the blank piece of paper, leaving room to the left for the predator (see fig. 9.13).

9. Ask students to color the entire piece of paper, using the same colors and patterns used on the prey outline. The trick is to make certain the background color and pattern exactly match the prey dinosaur outline (again, see fig. 9.13).

10. When the background is completely colored, have students staple the predator onto the sheet of paper so it appears to chase the prey animal.

11. Have students write their names on the back of the completed drawings.

12. Have students give you the drawings as they are completed and place a number in the lower left corner.

13. Post the completed drawings around the room so they can be seen by all students in the class.

(Text continues on page 189.)

Fig. 9.11. Dinosaur silhouettes of predator and prey.

Fig. 9.12. Dinosaur silhouettes of predator and prey, each colored with a different pattern.

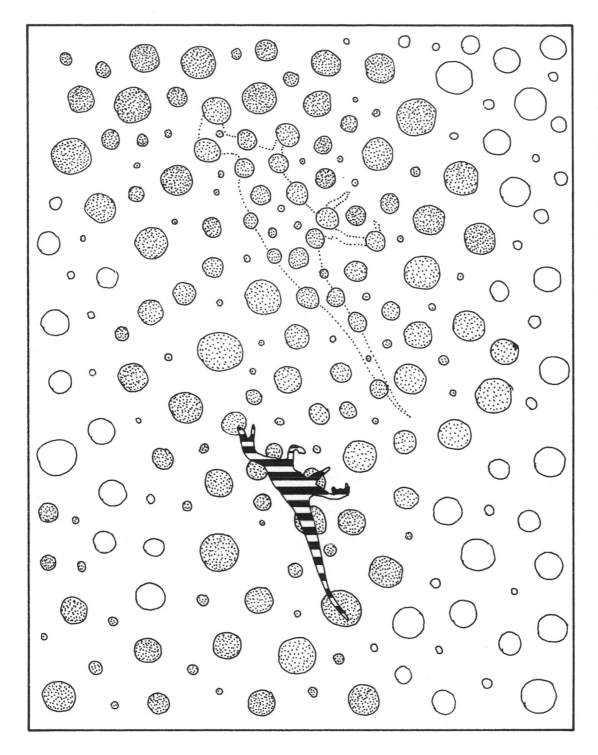

Fig. 9.13. Prey and predator silhouettes placed against a background that matches the prey. Notice that the prey animal seems to disappear.

TRIASSIC

230–208 million years ago

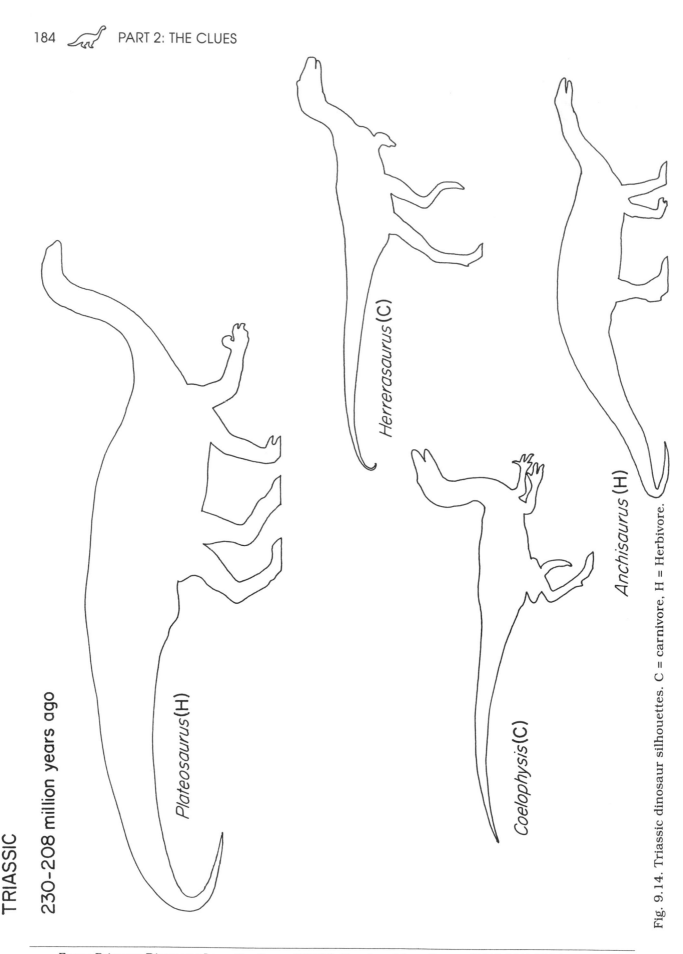

Plateosaurus (H)

Herrerasaurus (C)

Coelophysis (C)

Anchisaurus (H)

Fig. 9.14. Triassic dinosaur silhouettes. C = carnivore, H = Herbivore.

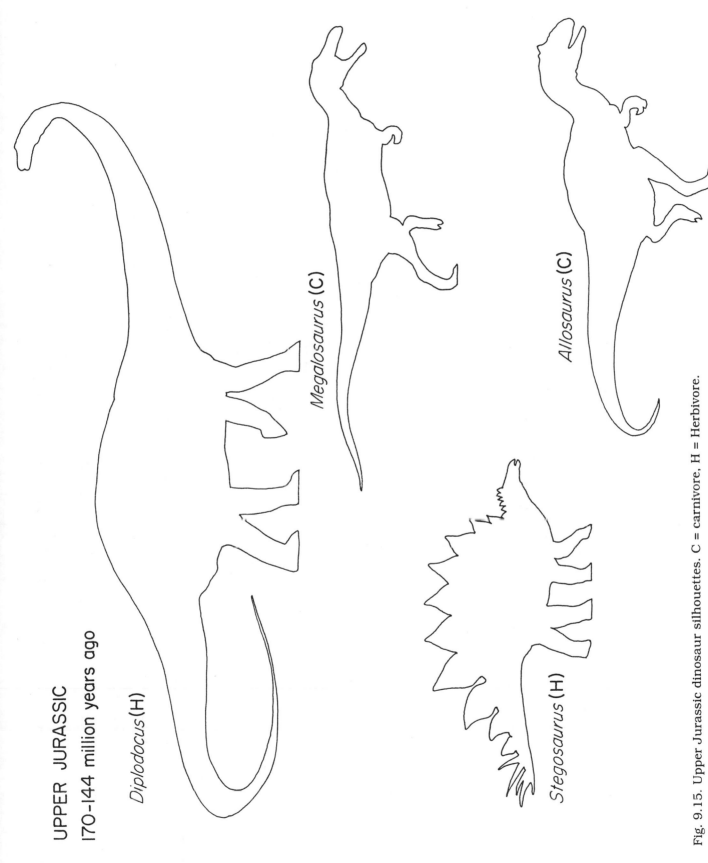

UPPER JURASSIC
170-144 million years ago

Diplodocus(H)

Megalosaurus (C)

Allosaurus (C)

Stegosaurus (H)

Fig. 9.15. Upper Jurassic dinosaur silhouettes. C = carnivore, H = Herbivore.

UPPER CRETACEOUS
100-66 million years ago

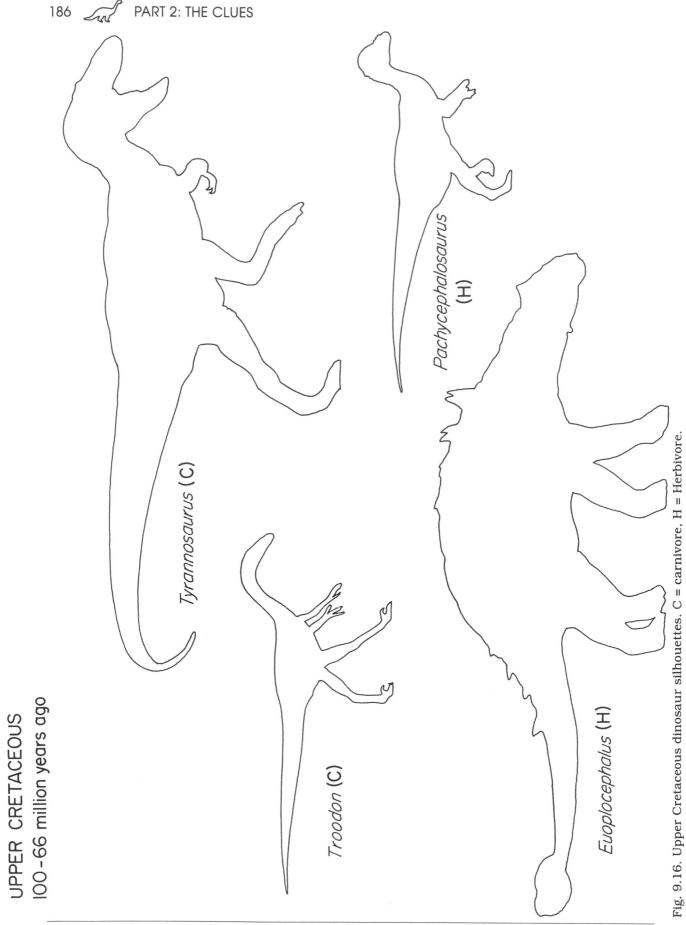

Tyrannosaurus (C)

Pachycephalosaurus (H)

Troodon (C)

Euoplocephalus (H)

Fig. 9.16. Upper Cretaceous dinosaur silhouettes. C = carnivore, H = Herbivore.

LOWER CRETACEOUS
144–125 million years ago

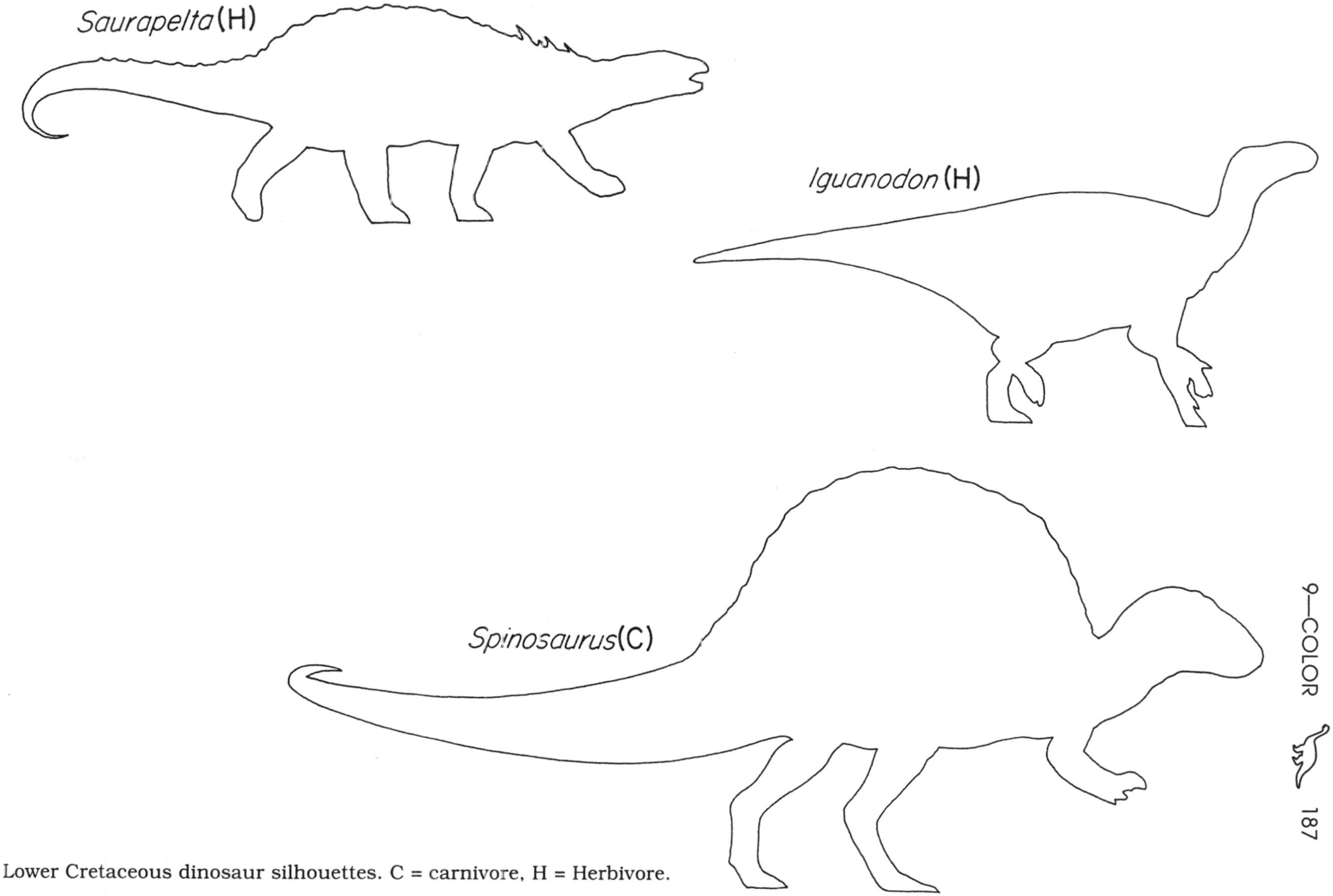

Saurapelta(H)

Iguanodon(H)

Spinosaurus(C)

Fig. 9.17. Lower Cretaceous dinosaur silhouettes. C = carnivore, H = Herbivore.

LOWER JURASSIC
208–180 million years ago

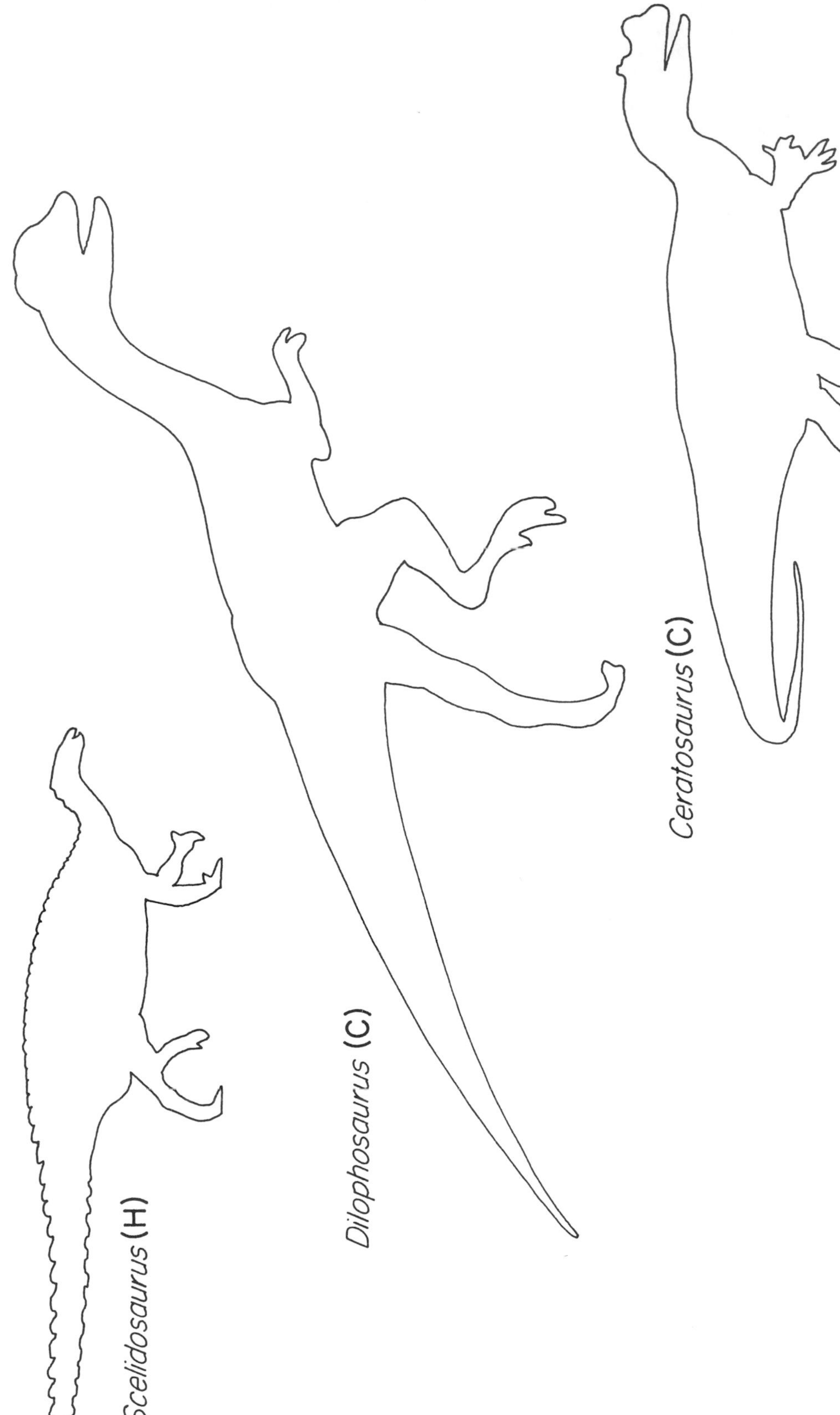

Scelidosaurus (H)

Dilophosaurus (C)

Ceratosaurus (C)

Fig. 9.18. Upper Jurassic dinosaur silhouettes. C = carnivore, H = Herbivore.

REFERENCES

Bakker, Robert T. 1986. *The Dinosaur Heresies.* New York: William Morrow.

Brown, Ruth. 1982. *If at First You Do Not See.* New York: Holt.

Powzyk, Joyce. 1990. *Animal Camouflage.* New York: Bradbury Press.

SUGGESTED READING

Dixon, Dougal. 1993. *Dougal Dixon's Dinosaurs.* Honesdale, Pennsylvania: Boyds Mills Press.

Ferrell, Nancy Warren. 1989. *Camouflage: Nature's Defense.* New York: Franklin Watts.

Hoffman, Mary. 1985. *Animals in the Wild: Zebra.* Milwaukee, Wisconsin: Raintree Children's Books.

Larrick, Nancy, and Wendy Lamb. 1991. *To Ride a Butterfly.* New York: Bantam Doubleday Dell.

McClung, Robert M. 1973. *How Animals Hide.* Washington DC: National Geographic Society.

Norman, David. 1991. *Dinosaur!* New York: Prentice Hall.

Sowler, Sandie. 1992. *Amazing Animal Disguises.* New York: Alfred A. Knopf.

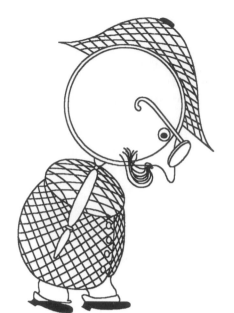

Sounds

INTRODUCTION

Animals make sounds for a variety of reasons. Some of these reasons are thought to be well understood by humankind; others are best known to the animals themselves. Animals create a broad range of sounds: snakes and turtles hiss; small cats meow; large cats growl; wolves howl; birds chirp and sing; elk bugle; elephants trumpet; bats click; whales and dolphins "sing." Some sounds are incidental (the hum of hummingbirds is caused by the vibration of the wings as the bird flies); other sounds are intentional (the growl of jungle cats or the chirping of birds and crickets).

We can hear noises modern animals make, and we can analyze their bodies—particularly their soft body parts (voice boxes in primates, the trunk in elephants)—to see how such sounds are made. Unfortunately, no one has ever heard a dinosaur make a sound. Even worse, dinosaur soft body parts that might be analogous to those that produce sound in modern animals are rarely preserved as fossils. Therefore, much of our information about dinosaur sounds is assumption and speculation, although some of it is based upon certain dinosaur features. Before discussing dinosaur sounds in more detail, we feel it is worth spending a little time discussing sound in general.

SOUND

Imagine someone slapping a hand on the water's surface. Two similar disturbances are immediately created. One is the vibration or wave that moves across the top of the water and is seen by the human eye as a ripple. It moves away from the hand in all directions. At the same time the ripple is started by the hand hitting the surface, a second wave is also created. It, too, travels away from the hand in all directions. It moves through the air and cannot be seen. Fortunately, humans have another sensory organ that can detect things—specifically, certain kinds of waves—that are not visible. Waves detected by the ears are called sound waves. The sound waves produced by the hand hitting the water are heard by the ear as a slap. As the sound waves travel through the air, others travel down through the water in all directions; they cannot be heard by the human ear, but they can be detected below the surface (by fish, for example).

Sound is one of the ways that we can tell that a substance is moving or vibrating. In the preceding example, the hand hitting the water rapidly moves the water surface. That movement then causes the air immediately above the water to vibrate. When the vibration of the air reaches the ear, it causes the eardrum to vibrate, ultimately sending a signal through the auditory nerve to the brain. The brain perceives the vibration as sound, and by comparing it to all the other sounds it has catalogued, it can identify its source.

ACTIVITY: WHAT'S A WAVE?

As a wave passes beneath a boat sitting on the water's surface, the wave clearly moves across the surface, yet the boat moves only up and down. Similar wave motion can easily be demonstrated in the classroom, showing that even though the wave travels horizontally (for example, along the length of a piece of string or rope), an object on the wave does not.

REQUIREMENTS

Time

Less than five minutes

Materials (any or all of the following)

- 30-foot length of relatively stiff, thin rope (such as clothesline)

- Long, coiled telephone cord (the longer the better)

- Slinky (steel spring toy)

Grouping

Pairs to demonstrate to the whole class

DIRECTIONS

1. Select two students to stand in front of the class.

2. Stretch the wire or rope as tightly as possible between the two students.

3. Have a student at one end *rapidly* move that end up and down to send a wave or pulse down the length of the rope.

4. Discuss with students that although there is movement along the rope, the rope itself is still in the same position. If the rope were moving, the students at the ends would have to be moving, too, and they are not.

5. To demonstrate more clearly, take a clothespin, clip, or piece of colored tape and attach it to the rope.

6. Ask the class to keep their eyes on the object on the rope and watch carefully as a pair of students repeats Steps 2, 3, and 4.

7. Discuss again how the wave moves from one end of the object to the other, but the object itself moves only up and down.

8. Survey students to see whether any have been to a beach and played in the waves. Ask them whether they have experienced the sensation of floating while a wave goes by. They are lifted up and float back down, but they do not move horizontally. The experience is the same when a small boat encounters the wake made by another boat.

EXTENSIONS

1. A short field trip to a nearby body of water could make the notion of waves more real to students (a shallow, plastic children's wading pool gently agitated by the teacher can also be used in the classroom). Float a buoyant object such as a rubber duck or cork on the water to show the vertical motion of the water, as opposed to the horizontal motion of the wave.

2. An oscilloscope, which converts audible sound to visible sound waves on a screen, can help students "see" sound; a high school physics teacher may be willing to loan you one. The best waves are those obtained from a single frequency or pitch; classroom sounds will produce a jumble of mixed noise. A tuning fork or musical instrument (like a recorder) should produce a single wave the characteristics of which will depend on the frequency (pitch) and amplitude (volume) of the sound. Students can create their own sounds by whistling, humming, or attempting to match the pitch of a tuning fork or recorder.

THE PHYSICS OF SOUND

The physics of sound are complicated, and much has been written on the subject. For those who would like to explore the subject, *Musical Sound* by Michael J. Moravcsik (1987) provides detailed explanations of sound creation and transmission for various types of musical instruments.

According to Moravcsik, the human voice is like a wind instrument. Most wind instruments vary the pitch of a sound by opening and closing valves that adjust the length of the tube through which air moves to produce the sound. If the human voice were truly a wind instrument, the sounds we produce would be varied by "opening or closing side holes in our necks or heads, or opening and closing secret bypass passages inside our heads" (Moravcsik 1987, 199). Humans, however, lack such holes and bypasses. To overcome such anatomical shortcomings, we use muscular control of the vocal chords and sound chambers. The size and shape of the larynx and oral and nasal cavities can be adjusted by muscle control, thus varying the sound.

It is almost certain that dinosaurs made sounds. Exactly why or how can only be speculated upon. The conjecture that they made sounds is based on behaviors of animals that exist today; how such sounds might have been made is based solely upon fossil evidence. Although there are commercial recordings available of the "songs" of whales and the howls of wolves, there are none of the trumpeting (or any other sounds) of hadrosaurs. If the dinosaurs produced sounds using soft parts of their bodies (the way humans use vocal chords, lips, and cheeks), we may never know how, because soft parts are rarely preserved as fossils. If, on the other hand, the number and shapes of chambers in the skull (see fig. 10.1) were "instrumental" in sound production, the possibilities for sound production are many. Any combination of soft and hard parts could have provided a broad range of sounds from a single animal.

In producing sounds, a dinosaur skull may have functioned much in the same way as an ocarina, a small, hand-held, egg-shaped ceramic instrument similar to a short, fat flute. Consult with the school librarian or music teacher for a picture of the actual instrument. In an ocarina, air is blown in one end as any of the several finger holes are covered to produce the desired note. Fingering obviously would not have occurred in dinosaurs, but soft tissue could have directed air to various openings or changed the shapes of those openings. Trumpets produce a variety of sounds through the use of valves that control the passage of air through the tubes of the instrument (see fig. 10.2, p. 194). If the holes in a dinosaur skull function like the brass tubes of the trumpet, the soft parts of the animal might have worked liked the valves of the trumpet, directing air flow from one tube to another.

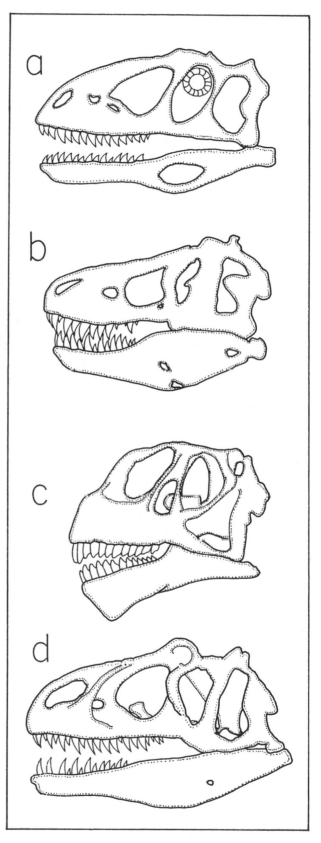

Fig. 10.1. Dinosaur skulls showing different numbers and configurations of holes (a. *Deinonychus*, b. *Tyrannosaurus*, c. *Camarasaurus*, d. *Allosaurus*).

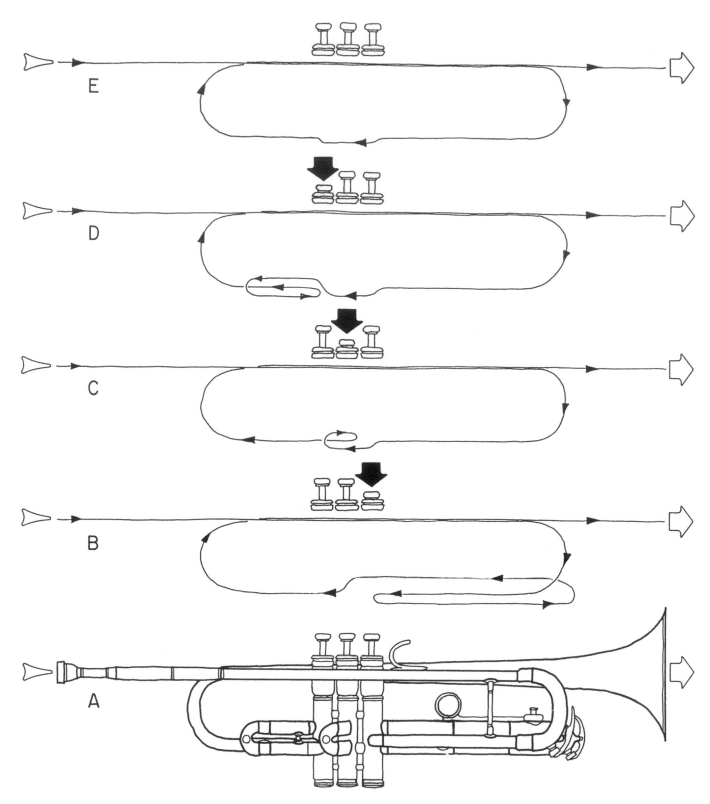

Fig. 10.2. Diagram showing how air passes through the tubes of a trumpet to produce different notes.

Without using anything other than their own bodies, people can make many kinds of sounds in many different ways. Some of these include:

a. clapping or rubbing hands together

b. whistling

c. tapping on the side of the cheek (the sound may be varied by opening and closing the mouth as you do so)

d. humming

e. singing and talking

f. expelling internal gases either orally or anally (students will be able to provide colorful names and descriptions for these two processes, so you might want to keep this for your own consideration only and avoid mentioning it to students)

ACTIVITY: HOW MANY CAN WE MAKE?

In this activity students will try to make as many different sounds as possible using only the soft parts of their heads (cheeks, lips, nasal membranes, etc.). The sounds need not be melodic. Whistles and snorts are certainly acceptable and may, in fact, be more realistic than other possibilities.

REQUIREMENTS

Time

Approximately 15 minutes

Materials

- None

Grouping

Whole class

DIRECTIONS

1. Seat the entire class in a large circle. You or a student recorder should stand by the blackboard to record the number of different sounds made by the students.

2. Discuss with students that dinosaurs only had a small number of holes in their skulls but could have made a large number of sounds using the soft parts of their heads. Ask students to name the holes in their heads (ears, nostrils, eyes, mouth) and the soft parts of their heads (cheeks, lips, noses, soft parts in the mouth). Vocal chords are in the neck, *not* in the skull, so sounds produced by them do not count.

3. Tell them they are dinosaurs and have them try to make as many different sounds as possible using only the soft parts of the head.

4. Have each student in turn make a sound, and have the rest of the class serve as a jury to determine whether this sound is different from those made earlier. If it is judged to be different, record it on the board in some descriptive manner.

5. As each student creates a sound, ask students what the sound might have been used for (sounding an alarm, attracting a member of the opposite sex, communicating, warning others about territory).

EXTENSIONS

Another resource when talking about animals sounds is the hunters in the community. There may be some excellent "buglers," "quackers," "honkers," and so on who would be happy to share their skills in the classroom by producing calls of various types. The local state wildlife office or Audubon Society chapter may be able to provide contacts.

ACTIVITY: HOW INSTRUMENTS MAKE SOUND

Despite the wide variety of sounds, they are all produced in the same way: they create a vibration in the air. Musical instruments are divided into four types based upon the way they produce sounds:

Percussion—Sound is produced by striking an object. Examples include drums, cymbals, xylophone, and piano (the hammer hits the strings).

String—Sound is produced by vibrating or plucking a string. Pitch is dictated by the length of the vibrating string. Examples include banjo, violin, viola, cello, bass, and harp.

Brass—Sound is produced by blowing into a mouthpiece. Pitch is changed by using valves to vary the length of the vibrating air column. Examples include trumpet, tuba, slide trombone.

Wind—Sound is produced by blowing through a reed. Pitch is determined by using a system of keys and holes to vary the length of the vibrating column of air; the longer the instrument, the deeper the sound (compare the alto saxophone to the tenor saxophone or the clarinet to the oboe).

To emphasize the importance of shape and size in sound production, show students various musical instruments. Invite community musicians and personnel from local music stores to share their expertise (see the sample invitation letter in fig. 10.3).

Music Volunteer Letter

(date)_____

Dear Community Musicians,

My class is involved in the study of animals and how they use sound. We would appreciate having any musicians from the community come into the classroom for a demonstration of an instrument or instruments. The connections that we are hoping students will make are the following:

1. Sound production is dependent on the size, shape, and design of instruments.

2. Sound production is dependent on the musician's knowledge of music and/or sound.

3. Sound production is affected by the materials used in the construction of instruments.

If you have an interest in sharing your musical talent and expertise with the class, please let me know.

Sincerely,

(teacher name)

- -

(Please detach and return to school)

Yes, I am interested in sharing my musical talent and expertise with your class. I will be sharing the (instrument)_____.
I would like to come on (date)_____ at (time)_____.

Volunteer name:_____

For confirmation of date and time, please include your phone number.

(H)_____ (W)_____

Fig. 10.3. Sample Music Volunteer Letter.

EXTENSIONS

Many musical instruments are available that make use of natural materials, for example gourds, animal skins, clay, or carved wood. These can be tied to multicultural activities, cultural events, or museum field trips.

ACTIVITY: HADROSOUNDS

Hadrosaurs (duckbill dinosaurs) were among the last dinosaurs to appear during the Cretaceous, and they were characterized by variously shaped crests on the top of the skull. Many ideas have been offered for the use of the crests, one of which suggests that they were used to create and amplify sounds. Even a cursory examination of hadrosaur skulls shows air passages of various sizes (fig. 10.4).

In certain instances, portions of the skull may have functioned as a long, buglelike tube (Bakker 1986, 43-44; Czerkas and Czerkas 1991, 192). Robert Bakker (1986, 43) refers to *Parasaurolophus* as "the trombone duckbill" because of the double air passages within the animal's crest. Close examination of the U-shaped tube in the crest of a *Parasaurolophus* skull has shown it connects to the nasal passages of the skull, leading Bakker to speculate that it might have functioned much like a trombone. Much like elk bugling in the fall, *Parasaurolophus* probably trumpeted to attract mates. As R. McNeil Alexander (1989, 88) writes, "The females had evolved a preference for large crests and deep voices, and chose males partly for those qualities."

Bakker suggests that even duckbill dinosaurs without such pronounced tubes could generate sounds in the vaulted roofs of their mouths (1986, 43). Alexander (1989, 87-88) describes the frequencies such tubes might have made and indicates they probably were not very loud because the skulls are missing the large bell shapes of a trumpet or tuba that amplify sound.

Students can make comparisons between air passages in the dinosaur crests and air passages in brass and woodwind instruments. Like those produced by musical instruments, the sounds produced by the hadrosaurs probably varied in both pitch (frequency) and volume (amplitude), due to the diameter and length of the air passages. Pipe organs function in the same manner. Pan pipes, small, hand-held wind instruments that have been used around the world for thousands of years, are easy to construct and produce interesting variations in sound.

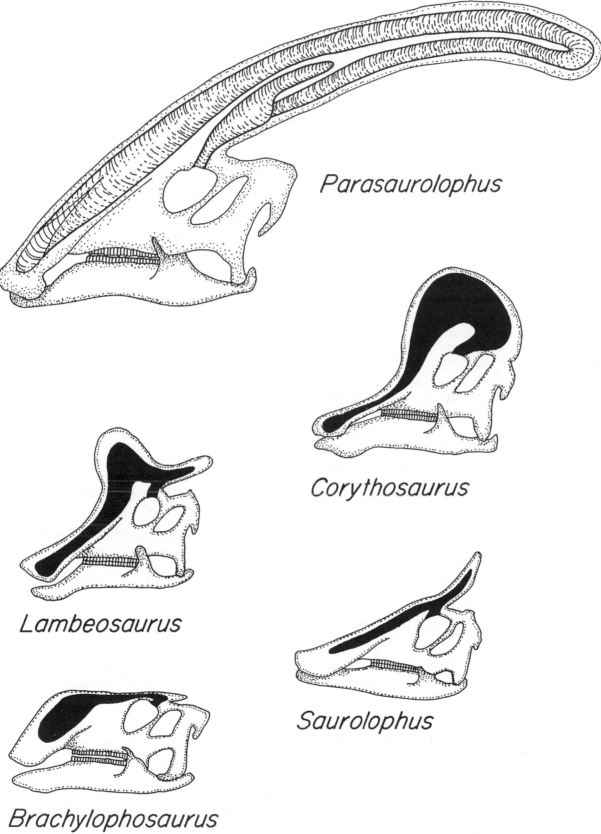

Parasaurolophus

Corythosaurus

Lambeosaurus

Saurolophus

Brachylophosaurus

Fig. 10.4. Examples of the air passages in hadrosaur skulls.

ACTIVITY: PAN PIPES

REQUIREMENTS

Time

Approximately 10-15 minutes for the construction of the individual instruments; allow time for playing the instruments

Materials

- ¾-inch PVC pipe (this can be purchased at a local hardware store) or copper pipe, which will produce better sound quality than the PVC; however, *be sure to smooth all sharp edges if copper is used*

- Three lengths of pipe (8 inch, 5 inch, 3 inch) per student

- Modeling clay

- Masking tape or other sticky tape

- Transparency of figure 10.5, page 202

- Overhead projector

Grouping

Individuals (each student should have his or her own instrument)

DIRECTIONS

1. Project transparency of figure 10.5 as you give directions.

2. Have students arrange the pipes in order of length, with the shortest pipe at one end and the longest at the other (see fig. 10.5).

3. Instruct students to tape the three lengths of pipe together, keeping the open ends level with one another on one side (see fig. 10.5).

4. Ask students to plug the other end of each pipe with a piece of modeling clay.

5. To play the pipes, tell students to place the edge of the open end of the pipe against the lower lip and blow gently across the opening.

6. Discuss with students what type of sounds are made by which tubes. (Low sounds are made by long tubes and higher sounds by short tubes.)

7. Discuss the implications for studies of hadrosaur sounds: hadrosaurs with long tubes may have made low sounds, and those with short tubes, high sounds. Do we know for certain? No, but it is possible.

EXTENSIONS

Arrange a visit to a local church that has an organ. A pipe organ will give students a dramatic demonstration of how pipe length affects sound.

ACTIVITY: BOTTLE BAND

Different sounds are created by different patterns of moving air. Through the use of valves or finger holes, a single instrument can produce many different notes by causing the sound to travel through tubes of different length. Because the tubes are of different length, the air within them vibrates at different frequencies, producing different notes. Air columns of any shape that are of different lengths will produce different sounds. Using this principle, a "pop organ" can easily be created in the classroom. Using this one instrument, two different types of sounds can be made. Take a pop bottle and add some water. If you blow across the top of the bottle, you will produce a sound; if you tap that same bottle with a hard object, you will get a different sound (see fig. 10.6, p. 202). If such a simple system can produce multiple sounds, imagine the variety a dinosaur skull, with its many holes, air passages, and soft tissues to control air flow, could generate.

REQUIREMENTS

Time

Approximately 30-45 minutes for initial setup, plus additional time for playing songs

Materials

- Overhead projector

- Transparency of figure 10.7, page 203

- For each student:
  —One 12-ounce or 16-ounce narrow-neck pop bottle. Bottles need not be from the same brand of pop, but they must be the same size and shape so that a given level of water will always produce the same note. The thinner the neck of the bottle, the better the sound will be when blowing across the top. Bottles should be rinsed thoroughly before they arrive in class.
  —One paper cup (nine ounces or larger)
  —Tap water (if you don't have access to a sink, use a large pitcher)
  —Two copies of figure 10.7
  —A "tapper": pencil, small metal spoon, or wooden dowel

Grouping

Students will practice in pairs, and the class will then function "in concert" as a large group

(Text continues on page 204.)

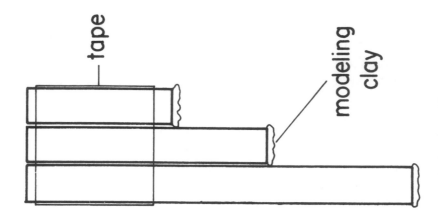

Fig. 10.5. Assembly diagram for pan pipes.

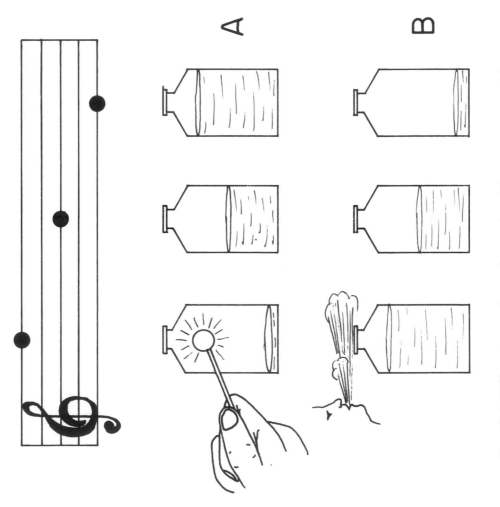

Fig. 10.6. Different sounds can be produced by tapping on or blowing across the openings of bottles filled with varying amounts of water.

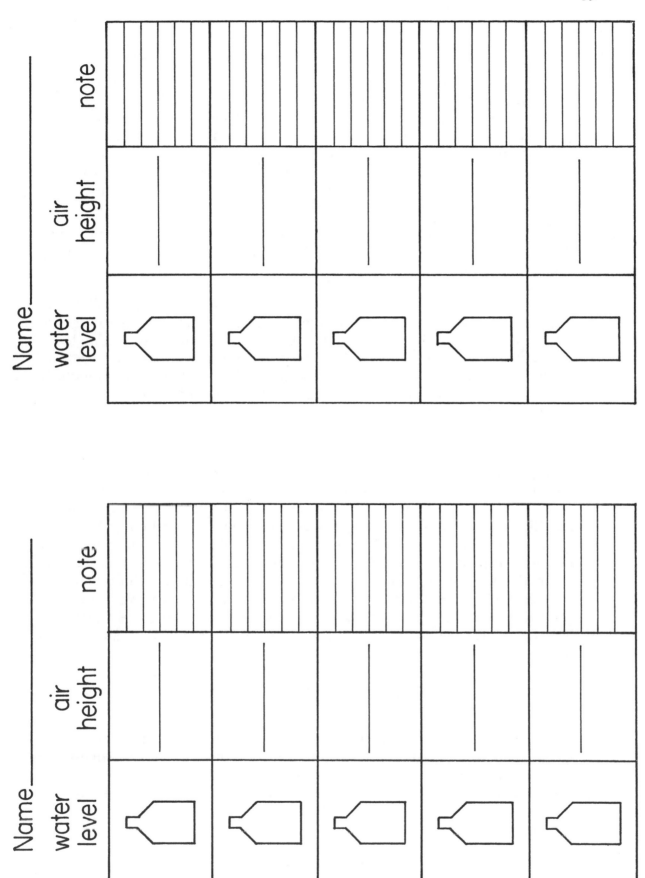

Fig. 10.7. Chart to be filled in by students showing water level, air height, and how they affect pitch.

DIRECTIONS

1. Have each student label his or her bottle with either a marker or stick-on label.

2. While they are seated at their desks, have students blow hard, straight across the top of the empty bottle, with their lips pursed. The air being forced out of their mouths and across the top of the bottle will cause the air column in the bottle to vibrate. Because all the bottles are the same, the air columns will be the same length (or height), and the notes produced will be the same. Practice this step with students until they are consistently able to create a whistlelike sound and are having fun.

3. Discuss the sounds with students. Are they all the same? Are they different? Why? How could different sounds be made? Students might suggest using different bottles: a good answer, but point out that these are the only bottles the class will be using for this activity and ask for other suggestions. Lead the discussion to the topic of different heights of air columns. Once this concept is agreed upon, discuss how the height of the air column in the bottles might be varied. If the discussion leads nowhere, ask students how water might be used to change the height of the air column. With continued guidance, the students will hopefully arrive at the conclusion that adding water to the bottle will change the height of the air column.

4. Distribute one copy of figure 10.7 to each student and show the transparency on the overhead. Ask students to fill in their name at the top. Review the figure with them and be certain they know what you expect. For your reference, figure 10.8, page 206, shows a completed student chart.

   A transparency of figure 10.8 could be used at the completion of the activity to review results with the students. The left-hand column (Water Level) indicates the level of water in the bottle (shown by coloring in the bottle). The second column (Air Height) describes the air column: with no water, the air column fills the bottle and is tall; with a lot of water, the column is short; and with a medium amount of water, the air column is of medium length. The right-hand column (Note) requires the student to describe on the five lines shown the note produced as they blow: a high note is indicated by placing a circle on the top line; a low note, on the bottom line; and others on the lines in between. You might want to ask students to model examples and show them how to fill in their charts.

5. Group the students in pairs.

6. Allow students to use paper cups to add various amounts of water to their bottles and blow across the opening, as they did in Step 2. Encourage them to experiment with different amounts of water and the notes they produce. Have students work together to complete their charts as they vary water levels and blow across the bottle openings. Repeat as often as you like.

7. Discuss with the class how the notes change with the amount of water in the bottle: low notes are produced with a low level of water and a tall air column; high notes are produced with a high level of water and a short air column.

8. Distribute the second copy of figure 10.7.

9. Have students empty their bottles and repeat the procedure of adding water and making notes. However, instead of blowing across the bottle openings, this time students should take a pencil or other "tapper" and tap the side of the bottle. Notes produced should be recorded on the new chart in the same manner as before.

10. Ask students to compare the two charts. The note results should be exactly opposite: when there is a low level of water in the bottle, a low note will be produced by blowing, but a high note will be produced by tapping; when there is a high level of water in the bottle, a high note will be produced by blowing, but a low note will be produced by tapping. Ask students how they might account for the differences. Remind them sound is produced by vibration. When they blow across the top of the bottle, the only thing vibrating is the air above the water. When the bottle is tapped, the glass, water, and air all vibrate, producing an entirely different sound.

EXTENSIONS

1. If an oscilloscope is available during this activity, students will be able to "see" the note they produce and possibly draw the screen image on their charts to visualize the difference between a high and low note.

2. The five lines that students used to plot the pitch of notes on figure 10.7 are much like a musical staff, with the high notes at the top and the low notes at the bottom. Students can play songs by adjusting the water level in the bottles and producing notes in the proper sequence indicated by a simple piece of sheet music.

3. Play "Tuby the Tuba" or Prokofiev's "Peter and the Wolf" to let students hear examples of high and low notes. As they listen to the recordings, they can place notes in the appropriate positions on a blank musical staff.

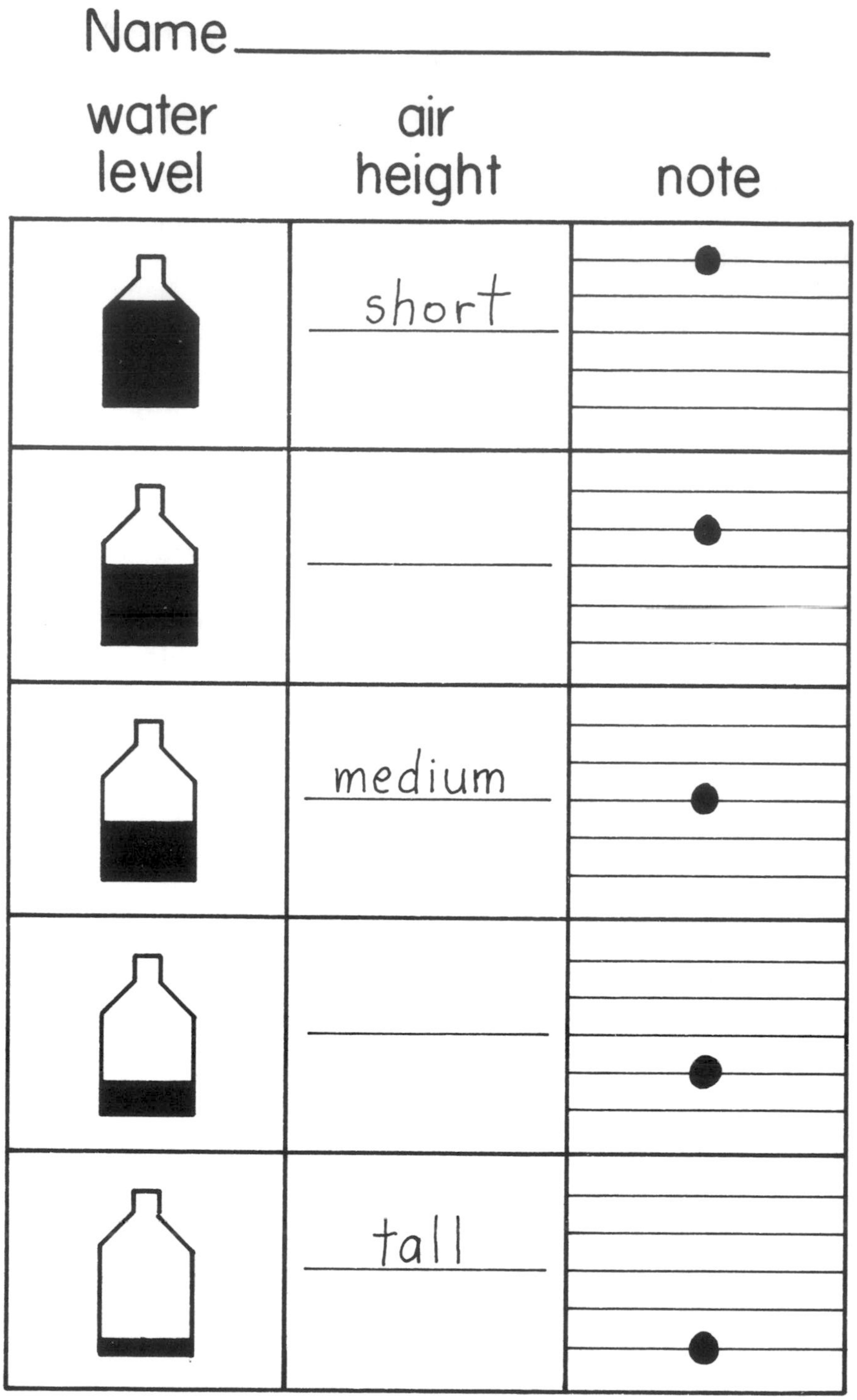

Name_____

water level	air height	note
	short	•
	_____	•
	medium	•
	_____	•
	tall	•

Fig. 10.8. Completed chart showing relationship between water level, air height, and note produced.

REFERENCES

Alexander, R. McNeil. 1989. *Dynamics of Dinosaurs and Other Extinct Giants.* New York: Columbia University Press.

Bakker, Robert T. 1986. *The Dinosaur Heresies.* New York: William Morrow.

Czerkas, Sylvia J., and Stephen A. Czerkas. 1991. *Dinosaurs: A Global View.* New York: Mallard Press.

Moravcsik, Michael J. 1987. *Musical Sound.* New York: Paragon House.

SUGGESTED READING

Benton, Michael J. 1989. *On the Trail of the Dinosaurs.* New York: Crown.

Berger, Melvin. 1978. *The Trumpet Book.* New York: Lothrop, Lee & Shepard.

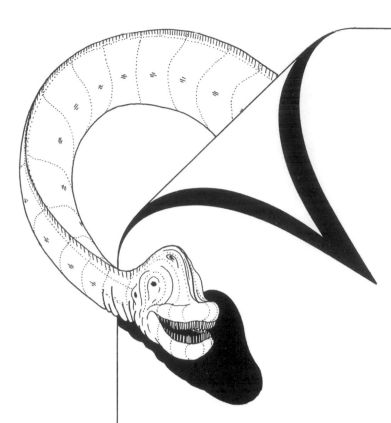

Stories about dinosaur discoveries read like great adventure or detective novels: Roy Chapman Andrews taking a motorized safari across the deserts of China; birdlike "missing links" being discovered in cracked-open slabs of German limestone; strange teeth being found by a doctor's wife in an English rock quarry; a botanist serendipitously finding large animal bones during a hunt for leaves in Colorado. Much of what we know (or think we know) about dinosaurs, we take for granted. We take our students to museums and nonchalantly announce, "There's a *Diplodocus!* It was a giant four-legged plant eater that lived during the Cretaceous, when parts of this country were much warmer than today." Despite the fact that no one has ever seen, photographed, or heard a *Diplodocus*, we feel awfully confident that the information we tell our students is correct.

Once many facts are known about dinosaurs, a basic question can finally be addressed: what is a dinosaur, and what makes dinosaurs distinct from other animals that coexisted on earth during the Mesozoic? Many misconceptions about dinosaurs exist, and they can be discussed with students and refuted based upon available information.

The process of scientific investigation that has led to our present understanding of these magnificent, extinct animals is open-ended enough to allow virtually continuous application of existing theories to new information while at the same time encouraging abandonment of existing theories should they prove incorrect. Nothing in science is sacred—except the truth. The constant search for that truth is the foundation of all science. In the following chapters, students will complete activities that will help them gain a stronger appreciation of how we know what we know about dinosaurs and the world they inhabited.

During any discussion about dinosaurs, we must always remember that whatever we know is based not on the animals themselves but on the fossils that have been found. One estimate (Dodson and Dawson 1991, 13) suggests that only 24 to 32 percent of the dinosaur genera that probably lived are represented by the fossil evidence discovered in the past 170 years. This means that three-quarters to two-thirds of the genera that existed remain to be discovered. In short, all of the knowledge we have today pertains to only a relatively small fraction of what actually lived. Given these figures, it is encouraging to find that there are three times as many dinosaur paleontologists active today than there were from 1900-1940 (Dodson and Dawson 1991, 3). Considering how far our knowledge of dinosaurs has come since the 1820s, it is difficult to imagine what information the future will reveal.

REFERENCES

Dodson, Peter, and Susan D. Dawson. 1991. Making the Fossil Record of Dinosaurs. *Modern Geology* 16:3-15.

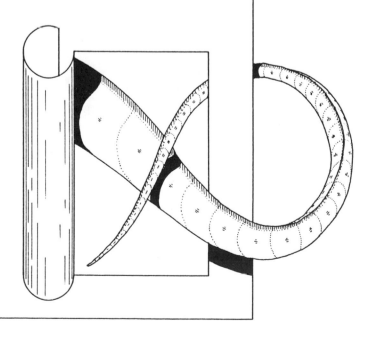

11

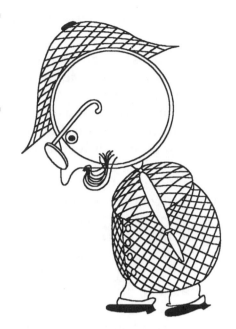

What and When

INTRODUCTION

The best way to begin this chapter is with a pretest—for the teacher! Why do you have to take a test? You may be surprised by what you know and don't know about dinosaurs. Please don't skim the chapter for answers; just answer the questions as best you can.

Pretest

		yes	no	maybe
1.	Dinosaurs are reptiles.	____	____	____
2.	Dinosaurs are cold-blooded.	____	____	____
3.	All dinosaurs laid eggs.	____	____	____
4.	Some dinosaurs could fly.	____	____	____
5.	Some dinosaurs could swim.	____	____	____
6.	All dinosaurs were large animals.	____	____	____
7.	All dinosaurs are extinct.	____	____	____
8.	Dinosaurs and people coexisted.	____	____	____
9.	All dinosaurs became extinct simultaneously.	____	____	____
10.	All dinosaurs appeared at the same time.	____	____	____

We won't give you the answers. As you read this chapter and the ones that follow, the answers will be revealed.

Many native peoples discovered large bones of animals that they were unfamiliar with. These bones were probably exposed by erosion of a rock formation. Although no documentation is available, these people probably reacted to the bones much as we would today: "Wow, what in the world is this?" They knew that the bones were strange and, most likely, that the animals they came from were strange as well, but they were unable to identify them.

Today, we believe we are much more sophisticated. We live in the Information Age of computers, instantaneous electronic media, and shelves full of encyclopedias that can be contained on tiny microchips. We are given the false impression that we know all that information saturation produces. We are, in fact, being bombarded by so much information that in an effort to stay current with the new data being produced, we often lose the basics in the shuffle. Many readers are aware of current dinosaur controversies: were they warm- or cold-blooded? Did they all hatch from eggs? Could they be cloned from fossil DNA? It is important to be aware of such questions. On the other hand, the most fundamental question often gets overlooked: what is a dinosaur?

How can dinosaurs be uniquely defined for students? They're old, but other animals are older. They're extinct (maybe), but so are many other animals. They're generally large, but some were as small as chickens. They're cold-blooded like other reptiles (well, maybe—we'll talk about that in a moment). They lived only during a specific period of earth history. As far as we know, this is true, but we probably have not discovered all dinosaur species, and new discoveries might invalidate that claim. In fact, some scientists believe that birds are the descendants of dinosaurs, and if this is true, then the dinosaurs did not become extinct 66 million years ago.

Dinosaurs are considered to be members of the class Reptilia and are subdivided into two orders distinguished solely on the basis of hip structure: the bird-hipped dinosaurs and the lizard-hipped dinosaurs. The fact that only certain skeletal structures are considered dinosaurian features eliminates many animals often thought to be dinosaurs. In dinosaurian skeletal structure, legs are positioned directly below the body for both support and speed, distinguishing them from coexisting reptiles that flew (pterosaurs), swam (plesiosaurs, mosasaurs, and ichthyosaurs), or had legs positioned to the sides (crocodilians and lizards).

Sounds simple, right? Wrong! Remember that part about dinosaurs being reptiles? Reptiles are animals that are ectothermic (cold-blooded), absorbing external heat. They are covered by scales, and most lay eggs on land. Other reptilian characteristics include generally small body size and bodies that are low to the ground and only move at high speeds for relatively short distances.

If we compare dinosaurian characteristics to those of reptiles, dinosaurs don't quite fit. Dinosaurs may be warm- rather than cold-blooded; dinosaurs probably did not have scales; at least some, but perhaps not all, laid eggs on land; body sizes were generally large (not small); bodies were often supported far above the ground; and, at least in some instances, dinosaurs may have been able to travel at reasonable speeds for fairly long distances. Were they reptiles? Maybe not. Strong evidence exists that they may have been an entirely different class of animal from the reptiles.

As far as we know at this time, all dinosaurs lived during the Mesozoic Era (245-66 million years ago—see appendix E); the oldest dinosaur known (recently discovered in Argentina) is approximately 228 million years old (Psihoyos 1994, 50) and the youngest approximately 66 million years old. Most people correctly believe dinosaurs lived a long time ago; they also incorrectly believe they all lived at the same time. During the 164-million-year tenure of dinosaurs on earth, new genera of dinosaurs appeared and existing genera became extinct (see fig. 11.1) with some regularity. Many of the genera appear to have existed for only 10 million of the total 164 million years of dinosaur presence on earth.

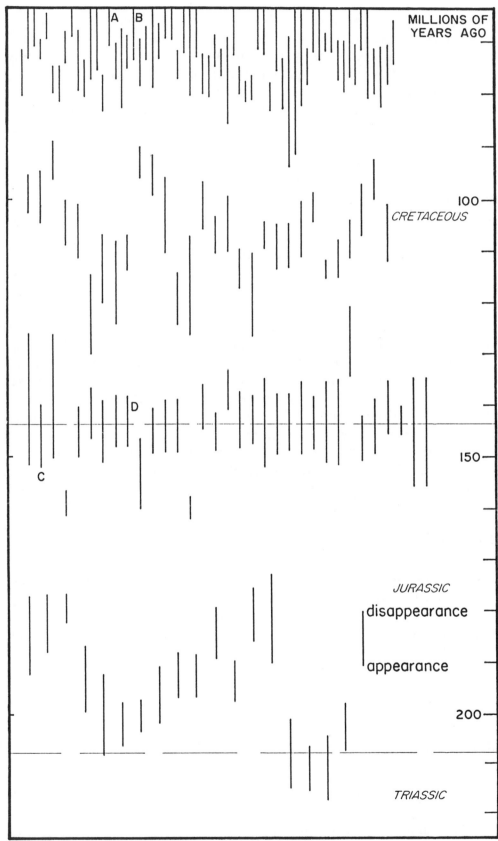

Fig. 11.1. Chart showing the appearance and disappearance of various genera of dinosaurs during the course of the Mesozoic (A is *Tyrannosaurus*, B is *Triceratops*, C is *Stegosaurus*, and D is *Diplodocus*).

If this book accomplishes nothing else, we offer our fervent hope that it will convince students that people and dinosaurs did not coexist. Unfortunately, both children and adults often believe they did. In 1991, Stephen Jay Gould reported a survey showing that approximately 30 percent of adults in the United States believed dinosaurs and humans were contemporaries (Gould 1991, 96). Many of us have grown up with *The Flintstones,* "Alley Oop," and movies showing cavemen fighting dinosaurs: what else are we to believe? The great dinosaur extinction presumably occurred approximately 66 million years ago. Humans are considered to have lived on earth for approximately 1½ to 2 million years. Dinosaurs, therefore, became extinct approximately 64 million years before our closest ancestors appeared. Clearly, they never set eyes on one another.

Young students, however, believe what they see on television, at the movies, and in books. In many excellent books, dinosaurs are shown with people to illustrate comparative sizes; younger children, unfortunately, remember the image of people and dinosaurs together. For the sake of an entertaining story, otherwise excellent children's books show people and dinosaurs in all kinds of improbable interactions. Children see the interactions, not their improbability and certainly not their impossibility. On the back cover of *Little Grunt and the Big Egg,* Tomie dePaola advises the reader that people and dinosaurs did not coexist; young children, however, rarely read the back cover. The book and movie *Jurassic Park* capitalize on an unlikely scenario in which people and dinosaurs coexist. Most adults recognize the story as science fiction; younger children are more likely to feel that seeing is believing.

The Mesozoic Era is divided into three periods: the oldest (245-208 million years ago) is called the Triassic; the middle (208-144 million years ago) is called the Jurassic (as in *Jurassic Park*), and the most recent (144-66 million years ago) is called the Cretaceous. The names are descriptions of the rocks or characteristics of the rocks themselves such as where rocks of that age were first described.

ACTIVITY: DINOMOES

In this activity students will become aware that all dinosaurs did not live at the same time, learn which dinosaurs did in fact coexist, and reinforce the fact that certain animals are not dinosaurs.

The activity is similar to dominoes, only in this case, students will be matching cards.

REQUIREMENTS

Time

20-30 minutes

Materials

- Set of "Dinomoes" made from figures 11.2-11.6, pages 215-19. Cut figures 11.2-11.6 along the lines indicated by the symbol >. Each cut piece will include two pieces like a domino. For durability, cards could be reproduced on card stock (rather than standard copying paper) and laminated. If time is available, each card symbol may be colored a different color to reinforce distinctions.

(Text continues on page 220.)

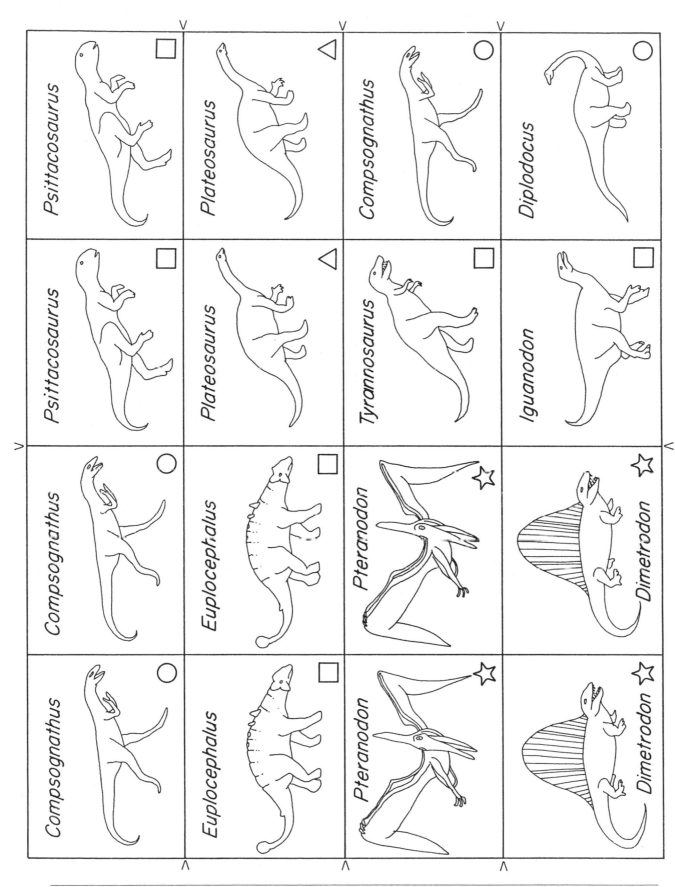

Fig. 11.2. Dinomo cards.

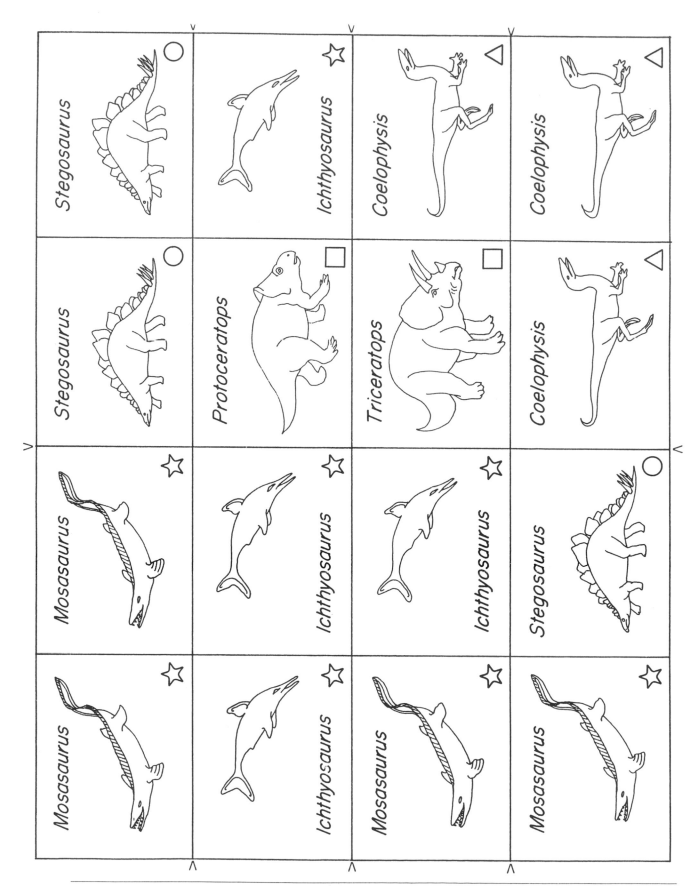

Fig. 11.3. Dinomo cards.

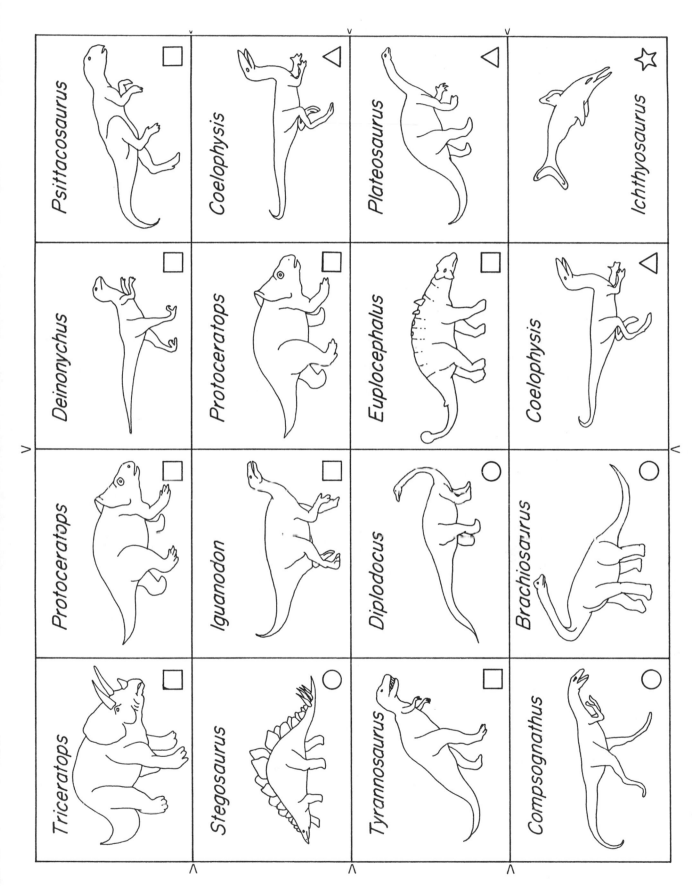

Fig. 11.4. Dinomo cards.

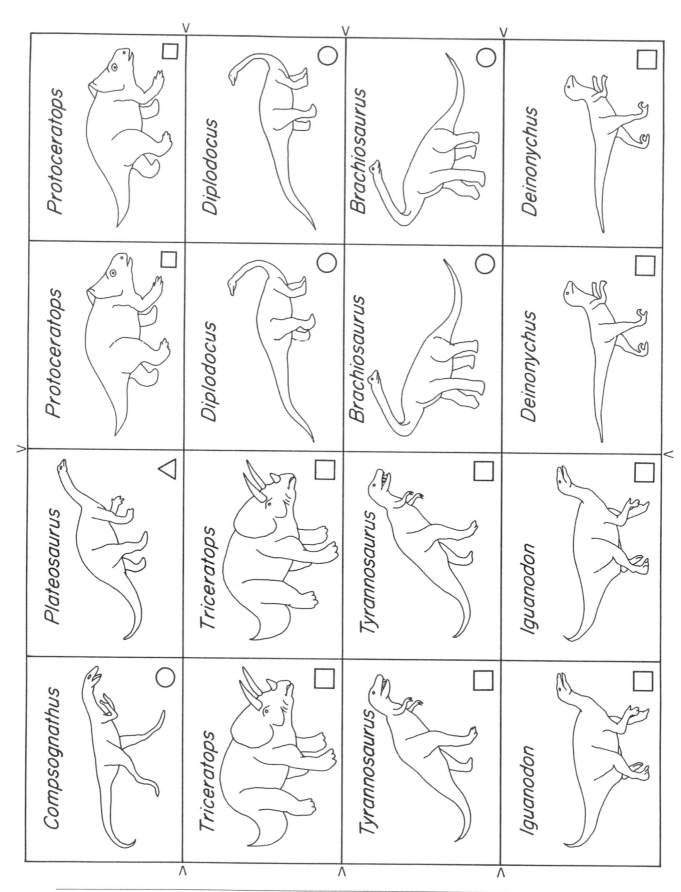

Fig. 11.5. Dinomo cards.

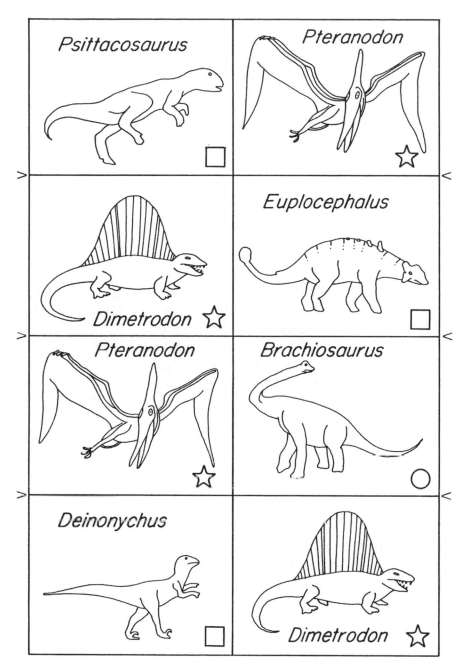

Fig. 11.6. Dinomo cards.

- Transparency of figure 11.7, showing how Dinomoes is played
- Transparency of figure 11.8, page 222, showing the Mesozoic Era and its three periods
- Overhead projector

Grouping

Flexible: the activity can be done in pairs, as small groups, or as a whole class; the cards can be kept in a box and brought out for students to play with as a reward or when they complete their work early.

DIRECTIONS

1. Duplicate figures 11.2-11.6 and cut them apart as shown (they should look like dominoes, but with two dinosaur pictures instead of dots).

2. Discuss with students when dinosaurs lived. Explain that the Mesozoic Era is divided into three periods (show transparency of figure 11.8). Explain that all dinosaurs did not live at the same time and that some died, never to return (this might be a good time to introduce the concept of extinction), and new ones appeared (you might want to make a transparency of figure 11.1 and show it at this point). Introduce the terms *Mesozoic, Triassic, Jurassic* (relate to *Jurassic Park*), and *Cretaceous*. Have students repeat the terms aloud as a class. Explain that some dinosaurs coexisted and some lived during completely different times. Tell students that on the game cards they will receive, dinosaurs that coexisted will be keyed with the same symbol.

3. Distribute some of the Dinomoes to students so they can follow along as you explain the game. The cards have the following symbol codes:

   a. If the animal is *not* a dinosaur, the card has a star.

   b. If the animal *is* a dinosaur, the card has either a circle, a square, or a triangle to indicate the period when the animal lived.

      i. If the animal lived during the Triassic Period (245-208 million years ago), the card has a triangle.

      ii. If the animal lived during the Jurassic Period (208-144 million years ago), the card has a circle.

      iii. If the animal lived during the Cretaceous Period (144-66 million years ago), the card has a square.

   Each card also includes the animal's name and a picture of the animal.

4. Explain to the students that they will be playing a game called Dinomoes that is very much like dominoes. The idea is to match similar items: Triassic dinosaur to the identical Triassic dinosaur; nondinosaur to the identical nondinosaur (show transparency of figure 11.7). Be certain the class understands how to play the game before continuing (younger students might match dinosaurs with similar symbols rather than identical animals).

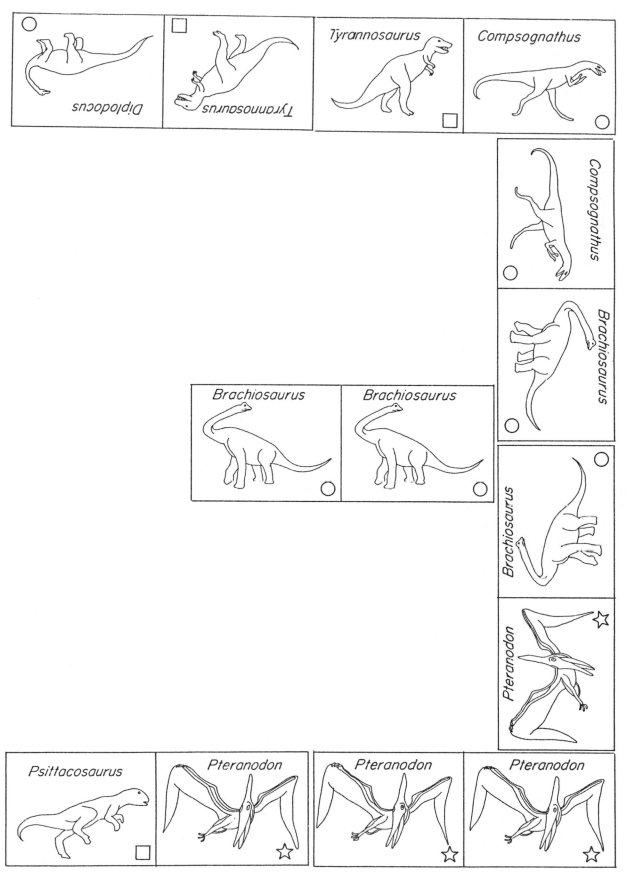

Fig. 11.7. Dinomoes is played by matching up animal cards.

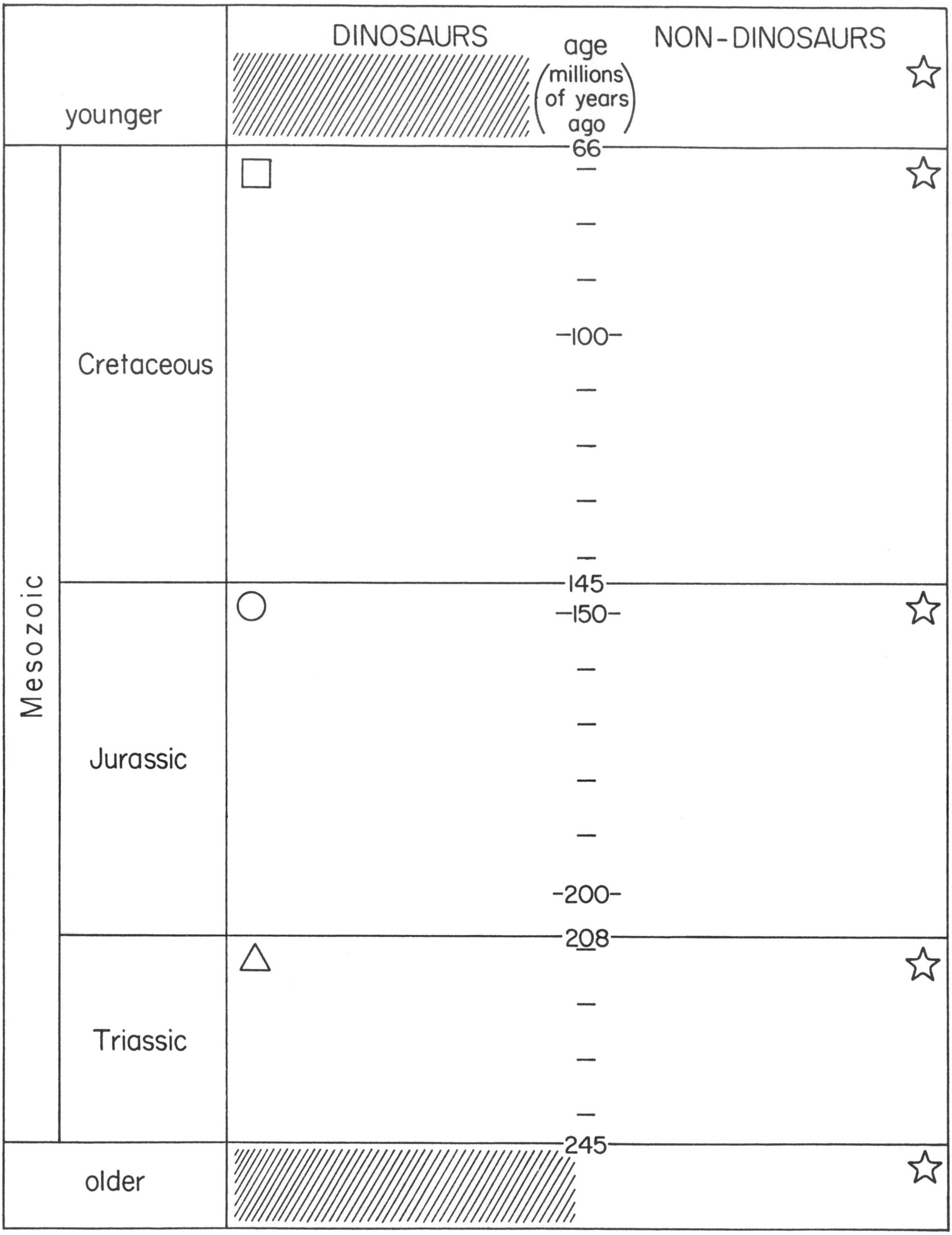

		DINOSAURS	age (millions of years ago)	NON-DINOSAURS	
	younger	░░░░░░░			☆
Mesozoic	Cretaceous	□	66 — — — —100— — — — — —145		☆
	Jurassic	○	—150— — — — — —200—208		☆
	Triassic	△	— — — —245		☆
	older	░░░░░░░			☆

Fig. 11.8. Diagram showing the Mesozoic Era and its subdivisions: the Triassic, Jurassic, and Cretaceous.

From *Primary Dinosaur Investigations.* ©1995. Teacher Ideas Press. (800) 237-6124.

5. Once you have completed the explanation, collect the cards from the students so that you now hold the complete set.

6. Arrange the entire class in a large circle around an open central area. Keep one card for yourself and distribute all the other Dinomo cards to the class.

7. Place your card on the floor in the middle of the circle and ask the students which cards would match. Select a student to begin the game (you might choose to go around the circle or to take turns alphabetically). If that student can exactly match one of the two pictures on the Dinomo card on the floor (both the symbol and the animal), have the student place his or her card on the floor so that the matching pictures are touching. If he or she cannot find a match, continue to the next student. If the skill level of the class allows, have each student read the name of the matching animals; if not, you might want to read the name of the animals on the matching cards. Continue until as many cards as possible have been played. Make the game a contest by seeing (1) how quickly the class can play, (2) how few cards remain after an allotted period of time, or (3) which student can play all the cards first.

ACTIVITY: DINOMO WALL CHART

REQUIREMENTS

Time

Approximately 30 minutes

Materials

- Enlargement (as big as possible) of figure 11.8 for a wall chart

- Set of single Dinomo cards (see Directions)

- Masking or clear cellophane tape

Grouping

Individuals or whole group

DIRECTIONS

Once students have become familiar with the concept of Dinomoes, it is possible to translate the information on the cards to a chart that students may use as a reference during dinosaur units in class. Make a large wall chart as shown in figure 11.8 (laminate if possible). Reproduce copies of the Dinomoes, cut them in half so that only a single animal appears on each card. Distribute cards to students. Ask students to come up one at a time and place the card in the appropriate position on the chart (if a dinosaur, in the correct time period in the Dinosaurs column; if a nondinosaur, in the Nondinosaur column). Double-sided tape or a loop of tape can be placed on the back of each card to affix it to the chart.

EXTENSIONS

The wall chart has been prepared with a vertical time scale in millions of years ago. Have students visit the library or consult classroom books to determine more precisely the years when the animals lived. This information can be added to the cards and the cards then placed more precisely on the wall chart. This extension will reinforce the concept that even during the Jurassic, for example, dinosaurs lived at different times.

ACTIVITY: WHAT'S NEW?

Like other scientific disciplines, dinosaur research is not static. New information about dinosaurs is constantly being discovered. Some research provides new ideas never thought of before while other research refutes earlier "facts." As field discoveries continue or older museum collections are re-examined with a critical eye, new animals are also being discovered and named.

REQUIREMENTS

Time

Two to three class periods; may also be done as an ongoing activity to be completed during a classroom dinosaur unit

Materials

- Blank Dinomo cards
- Library books, student resources, periodicals
- Figure 11.9 for each student or pair of students

Grouping

Pairs

DIRECTIONS

1. Schedule trips to the library or accumulate resources in class from the library collection, students' own collections, magazines, and newspapers. Videos can also be included. Emphasis should be placed on newer resources.

2. Working in pairs, have students review the assembled materials, looking specifically for Mesozoic animals that are not shown on the Dinomo set (these may be newly discovered animals or known animals not included in the set).

3. Ask students to record both the animal's name and the time period during which it lived (by period and in millions of years, if possible) on figure 11.9.

4. By filling in blank Dinomo cards, students can both increase the Dinomo set and add to the wall chart. The new cards should include a drawing of the animal, the animal's name, and the appropriate symbol for when it lived (square, circle, or triangle). Nondinosaurs should also be included and shown with a star.

student names _____ , _____

Mesozoic animals

Dinosaurs △ ○ □		Non-dinosaurs ☆

name	symbol	age	name	age
_____	_____	_____	_____	_____
_____	_____	_____	_____	_____
_____	_____	_____	_____	_____
_____	_____	_____	_____	_____
_____	_____	_____	_____	_____
_____	_____	_____	_____	_____
_____	_____	_____	_____	_____
_____	_____	_____	_____	_____
_____	_____	_____	_____	_____
_____	_____	_____	_____	_____
_____	_____	_____	_____	_____
_____	_____	_____	_____	_____
_____	_____	_____	_____	_____
_____	_____	_____	_____	_____
_____	_____	_____	_____	_____
_____	_____	_____	_____	_____
_____	_____	_____	_____	_____

Triassic △   Jurassic ○   Cretaceous □

Fig. 11.9. Mesozoic animal classification chart.

EXTENSIONS

Libraries include many older books as well as newer works. Students should be encouraged to find the same dinosaurs shown in both newer and older books. As new information about the animals is discovered, their portrayal evolves. In some older books, for instance, *Brachiosaurus* is shown semisubmerged in deep water, using its long neck and nostrils as a snorkel. More recent interpretations suggest that such a lifestyle would have been unlikely because the water pressure would have made it impossible for the animal to breathe in such a manner. More recent publications show *Brachiosaurus* living on land and eating from trees, much like a giraffe. Comparisons of new and old interpretations can be included in a written report or as part of a bulletin board display. (Suggestion: use varying interpretations of *Brachiosaurus, Iguanodon,* and the German *Diplodocus.*)

REFERENCES

Gould, Stephen Jay. 1991. *Bully for Brontosaurus.* New York: W. W. Norton.

Psihoyos, Louie. 1994. *Hunting Dinosaurs.* New York: Random House.

12

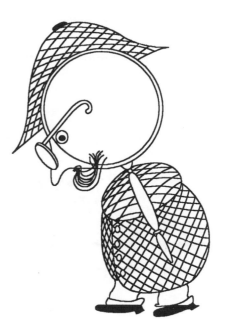

Correlations

INTRODUCTION

One way to find out more information about dinosaurs is to discover more dinosaur fossils. The type of rocks in which dinosaur fossils (and almost all other fossils) are found is called sedimentary rock. Sedimentary rock occurs as generally flat layers called *strata* (a single layer is called a *stratum*). Imagine that you have a handful of coarse sand, a handful of very fine sand, and a bucket of water. If you were to drop both handfuls of sand into the water, two things would happen. First, the sand would settle to the bottom of the bucket. The coarse sand would settle quickly, and then the fine sand would settle out more slowly. Second, when the sand reached the bottom of the bucket, it would spread out, forming two flat layers, a layer of coarse sand covered by the layer of fine sand. The process of settling is called *sedimentation*, from the Latin *sedimentum*, meaning the act of settling. The layers formed across the bottom of the bucket are called strata, from the Latin word *stratum*, meaning covering.

Virtually the identical process occurs in nature. Imagine a river carrying lots of sand and other eroded material emptying into a large body of water like a lake or ocean. As the materials settle out of suspension, flat layers are created at the bottom of the body of water. Dinosaur bones carried by the river would also settle out and be found in one of the layers on the lake or ocean bottom. Eventually, this layer would be covered by subsequent layers. Over time, the soft layers would be turned into rock, the bones would be preserved within the layers, and finally they might be raised to the surface, where a lucky paleontologist might recover them for a museum (the entire process is shown in figure 12.1, pages 228-29).

1. A solitary, perhaps injured or sick, animal was tracked by predators (fig. 12.1a).

2. The animal was attacked, in much the same way a pack of wolves attacks a moose (fig. 12.1b).

3. (Minutes to hours later) Cruelly, even as the prey was dying, the gorging and dismembering by the attackers began. Eventually the carcass was completely torn apart, and some bones were carried away from the killing site (fig. 12.1c).

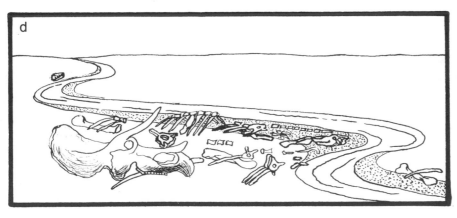

4. (Days or weeks after the kill) As the skeletal remains lay exposed on the surface, they were assaulted by the weather, and the bones were further disturbed. Bones were washed away by streams or heavy rains, and new bones, from other kills, were carried into the site by streams (fig. 12.1d).

Fig. 12.1. Sequential diagram of bone-site formation, burial, and exposure.

5. (Weeks or months after the kill) Rivers that carried bones to the original site also transported sand and mud, which buried the bones. In some places, windblown sand covered the skeletal remains with thick layers of sediment (fig. 12.1e).

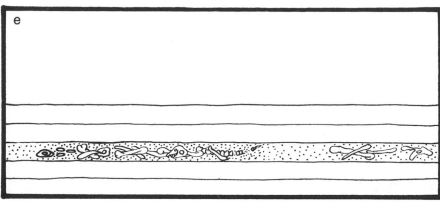

6. (Thousands or millions of years after the kill) Over time, additional sand and mud layers further buried and compressed the bones and the earlier sediments, turning the sediments into rock and possibly deforming the bones (fig. 12.1f).

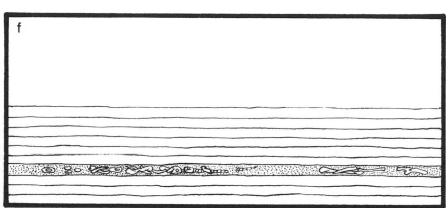

7. (Tens of millions of years after the kill) Tectonic activity (deformation of the earth's crust) tilted and uplifted the previously buried layers and exposed the bone layer at the surface (fig. 12.1g).

8. (Tens of millions of years after the kill) Weathering and erosion removed some of the enclosing rock material partially separating the bones from the materials in which they were encased during burial. Careful collection will recover as much of the original material as possible. In the excitement of the moment, however, casual collectors might take a single bone without even thinking other bones might be nearby, further dispersing the remains (fig. 12.1h).

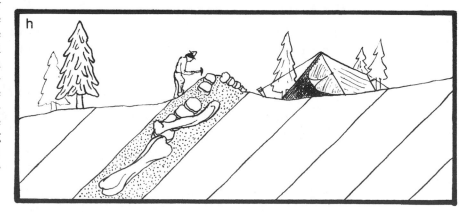

Fig. 12.1—*Continued*

ACTIVITY: WATCH IT HAPPEN

The processes of sedimentation, strata formation, and bone preservation are easily demonstrated in the classroom. The container is critical to the success of this activity: it must be clear, and the taller the better. Something tall and skinny (like a clear juice bottle) will produce better results than something wide and low (like a fish tank). It might be possible to borrow a large graduated cylinder from a high school or middle school science department.

REQUIREMENTS

Time

15-30 minutes, depending on classroom discussions

Materials

- A clear, upright container

- Approximately two handfuls of sediment (amount is not critical). Sediment can be easily obtained by scooping up some nearby stream bottom; if this is not possible, prepare a dry mix composed of aquarium gravel, coarse and fine sand, and powdered clay (proportions are not critical).

- "Dinosaur bones" (use two types: one represented by pennies and one represented by nickels or washers, approximately 5-10 of each)

- Sufficient water to almost fill the container (leave enough room at the top so that it does not overflow when the other material is added)

- Transparencies of figure 12.1

- Overhead projector

Grouping

Whole class

DIRECTIONS

1. Gather the students in a circle around the clear container partially filled with water.

2. Explain the process of sedimentation and bone preservation as described in the chapter introduction and illustrate with transparencies of figure 12.1.

3. Mix the "dinosaur bones" (coins) with the rest of the material.

4. Explain that you will be dropping the mixture into the water and it will all immediately start settling to the bottom (the process of sedimentation). Ask students to predict what will settle to the bottom first (largest size material). Tell them to focus on the "bones" and watch how the "bones" behave. The coins should fall slowly because of their flat shape. At the bottom of the container, the material will spread out, forming flat layers called strata. The coarser material will fall very quickly, but the finest materials may stay in the water for several minutes, hours, or even days,

making the water appear cloudy. Keep the container somewhere where it will remain undisturbed. Ultimately, the water will become clearer and clearer, and the finer particles will form the uppermost layer on the bottom of the container.

5. Look for the "bones" in the sediment layers. Are they in one layer or scattered? Are all the "bones" of the same type in the same layer? As scientists search for fossils, they focus on those layers where the bones seem to be concentrated.

ACTIVITY: FINDASAURUS

Looking for bone layers is much like playing detective. If the age of the earth is 4.6 billion years and dinosaurs existed for only 164 million years, it is clear that dinosaurs existed during only a very short period (3.6 percent) of earth history. Arthur Holmes (1965, 157) suggests a maximum total thickness of 452,000 feet of rocks that are known to contain fossils of animals with hard parts, and only 125,000 feet of these were deposited when the dinosaurs existed. If only 28 percent of the fossil-bearing rock thickness may contain dinosaur fossils, how do we search for them?

The first thing we must do is narrow the search. We must first locate the 28 percent of sedimentary rocks in which dinosaur fossils may be found. Consider the following situation: a paleontologist from Texas goes on vacation to Montana, where he discovers dinosaur bones in a particular layer of rock. He wonders whether the same layer exists in Texas, where he would be able to find bones much closer to home. In an ideal situation, that rock layer would be exposed at the surface continuously, and he would be able to follow it all the way from Montana to Texas. However, it is rarely the case that a rock layer is exposed continuously in this fashion. In many cases the bone layer might be covered by layers of younger rocks, and in other cases the bone layer might be worn away by erosion. Both covering and erosion would make it impossible to follow the layer from Montana to Texas.

Clearly, another method must be found for locating particular fossil-rich rock layers. One of the most reliable ways to locate particular fossils is with other fossils. Certain widely found fossils represent animals that lived on earth for a very short and very specific time; such fossils are called *index fossils*. When found in two geographically separated layers, such fossils allow scientists to say with some confidence that the layers are the same age. Index fossils can be used to track a layer from Montana to Texas, or from Montana to France. The process of determining whether layers in different places are the same is called *correlation*.

Once the layer is found, more work needs to be done. Dinosaurs probably did not live everywhere in that layer. Chapter 2 explained how fossils can be used to determine the environment at the time the animal was alive. We know that dinosaurs did not live in the oceans, so we can avoid searching in areas that fossils tell us were oceans at the time of the dinosaurs. Fish and marine reptiles (such as plesiosaurs) did not live in the same places as dinosaurs; if paleontologists find the former, they won't find the latter. Index fossils allow us to determine not only which layers contain which fossils, but also where in a particular layer certain fossils may be found.

Using fossils to correlate and locate the correct strata and to determine where in those strata dinosaurs might be found, students will learn in this activity how dinosaur fossils can be traced from one place to another.

REQUIREMENTS

Time

30-45 minutes

Materials

- Transparencies of figures 12.2 and 12.4, page 235

- Overhead projector

- For each student:
  —Drawing pencil with eraser
  —Two colored pencils
  —Copies of figures 12.2 and 12.3, page 234

Grouping

Individuals

DIRECTIONS

1. Distribute figure 12.2 to students. Explain that the figure shows two stacks of rock layers, one in Montana and one in France. Their job is to determine by matching letters (1) which layers in Montana correlate with which strata in France and (2) which layer in France would contain the same dinosaur fossil as layer "d" in Montana.

2. Have students use one of the colored pencils to connect the rock layers in Montana with those in France. Use the transparency of figure 12.2 to model one connection for the class. Students will often be reluctant to make connections because of the uncertainty involved; they do not want to make a wrong connection. Explain that this is what happens to scientists, too. The connection that they draw is called a *hypothesis*, or best guess. Will it be correct? Probably not, but that's all right. Once students add the information from the fossils (see Step 3), they will see whether they are on the right track. On the back of figure 12.2 ask students to write the letter of the layer in France they predict will contain the dinosaur bone found in layer "d" in Montana.

3. Distribute figure 12.3 to students. Figure 12.3 is a chart showing index fossils found in certain layers. Each fossil will be found in only one layer in Montana and only one layer in France; that is how the students will determine how the strata correlate. Have students use their drawing pencils and the information shown in figure 12.3 to draw the fossils in the layers shown on the chart. For instance, index fossil 2 should be drawn only in layers "c" and "i." Students should make their best efforts at reproducing the drawing accurately, but they should also be made aware

(Text continues on page 236.)

Name_____

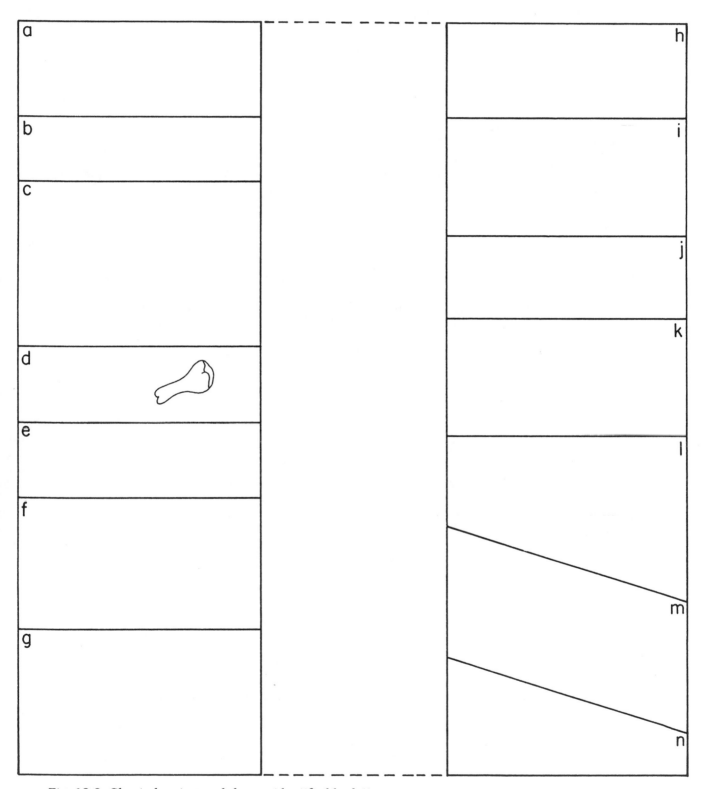

Fig. 12.2. Chart showing rock layers identified by letter.

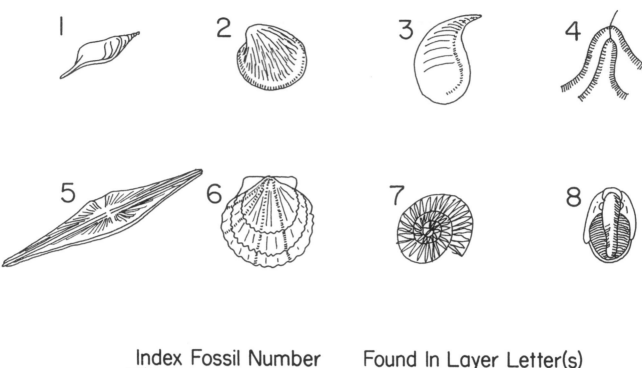

Index Fossil Number	Found In Layer Letter(s)
1	b,h
2	c,i
3	l
4	f,m
5	e,k
6	a
7	d,j
8	g,n

Fig. 12.3. Chart indicating index fossils and which rock layer they can be found in.

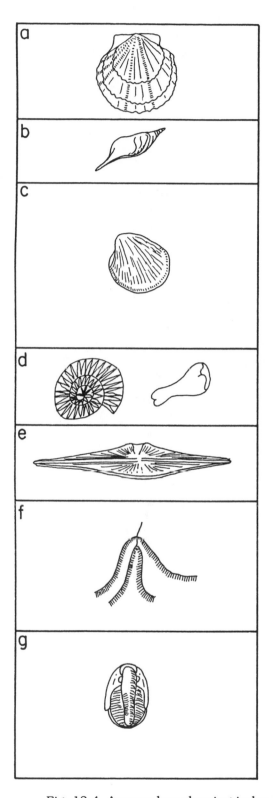
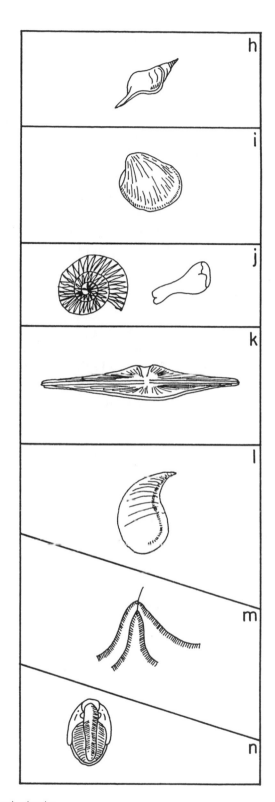

Fig. 12.4. Answer key showing index fossils placed in the correct strata.

that they will not be judged on their drawings. The drawings, like the fossils, are clues to help them determine how the layers correlate; they are not works of art. Only one fossil will be drawn in each space. Time to complete this part should be flexible, depending upon the skill level of the students.

4. Ask students to use the remaining colored pencil to connect the layers, relying on the fossil evidence they have just drawn. Have them compare these connections with those made in Step 2. Do they match? If not, which guess is most accurate, and why?

5. Ask students which layer in France they now believe contains the dinosaur fossil found in Montana layer "d" (the answer is "j"). Is it the same one that they guessed earlier? What fossil made the biggest difference?

6. Once students have completed their efforts, show them the transparency of the solution (fig. 12.4).

REFERENCES

Holmes, Arthur. 1965. *Geologic Time.* New York: Ronald Press.

Newman, William L. 1991. *Geologic Time.* Denver, Colorado: U.S. Geological Survey.

13

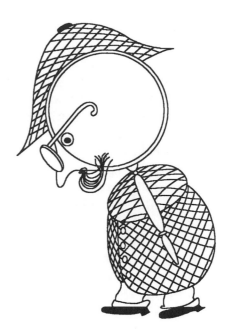

The World in the Time of the Dinosaurs

INTRODUCTION

As any geologist will tell you, the one constant about the earth is that it is always changing. Most of the changes in the earth occur at rates too slow to observe on a day-to-day basis. The global climate is possibly getting warmer; mountains and oceans are rising and falling; the rotation of the earth on its axis is slowing down; Europe and North America are moving farther apart; and the sun is getting cooler. Science fiction? No! These things are all happening as you read this book, but at rates of change so slow they have almost no impact on our daily lives. Such changes are observable only over relatively long periods of time. They are studied over years, tens of years, hundreds of years, and even thousands of years. Over such extended periods of time, the changes can be dramatic. Imagine what those changes might have produced over 65 million years and you have some idea that the earth at the time of the dinosaurs was quite a different place.

The first dinosaurs appeared on earth approximately 230 million years ago in a world that was much different than it is today. The world's large landmasses were not scattered around the globe as they are today; rather, they were connected to form a single large landmass called Pangaea, which sat in a single hemisphere, with land distributed fairly equally north and south of the equator. Animals and plants could spread freely from one portion of the landmass to another. Because there were no large bodies of water between what are now the continents, large areas of these compacted landmasses were drier than they are today. Because Pangaea straddled the equator, temperatures were generally much warmer than they are today on the now separate continents, and in many areas the landmass was covered by dense vegetation. Evidence of such climatic changes can be found in the Petrified Forest of the modern Arizona desert; the massive trunks of redwood trees in Florissant, Colorado; coal in Antarctica; and fossils of mixed hardwood forests in the badlands of Alberta, Canada, and the Dakotas.

Reptiles, some very large, adapted rapidly to this evolving world and proliferated, becoming the dominant animal form on land and in the seas. Twenty-foot crocodilians roamed the wetlands while their 40-foot finned counterparts prowled the seas. The mammals that dominate the world today had only recently emerged and, far smaller than their modern counterparts, were scurrying around the floors of the forests, hoping to avoid becoming a link in the food chain during this Age of Reptiles. The reptiles of the time, much like crocodilians and lizards of today, stood low to the ground, with long bodies supported by legs that sprawled to the side. This inefficient skeletal structure permitted only short bursts of speed over relatively small distances and limited feeding to low-growing plants and generally slower animals. Large ecological niches remained, and these were filled by the animals that would dominate the earth longer than any other—the dinosaurs.

As a life form, dinosaurs were once considered a failure of the evolutionary system because they no longer exist. The reality is that dinosaurs were a glowing success. These animals not only lived on this planet for approximately 164 million years (humankind has existed on earth for only one to two million years and has dramatically changed the planet) but absolutely dominated the world around them. That the Age of Mammals began after the dinosaurs became extinct is not coincidence; while the dinosaurs existed, the mammals simply never had a chance.

Prior to the early 1960s, much of what earth scientists studied was a series of seemingly unrelated geologic events and physical features. Earthquakes shook houses and volcanoes erupted. Scientists noticed that parts of the landmasses seemed to fit together, that high mountains on land seemed to parallel deep trenches in the ocean floor, that rocks and fossils of similar types were found on landmasses separated by thousands of miles of ocean. As scientists studied these diverse features and events and plotted them on maps, certain patterns appeared. Earthquakes, volcanoes, and mountains seemed to arise in narrow bands that could be traced around the earth, somewhat like seams on a baseball. At the same time, new technology developed during World War II permitted detailed study of the ocean floor, and what scientists discovered seemed related to the patterns they had already discovered on land. All this new information was rolled into a new theory that tried to tie all of these diverse events into a single, unifying geologic process: the theory of plate tectonics.

A theory is to earth scientists what a syndrome is to a doctor. It attempts to attribute a collection of apparently diverse facts to a single cause. Is it always correct? No. Will it be revised as new information becomes available? Absolutely. That's how science works. In science there is a sequence of confidence that is gained as information is explored. The list that follows is one example of that sequence:

idea   least confidence
concept
hypothesis
theory
law   most confidence

In the minds of some, the scientific process seems similar to the machinations of Merlin the magician: incantations shrouded by mystery, producing some magical, incomprehensible result that affects our lives in ways we cannot hope to control. In fact, if you look in *Roget's Thesaurus,* you will find *sciences* sandwiched in among *sorcery, occult, hoodoo,* and *voodoo.* The impact of this prejudice is that studies made and conclusions drawn by scientists are often suspect.

Scientists cannot turn lead into gold; if we could, we would all be much richer than most of us are. Science does, however, search for the truth about the world around us; it strives for confidence in conclusions and repeatability of effort. That sounds incredibly grandiose, but it is the simple premise that drives the scientific process.

Students must become aware of differences between an idea, a theory (for example, humans evolved from life forms that existed at the time of the dinosaurs) and a law (when a dinosaur died, gravity caused it to fall down). Any idea is valid until tested information proves it wrong. If proven wrong, it must be revised or discarded. If proven correct, enough evaluation and testing will cause it to become accepted as a fact. If a collection of facts withstands the verification process, it becomes a theory. Sustained testing and verification to the point of certainty will cause the theory to be accepted as a law.

The key to acceptance and verification is scrutiny and review by fellow scientists. Scientists are an extremely competitive lot, driven frequently by one-upmanship. The drive to be first in such competition can result in the creation of false claims and less-than-rigorous proofs by the claimant. However, a rigid and public peer review process is immediately undertaken by all those who were ostensibly outdone. It is after discoveries are announced in scientific journals that this process of scrutiny begins.

ACTIVITY: THE PUZZLING PAST

Some 400 years ago, early explorers noticed that the coastlines of the continents looked as though they might fit together like a giant jigsaw puzzle. A few people even wondered whether it was possible that at one time the earth's dry surfaces had been connected and then broken apart to form the landmasses as we know them today. This idea was dismissed because there was no evidence at the time to support such a theory. Three hundred years passed before the fossil evidence became available to reopen the discussion.

In this activity, students will be presented with pictures of the fossil remains of *Glossopteris,* a large-leafed plant, and *Mesosaurus,* a small reptile that lived in fresh or slightly salty water. Students will try to determine how these fossil remains came to appear in diverse locations identified on a map.

REQUIREMENTS

Time

One 10-minute modeling lesson by teacher, plus two sessions

Materials

- Large world map for demonstration lesson

- Transparency of prediction guide for teacher demonstration (fig. 13.1)

- Transparency of world map (figure 13.3, p. 243)

- Overhead projector

- For each pair of students:
  —Copy of prediction guide (fig. 13.1)
  —Pictures of *Glossopteris* and *Mesosaurus* (fig. 13.2, p. 242)
  —World map with legend showing the locations of *Glossopteris*
     and *Mesosaurus* fossil discoveries (fig. 13.3)
  —One pencil for each student

Grouping

Whole class for model lesson, then pairs of students working together for the prediction activity and the map activity

DIRECTIONS

1. Gather students together to look at the sample prediction guide (fig. 13.1) on the overhead projector.

2. Ask students how the same type of fossil might have come to be deposited in two far-apart places (for example, on the east coast of the United States and the west coast of Great Britain). Emphasize to students that they will be making predictions or guesses based on any information that they may have. Encourage them to refer to the world map and think about the location of the two countries.

3. Once you have received three different responses, write them down in the three large targets on the prediction guide transparency.

4. Explain to students that they will be receiving their own prediction guides and other materials and that they will be writing down their predictions in the large targets in the same manner. Tell them to ignore the small targets at the bottom for the time being.

5. Distribute the fossil pictures, the map and legend, and the prediction guides (figs. 13.1-13.3) to each pair of students.

(Text continues on page 244.)

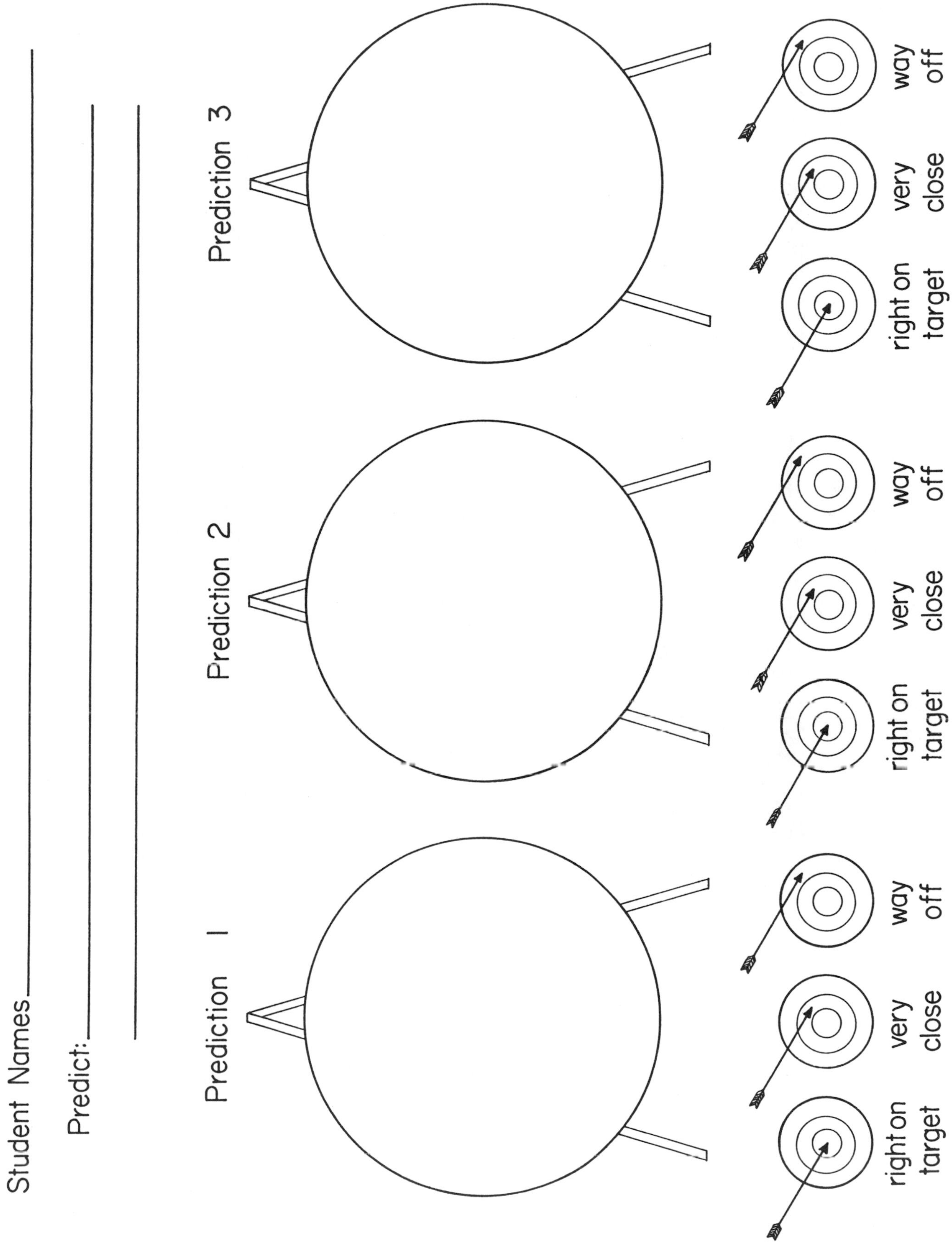

Student Names

Predict:

Prediction 1

Prediction 2

Prediction 3

right on target   very close   way off

right on target   very close   way off

right on target   very close   way off

Fig. 13.1. Prediction guide.

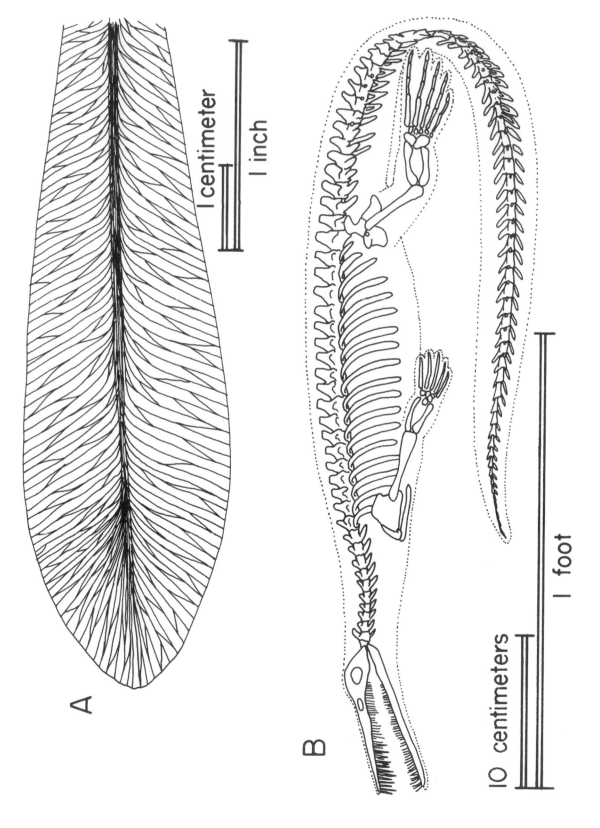

Fig. 13.2. Fossil remains of *Glossopteris* (A) (From Leet and Judson) and *Mesosaurus* (B) (From Czerkas and Czerkas).

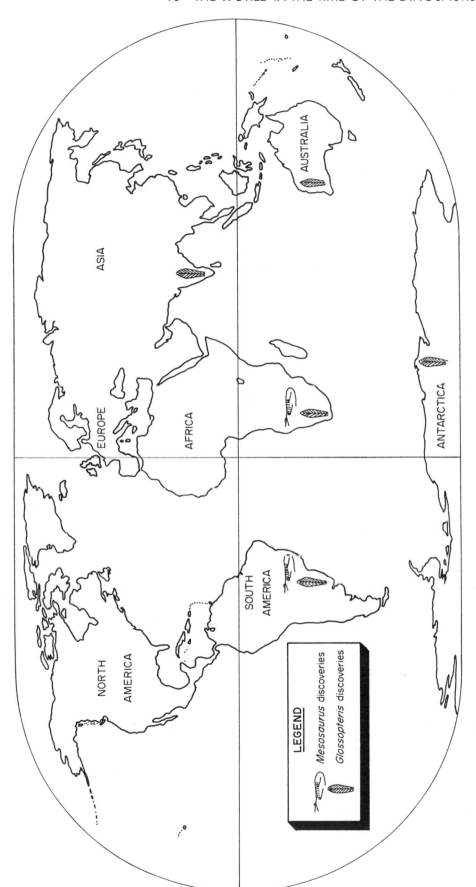

Fig. 13.3. World map showing locations of *Glossopteris* and *Mesosaurus* fossil finds.

6. Project world map (fig. 13.3) and introduce map legends if students are unfamiliar with them. Explain that the small pictures on the legend represent *Glossopteris* and *Mesosaurus* fossils and that when the small pictures appear on the world map, it means that the fossils can be found in that location. Point out a few examples on the map.

7. Have each student pair write down their names and enter the following question at the top of their prediction guide: How do you predict the fossil remains of *Glossopteris* and *Mesosaurus* came to be discovered in all of the areas identified on the map?

8. Have each pair make one prediction about how these two ancient organisms came to be on different continents. When pairs think they have a good prediction, have them write it down in the first large target on the prediction guide.

9. After students have recorded their prediction, give those who choose to, an opportunity to share their predictions.

REQUIREMENTS

Materials

- World map
- "Our Earth Has Changed" (copy follows)
- Prediction guides
- One crayon or marker for each pair of students
- One pencil for each pair of students

Grouping

Whole class for the initial reading, then partners for the prediction activity

DIRECTIONS

1. Tell students they will be listening to information that will help them make two more predictions.

Our Earth Has Changed

When we look at a map of the earth's surface, we are able to see how some of the continents seem to fit together like pieces of a giant jigsaw puzzle. Scientists and explorers made this same observation nearly 400 years ago. No one could explain how the continents could have been connected and then broken apart, so the idea was forgotten for the next 300 years.

The idea that the continents might have been connected came up again when scientists started making some interesting fossil discoveries. How was it possible for a large-leafed plant like *Glossopteris* to have left fossil remains in South America, South Africa, Australia, India, and Antarctica? All of these places have very different climates, and they are thousands of miles apart. Had *Glossopteris* grown in all these different places? Scientists did not think this was very likely. Was it possible that this plant had grown on one very large body of land that later broke apart to form the different landmasses the fossils were found on? Scientists liked this solution better, but they could not explain how this might have happened.

At about the same time *Glossopteris* flourished, a small reptile called *Mesosaurus* also lived. Its fossils have been found in two places: the east coast of Brazil and the west coast of South Africa. Once again, scientists wondered how the fossils of this small reptile came to appear in two very different places. Again they asked themselves whether the continents had been joined at one time.

Many more fossils have been discovered that help scientists to understand changes in the earth's climate and the positions of the continents.

(Pause: tell students to enter a
second prediction in the second large target.)

Finally, in the 1960s, earth scientists developed a theory about how the earth's surface may have changed over millions of years. Scientists now believe that the earth's outer layer (crust) is made up of a number of huge plates. The plates float on denser material in the earth's mantle (the layer below the crust). As these plates move, everything that is on them moves, too. That means that the oceans, continents, and islands are all moving! This motion is very slow, so we do not feel it. Parts of the earth's surface are moving one or two inches every year—about as quickly as fingernails grow. Other parts move twice as fast. This theory—called plate tectonics—helps scientists explain how the surface of the earth has changed over millions and millions of years.

(Pause: tell students to enter their
third prediction in the third large target.)

2. Have students look at their predictions and decide whether they were right on target, close to target, or way off target.

3. Have students color in the appropriate small target under each large-target prediction.

4. Discuss with students how their predictions changed as they listened to "Our Earth Has Changed."

EXTENSIONS

Prediction guides may be used anytime a new question is posed. The more frequently students use the guides, the more accurate their predictions will become. Divide the class into three or four groups and assign each group a question such as the following: Why couldn't dinosaurs live in your backyard? Why were there more herbivores than carnivores? How did climatic changes affect the dinosaurs' habitat? After students have completed a prediction guide, direct them to the library to research the answers.

ACTIVITY: PLATE PUZZLE

It is difficult for students to imagine the world ever looking any different than it does on today's maps. In this activity, students will reorganize the earth's surface to look as it did in the time of the dinosaurs.

REQUIREMENTS

Time

45 minutes

Materials

- For each student:
  —Copies of figures 13.4 and 13.5, pages 248 and 249
  —Scissors
  —Glue
  —Pencil

- For the teacher:
  —Globe
  —World map (other than Mercator projection)
  —Transparencies of figures 13.6 and 13.7, pages 250 and 251
  —Overhead projector

Grouping

Students may work together or individually, but each child will have a finished product at the end of the session

DIRECTIONS

1. Introduce students to plate tectonics by looking at a globe and comparing the shapes and sizes of the landmasses. Compare the globe to a giant jigsaw puzzle.

2. Direct their attention to the equator, the prime meridian, the north pole, and the south pole.

3. Point out the four cardinal directions—north, south, east, and west—in relationship to the equator and the poles. To make sure students understand, ask questions such as, Which landmasses are north of the equator? Which are south of the equator? What ocean borders the western United States? What ocean borders the eastern United States?

4. Show students the global template (fig. 13.4). Ask them to identify the equator and the north and south poles.

5. Distribute figures 13.4 and 13.5. Have students cut out the continent puzzle pieces from figure 13.5 and glue them in the appropriate place on the global template. Explain that matching up the fossil pictures on the puzzle pieces will help. The end result will be a reconstruction of the world as it appeared during the time of the dinosaurs.

(Text continues on page 252.)

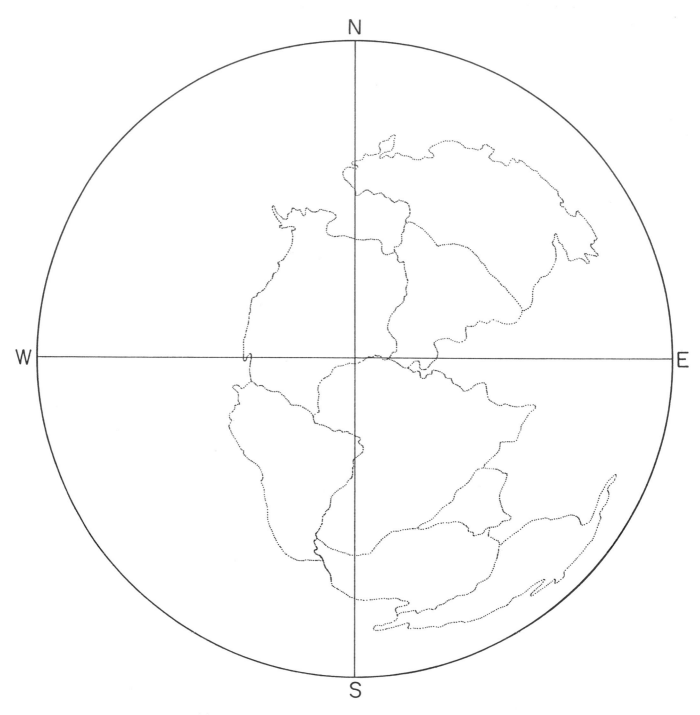

Fig. 13.4. Map template showing the outlines of the continental plates just before the time of the dinosaurs (Permian age). Modified from Czerkas and Czerkas.

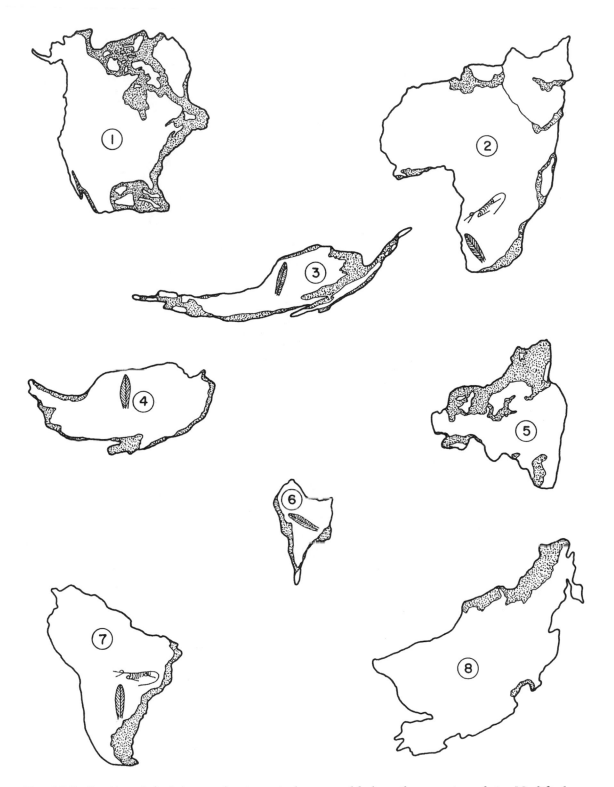

Fig. 13.5. Continental plate puzzle pieces to be assembled on the map template. Modified from Czerkas and Czerkas.

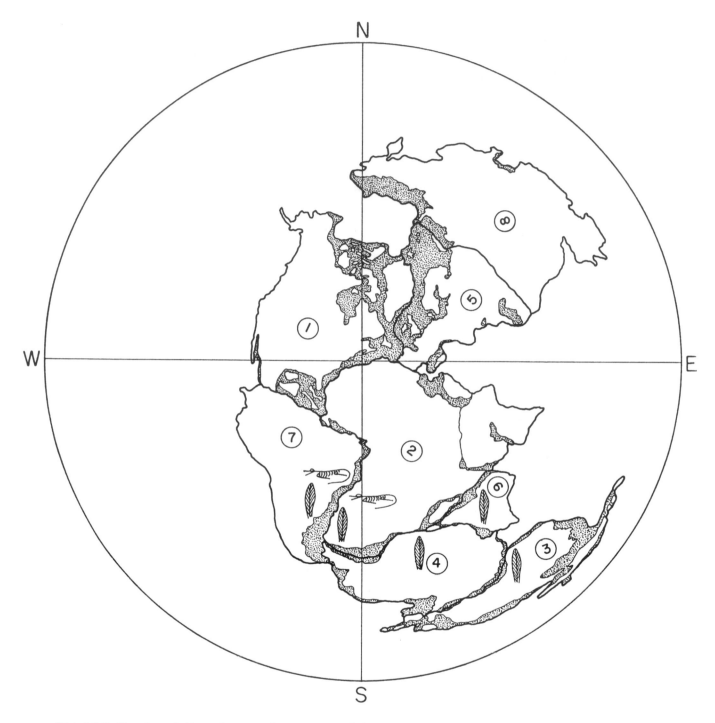

Fig. 13.6. Puzzle solution showing the position of the continental plates just before the time of the dinosaurs. Modified from Czerkas and Czerkas.

Fig. 13.7. Position of the continental plates during the late Cretaceous. Modified from Czerkas and Czerkas.

Closure

Show transparencies of figures 13.6 and 13.7. Have students make comparisons and discuss the arrows showing the shift of the landmasses.

EXTENSIONS

1. Once the world during the time of the dinosaurs has been re-created, ask students to explain why scientists have discovered the fossil remains of many tropical plants in Antarctica and Alaska.

2. Have students choose a dinosaur and research all of the different places its fossil remains have been found. Ask them to report on how they believe the animal came to be in so many different places.

REFERENCES

Czerkas, Sylvia J., and Stephen A. Czerkas. 1991. *Dinosaurs: A Global View*. New York: Mallard Press.

Lauber, Patricia. 1987. *Dinosaurs Walked Here and Other Stories Fossils Tell*. New York: Bradbury Press.

————. 1991. *Living with Dinosaurs*. New York: Bradbury Press.

Leet, L. Don, and Sheldon Judson. 1971. *Physical Geology*. Englewood Cliffs, New Jersey: Prentice-Hall.

SUGGESTED READING

Gallant, Roy A. 1986. *From Living Cells to Dinosaurs*. New York: Franklin Watts.

Kiefer, Irene. 1978. *Global Jigsaw Puzzle: The Story of Continental Drift*. Brattleboro, Vermont: The Book Press.

Munsart, Craig A. 1993. *Investigating Science with Dinosaurs*. Englewood, Colorado: Teacher Ideas Press.

Rossbacher, Lisa A. 1986. *Recent Revolutions in Geology*. New York: Franklin Watts.

14

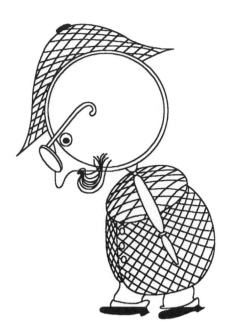

Strut Your Stuff: A Grand Celebration

ACTIVITY: A GRAND CELEBRATION

This culminating activity ties together all the animals and concepts introduced in *Primary Dinosaur Investigations*. The activity itself involves the creation of a cultural and scientific showplace where students can entertain their parents and other important people.

REQUIREMENTS

Time

This will largely depend on your school schedule and community participation. We recommend an evening activity that would last approximately two hours. Be sure to allow adequate set-up time to accommodate the number of activities to be showcased.

Materials

- A large space such as the school gymnasium, cafeteria, or a long hallway
- Wall and table space to display student activity projects
- Masking tape
- Staples
- Name tags
- Markers

Grouping

All students who have been involved in the *Primary Dinosaur Investigations* study

DIRECTIONS

Early in the dinosaur investigations study, start collecting student work to display at the celebration. As you begin the activities, you might want to provide each student with a portfolio to store flat materials in. It would also be handy to have several storage-size boxes for three-dimensional materials. Be sure to label the boxes as you place products in them; otherwise, they become the safe places that are lost forever (this may sound like the voice of experience; we'll let you draw your own conclusion).

Following is a partial list of items you may want to save (and how to use them) for the celebration. (While no specific activities are listed for chapters 7, 8, and 9, students may want to involve visitors in some of the activities that were completed in class):

Chapter 1: The Process of Dinosaur Discoveries

- KWL Graphic Organizer
- Group murals of the Montana dig

Chapter 2: Fossils

- Cross section of modern animal environments
- Fossil research outlines

Chapter 3: Bones, Bones, Bones

- Assembled bone pictures

Chapter 4: Full Size

- Set of footprints (arrange these to lead from the school's front door to the area where the celebration is taking place)
- Full-size dinosaur drawings—both skeletons and those with skin overlays (hang these along the route to the celebration)
- Full-size dinosaur drawings (incorporate these into the Mesozoic murals [chapter 7] showing camouflage and plant life)

Chapter 5: Eyes

- Experiments from the activities "Seeing Two Pictures at the Same Time" and "Two Are Better Than One" (repeat these with parents and guests)

Chapter 6: Tails, Legs, Feet, Arms, and Hands

- The animals created during the activity "Let's Buildasaur"

Chapter 10: Sounds

- Pan pipes and "bottle band" (display these so students can explain and demonstrate how they work)

- Enlargements of the hadrosaur crest drawings (have students explain that the crests may have been used in sound production)

Chapter 11: What and When

- Dinomo wall chart

Chapter 12: Correlations

- Findasaurus

Chapter 13: The World in the Time of the Dinosaurs

- Prediction Guide

- Pangaea maps

In addition to all the science that will be on display, set out some of the books that the students used for research. A quiet corner with some pillows and carpets might prove inviting to some young paleontologists and provide an opportunity for some of the more seasoned readers to familiarize themselves with current research.

Dinosaur Dances by Jane Yolen (1990) is a collection of poems written strictly for humor. Students might enjoy presenting these to parents and guests either as choral or individual readings. Other good choices include Jack Prelutsky's *Something Big Has Been Here* (1990) or *The Dragons Are Singing Tonight* (1993).

Students could use their paper bag masks from chapter 5 and stage their own dinosaur dance.

As you can see, the grand celebration is just that: an opportunity for students to share their enthusiasm and learning with others. It's an opportunity to share the exciting things that are happening in classrooms where literature is integrated into all areas of learning. It's time for everyone to enjoy.

REFERENCES

Prelutsky, Jack. 1990. *Something Big Has Been Here.* New York: Greenwillow Books.

———. 1993. *The Dragons Are Singing Tonight.* New York: Greenwillow Books.

Yolen, Jane. 1990. *Dinosaur Dances.* New York: G. P. Putnam's Sons.

Grouping Strategies

Many activities involve groups. Below are listed some ways of varying and selecting student groupings.

1. Select as many matched playing cards as there are students in your class. Deal cards to students. The two red jacks get together, two black fours get together, and so on.

2. Write all of the students' names on tongue depressors. Draw them out of a can and match them two by two.

3. Cut 2-x-8-inch strips of construction paper into matching puzzle pieces. Pass out all pieces and have students search to find their matching partner.

4. Form groups by cutting comic strips into sections. Students need to find their comic strip partners to form a group.

5. Number students one through five to create groups of five. All the ones stay together, all the twos stay together. This procedure can be varied for any number.

6. Attach four large cards to the wall, each with a job title and description written on it. Use a different color for each card. The four job descriptions might be (1) recorder—writes down group responses, decisions, concerns, (2) leader—keeps group members on task, (3) reporter—reports group member responses back to the entire group, and (4) encourager—gives positive feedback on ideas that are shared. With the same four colors used on the job cards, write down the numbers one through six (or whatever number comes closest to evenly dividing class size by four) on small pieces of paper. Mix these up and pass them out. All of the students who drew the same number will work together as a group; each student should end up with a different color-designated job.

7. Write each student's name on a strip of paper. Place all of the strips in a can, bag, or box. Draw one name from the container. That child will draw one or more names (depending on desired group size) from the container to form his or her group. Draw the first name for the next new group.

8. Arrange chairs in a circle, as for musical chairs. Start some music and remove three (number can vary, depending on desired group size) chairs. When you stop the music, children must sit down. Three children will be without chairs, and they are a group.

9. Peer partnerships or partnerships with older students. Invite older students to participate in activities that may require extra hands or better dexterity.

Annotated Book List

Aliki. *Dinosaurs Are Different.* New York: Harper Trophy, 1985.
Explains how the various orders and suborders of dinosaurs were similar and different in structure and appearance.

————. *Digging Up Dinosaurs.* New York: HarperCollins, 1988.
Briefly introduces various types of dinosaurs whose skeletons and reconstructions are seen in museums and explains how scientists uncover, preserve, and study fossilized dinosaur bones.

————. *Dinosaur Bones.* New York: Harper Trophy, 1988.
Discusses how scientists studying fossil remains provide information on how dinosaurs lived millions of years ago.

————. *Fossils Tell of Long Ago.* New York: Harper Trophy, 1990.
Explains how fossils are formed and what they tell us about the past.

Baylor, Byrd. *If You Are a Hunter of Fossils.* New York: Charles Scribner's Sons, 1980.
A fossil hunter looking for signs of an ancient sea in the rocks of a western Texas mountain describes how the area must have looked millions of years ago.

Brown, Ruth. *If at First You Do Not See.* New York: Holt, 1982.
A caterpillar has some scary adventures before becoming a beautiful butterfly. The reader needs to turn the book as he or she reads, because there is writing around the sides of the pages.

Carrick, Carol. *What Happened to Patrick's Dinosaurs?* New York: Trumpet, 1986.
Patrick imagines many different dinosaurs when he looks at things common to his surroundings.

Cash, Terry. *Sounds.* New York: Warwick Press, 1989.
Experiments with and explanations of sound production.

Farlow, James O. *On the Tracks of Dinosaurs: A Study of Dinosaur Footprints*. New York: Franklin Watts, 1991.
Describes the formation and discovery of fossilized dinosaur footprints and how paleontologists use them to learn about the probable nature and behavior of the animals who made them.

Ferrell, Nancy Warren. *Camouflage: Nature's Defense*. New York: Franklin Watts, 1989.
Discusses various forms of protective defenses used by animals, with an emphasis on camouflage phenomena such as disruptive coloration and concealing coloration.

Fornari, Giuliano. *The Great Dinosaur Atlas*. Englewood Cliffs, New Jersey: Simon & Schuster, 1991.
Beautiful illustrated text of many common and not-so-common dinosaurs.

Hagood, Allen, and Linda West. *Dinosaur: The Story Behind the Scenery*. Las Vegas, Nevada: KC Publications, 1992.

Hoffman, Mary. *Animals in the Wild: Zebra*. Milwaukee, Wisconsin: Raintree Children's Books, 1985.
Describes the life and habitat of the zebra, with emphasis on its struggle for survival.

Horner, John R., and James Gorman. *Maia: A Dinosaur Grows Up*. Philadelphia, Pennsylvania: Running Press, 1989.
Maia is a realistic account of the life of a young dinosaur, written by the first paleontologist ever to discover an extensive dinosaur nesting ground. This discovery, made by paleontologist John R. Horner in the Montana grasslands in 1978, enabled scientists to piece together a picture of a new species of peaceable, duckbilled dinosaur.

Larrick, Nancy, and Wendy Lamb (eds.). *To Ride a Butterfly*. New York: Bantam Doubleday Dell, 1991.
An illustrated collection of fables, folktales, stories, poems, songs, and nonfiction by a variety of authors and illustrators.

Lauber, Patricia. *Dinosaurs Walked Here and Other Stories Fossils Tell*. New York: Bradbury Press, 1987.
Discusses how fossilized remains of plants and animals reveal the characteristics of the prehistoric world.

———. *Living with Dinosaurs*. New York: Bradbury Press, 1991.
Re-creates life among the dinosaurs that inhabited North America 75 million years ago.

Most, Bernard. *Dinosaur Cousins?* New York: Harcourt Brace Jovanovich, 1987.
Examines 19 modern animals and describes the dinosaurs they resemble in appearance or behavior, making such comparisons as the giraffe to the long-necked *Brachiosaurus* and the armadillo to the armored *Ankylosaurus*.

Parker, Steve. *Dinosaurs and Their World.* New York: Grosset & Dunlap, 1988.
Provides good information about dinosaurs but makes too many comparisons to humans for size reference. This could be confusing for the very young reader because humans and dinosaurs did not coexist.

Patent, Dorothy Hinshaw. *The Challenge of Extinction.* Hillside, New Jersey: Enslow, 1991.
Focuses on the scientific, technological, and social impacts of plant and animal extinction.

Schlein, Miriam. *Discovering Dinosaur Babies.* New York: Four Winds Press, 1991.
Explains what paleontologists have been able to determine about how different varieties of dinosaurs cared for their young.

Selsam, Millicent. *Strange Creatures That Really Lived.* New York: Scholastic, 1987.
Provides pictures and brief descriptions of prehistoric animals.

Simon, Seymour. *The Largest Dinosaurs.* New York: Macmillan, 1986.
Surveys findings on *Brachiosaurus, Diplodocus,* and four other examples of the largest dinosaurs, including the locations of the discoveries and explanations of the dinosaur's names.

————. *New Questions and Answers About Dinosaurs.* New York: Trumpet, 1990.
Discusses current questions about dinosaurs.

Sowler, Sandie. *Amazing Animal Disguises.* New York: Alfred A. Knopf, 1992.
Introduces animal disguises involving camouflage and mimicry in such animals as the zebra, polar bear, and caterpillar.

West, Linda, and Dan Chure. *Dinosaur: The Dinosaur National Monument Quarry.* Jensen, Utah: Dinosaur Nature Association. 1989.
Good general resource.

Yolen, Jane. *Dinosaur Dances.* New York: G. P. Putnam's Sons, 1990.
Seventeen whimsical poems featuring *Allosaurus, Stegosaurus, Tyrannosaurus,* and other dancing dinosaurs.

Map and Globe Orders

MAPS

The United States Geological Survey provides a variety of maps, with an obvious focus on the 50 states and U.S. possessions and territories. USGS produces one of the few maps of the United States available showing Hawaii and Alaska in their actual positions, not as insets between Texas and Baja, California. Not only are most USGS maps inexpensive to begin with, but as of January 1995, educators can obtain any map products at half price by ordering on school letterhead or school purchase order. For details contact:

United States Geological Survey
Map Distribution
Box 25286
Denver, CO 80225
(303) 236-7477

Two good primary maps are available for purchase from Nystrom: Readiness World Map—Robinson Projection (INS99 $109.00) and Readiness World/U.S. Map Combination (INS991 $179.00). Contact Nystrom at:

3333 Elston Avenue
Chicago, IL 60618-5898
(312) 463-0515 or (800) 621-8086

GLOBES

A good primary globe is available through CRAM. The surface is made of an erasable material that can be written on with a wax pencil or crayon. The 16-inch Discovery Globe is guaranteed against peeling, cracking, or breaking and includes globe markers for markable surface. The metal mounting helps make this a good resource for hands-on activities. Order #1661 Swing Meridian, $135.00 (1994 price list), or #1601 Clear View Mounting, $98.00 (1994 price list).

Another useful globe is the 16-inch Sun Ray Mounting globe. This globe illustrates earth/sun relationships. Students can gain a better understanding of changing seasons, day and night, long and short days, earth rotation and revolution. Order #1657, $240.00 (1994 price list). Contact CRAM at:

George Cram & Company
301 S. LaSalle St.
Indianapolis, IN 42601
(317) 635-5564

Fossil Collections

Through three regional libraries the United States Geological Survey makes available fossil sets for free loan to educators. These sets contain a wide variety of hands-on fossils and casts, of both dinosaur and nondinosaur animals and plants. Contacts are listed below.

U.S. Geological Survey Library—National Center Geocenter
Mail Stop 950
12201 Sunrise Valley Drive
Reston, VA 22092-9998
Contact: Suellen Skinner
(703) 648-4476

U.S. Geological Survey Library Geocenter
Mail Stop 914
Box 25046
Denver, CO 80255-0046
Contact: Susann Powers
(303) 236-1015

U.S. Geological Survey Library Geocenter
Mail Stop 955
345 Middlefield Road
Menlo Park, CA 94025-3591
Contact: Diane Yassenoff
(415) 329-5028

Geologic Time

Time is a difficult concept for young students (and many adults). It is often measured in abstract ways: the earth moving around the sun, and the earth rotating on its own axis. When a young student's greatest temporal challenge is mastery of the analog (as opposed to the digital) clock, the idea that the motion of celestial bodies can be used to measure time really stretches the limits of his or her comprehension.

In the earth sciences, however, time is truly the fourth critical dimension. Length, width, and depth can physically delimit mountains, glaciers, and oceans, but to understand what is happening to those physical features, those dimensions must be placed within the framework of time. Time is important for two reasons:

1. Many events happen so slowly that instantaneous evaluation is almost meaningless. Plates move around on the earth's crust; mountains rise; resources are depleted; global sea levels rise and fall; pollution fills the atmosphere; trees are cut in the rain forest; ice caps melt: the impact of these generally slow processes can only truly be measured if enough time has passed.

2. Processes have been operating over a long period. The universe was formed sometime between 10 and 20 billion years ago (Sagan 1980, 246). Twenty billion is a huge number. On the clearest, pollution-free night, the naked eye can see approximately 2,000 stars in the star-filled sky. Twenty billion is 10 million times this figure. To study events that occur over such a long period, smaller intervals must be created to provide a framework for understanding time: hours, days, months, years, centuries, millennia.

For earth scientists, time becomes important at approximately 4.6 billion years ago, when the earth was formed (Holmes 1965, 380). On a time scale of this magnitude, dinosaurs do not appear until the relatively recent past (see fig. 1, p. 268). Geologic time from the earth's formation to the present is divided into four large intervals called eras (see fig. 2, p. 268), based upon life forms found within

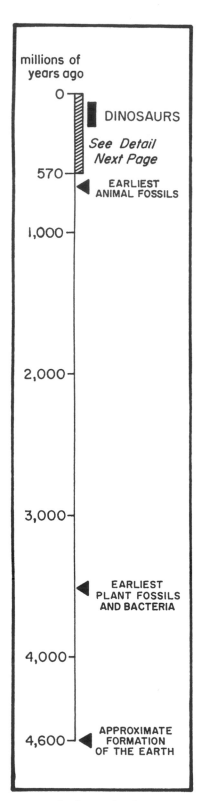

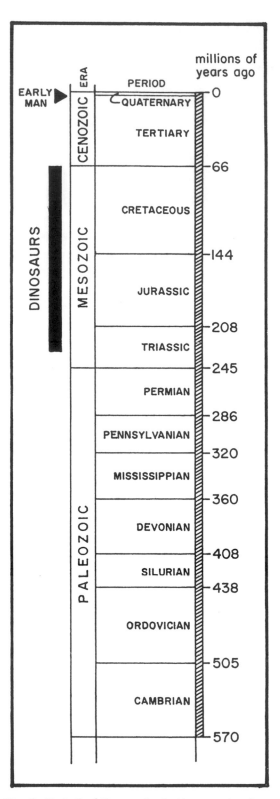

Fig. 1. Time scale from the formation of the earth to the present. The Paleozoic, Mesozoic, and Cenozoic eras are shaded. Notice that dinosaurs did not appear until the relatively recent past.

Fig. 2. Detail of the geologic time scale showing the Paleozoic, Mesozoic, and Cenozoic eras and the period during which the dinosaurs lived.

them: the Precambrian ("before old life"; 4,600-570 million years ago), the Paleozoic ("old life"; 570-245 million years ago), the Mesozoic ("middle life"; 66-245 million years ago), and the Cenozoic ("recent life"; 66 million years ago to the present). The eras are further divided into periods, epochs and ages. Considerably more detail about the formulation of the geologic time scale can be found in Arthur Holmes (1965, 154-157) and Allison R. Palmer (1983). An excellent (and free) brochure by William Newman (1991) is available from the U.S. Geological Survey.

As you study geologic time, you may become aware that the dates given for certain events, time spans, and fossil finds may vary from source to source. This is due not to scientific error but to different interpretations of the data on which the dates are based. In *Primary Dinosaur Investigations,* dates are based on Palmer (1983).

REFERENCES

Holmes, Arthur. 1965. *Principles of Physical Geology.* New York: Ronald Press.

Newman, William L. 1991. *Geologic Time.* Denver, Colorado: U.S. Geological Survey.

Palmer, Allison R. 1983. The Decade of North American Geology; 1983 Geologic Time Scale. *Geology* 11, no. 9:503-504.

Sagan, Carl. 1980. *Cosmos.* New York: Random House.

The Field Trip

As Alfred T. Collette and Eugene L. Chiappetta write, "Study indoors the things that are best studied indoors; study outdoors the things that are best studied outdoors" (1989, 189). Although it seems self-evident, this simple premise is often overlooked during much science instruction. With the abundance, convenience, and availability of videos as a resource, field trips to see the real thing are often ignored. Audiovisual materials are useful, but as a teaching resource, showing a student a picture of a dinosaur bone is not nearly as effective as placing one in the student's hand or in front of the student's face.

What we know about dinosaurs, we know from two sources: fossils the animals left behind and comparisons to animals that exist today. The former are most accessible in natural history museums, the latter in zoos; both are excellent resources for studying dinosaurs and both complement the use of library resources. Like a trip to the library, a trip to the zoo or museum can provide important information that may dramatically improve a student's performance and research products. With only minimal planning, students can be encouraged to examine, identify, compare, and answer questions based upon the resources available at the museum. Observation and recording information are critical steps in the scientific process; such activities should be incorporated in any visit to a field resource. As Rosalyn Yalow writes in *Science for Children* (1988, iii), "Science is not simply a collection of facts; it is a discipline of thinking about rational solutions to problems after establishing the basic facts derived from observations." The field trip should be considered part of a learning continuum that includes classroom studies, planning for what can be learned from the outside resource, the field trip, and incorporating what was learned in the field with what was previously known from classwork.

A scheduled visit to the school library without specific plans for student activity would be absurd. Students would wander aimlessly, be nonproductive, and probably exhibit behavioral problems. Yet that is precisely what happens on many field trips as a result of lack of planning. As John H. Falk and John D. Balling describe

(1980, 7), the field trip setting can create certain behaviors in the participants. Extreme novelty in a field trip site "causes fear, excitement, and nervousness." Sites that are too familiar "cause boredom, diversionary activities, and fatigue." A natural history museum or a zoo is a major attraction for any community, and preschool-age students may have already attended with family members. Pretrip discussions of plans and activities with the class can:

1. Alleviate the anxieties of those going to the resource for the first time. For very young students this may be the first field trip from school, and some extra discussion time may be worthwhile (perhaps students who have already been to the field trip destination can contribute).

2. Increase the interest of those students who may think, "Oh no! Not the museum again!" Discussion of a well-planned, structured visit with activities to maintain student interest may be able to involve even the hard-core skeptics (perhaps you could use them as leaders of student groups).

To utilize the field resource effectively, we believe it is important to have specific ideas for student activities (worksheets, scavenger hunts), prepare the students beforehand, and incorporate the knowledge gained from the field resource into subsequent lessons in the classroom. We also believe the students will function best within small groups. Unfortunately, such grouping will require additional supervision (parents, aides, high school students) that is often unavailable.

THE MUSEUM FIELD TRIP

Unfortunately for most of us, dinosaur resources in the field are often too far from the classroom to be used effectively as teaching tools. Museums provide a valuable alternative. Although the museums cannot duplicate the discovery experience of the field, they can display assembled, upright skeletons of several specimens, providing a perspective and variety that visitors to the field do not receive. They can also make a broad variety of dinosaur resources visible to students.

The typical visit to a natural history museum is often less than ideal. Once the reality hits that yours is the 43rd school bus in line in the parking lot, you realize that any desire to make yourself heard above the din surrounding every exhibit for the next four hours is mostly fantasy. The best you may be able to hope for is to get all the students back on the bus in a timely manner. Too often a class museum visit involves a cursory walk-through of a dinosaur exhibit, with students holding hands as they pass the skeletons and displays (which are often surrounded by hordes of other, often much older, students doing the same thing), or perhaps a lecture by museum staff members, with students sitting in small groups in a noisy, distracting exhibit hall. In most instances, the supporting text for exhibits is incomprehensible to students of younger grades, and the exhibit itself may be designed for an adult of average height, so that primary students are at a physical disadvantage as well. In this case, even the most outstanding museum display often yields only minimal information to young students. If arrangements for special classes conducted by the museum staff are not made, the student experience can often be passive and nonstimulating and involve little learning. Consequently, neither the teacher nor the student is satisfied with the visit, students become discipline problems, and the highlight of the day often becomes the lunch break. Correcting these problems—not only for the sake of the students but also because field trips are often expensive and difficult to schedule—is critical.

There is great variety in the magnitude and nature of dinosaur exhibits in museums. Some exhibits are collections of mounted dinosaur skeletons; others may address the finding, recovery, and assembly of specimens; and still others may focus on the nature of ancient life and how dinosaurs fit into the evolutionary continuum. Following are some features of dinosaurs that can help students identify dinosaurs in museum exhibits:

Carnivores	*Herbivores*
arms and legs ending in claws	hooves
sharp, long teeth	flat, crushing teeth
large head and mouth	small head and mouth

Bipedal Dinosaurs	*Quadrupedal Dinosaurs*
big back feet	equal-size feet
big back legs	different-size legs
body upright	body horizontal
very small arms	
"hands" that can grab	

Following are some comparisons you can ask students to draw as they view the dinosaurs (this is a good time to introduce observation, notetaking, and drawing skills, if you choose):

- Dinosaur eggs and the eggs of other animals

- Dinosaur bones and student bones (hands, feet, arms, legs)

- Dinosaurs with lizard hips and dinosaurs with bird hips

THE ZOO FIELD TRIP

The frustrations of the zoo field trip are similar to those of the museum: the same crowds in the parking lot and exhibits, often the same student passivity.

Large school groups traveling through the zoo are disconcerting to the animals, zoo staff, other zoo visitors and frustrating to the students as well. It is far better to organize enough parental support so that closely supervised groups of no more than four or five students can move from enclosure to enclosure, observe, make and compare notes, and ultimately meet at a predetermined place and time with the remainder of the class. We recognize that such parental support is often unavailable, so the bottom line is, the smaller the group, the better.

The zoo must be considered a living museum where animal features not found in a museum can be observed. Animal sounds, movement, visual systems, use of hands and feet, and behavior (which are not available in the fossil record) are all observable in zoos. Students can be asked to answer the following questions: Do animals behave as individuals or in groups? Do they run on two legs or four legs? Are the eyes located on the front or sides of the head? Are the animals carnivores or herbivores? Do the animals live in trees or on flat land? How do they use their arms and legs? How do they use camouflage and coloration?

CONCLUSION

Once the group returns to school, information gathered from the museum or zoo resource should be incorporated into classroom or subsequent library studies. The physical dinosaur resources seen during the field trips will provide students a broader framework within which to place printed references and information from videos or television. Field trips have the capability of making the classroom activities more real for the students.

REFERENCES

Collette, Alfred T., and Eugene L. Chiappetta. 1989. *Science Instruction in the Middle and Secondary Schools.* Columbus, Ohio: Merrill.

Falk, John H., and John D. Balling. 1980. The School Field Trip: Where You Go Makes the Difference. *Science and Children* 17, no. 6: 6-8.

National Science Resources Center. 1988. *Science for Children: Resources for Teachers.* Washington, D.C.: National Academy Press.

Glossary

GENERAL TERMS

Angiosperm—Flowering plants that form seeds found inside protected covering such as fruits.

Binocular—Pertaining to both eyes at the same time; the type of vision that has enhanced depth perception.

Cardinal direction—One of the four principal points on a compass: north, south, east, west.

Chisel—A metal tool with a sharp, beveled edge. Used to carefully chip away rock from bone material.

Climate—The general meteorological conditions of an area over a long period of time.

Coexisted—Lived together at the same time and in the same place.

Concealing coloration—The kind of camouflage where the colors of an animal match or blend well with its immediate suroundings.

Cretaceous—The third and most recent period (from 144-66 million years ago) of the Mesozoic Era. The name comes from the fact that Cretaceous rocks are often chalky (the Latin *creta-* means chalk).

Cross section—A view of an object created by cutting vertically through it, like a knife cutting down into a layer cake.

Disruptive coloration—The kind of camouflage that breaks up or disturbs the visual outline of an animal, making it difficult to see. A good example is stripes on a zebra.

Ectothermic—Having a body temperature that approximates that of the surrounding environment; cold-blooded.

Equator—The line of zero latitude formed by a great circle perpendicular to the earth's axis of rotation and passing through the earth's center.

Eroded—Worn away by abrasion.

Fresnel lens—A thin, flat piece of plastic containing small concentric circles that act as magnifiers. They are often used to concentrate light or images.

Genera—A group of species with similar characeristics.

Genus—In binomial scientific nomenclature, the first of two names designating a particular organism. The classification category between family and species.

Gymnosperm—Plants whose seeds are not enclosed within a special chamber, such as conifers or pine trees.

Habitat—The area or type of environment in which an organism or biological population normally lives.

Hand spade—A small shovel with a short handle, often used for gardening.

Hemisphere—Half of the earth, literally a "half ball." The earth is divided into northern and southern hemispheres by the equator, and eastern and western hemispheres by the prime meridian and the line of 180 degrees longitude.

Hypothesis—An explanation that accounts for a group of facts that can be tested by further investigation; an educated guess based upon the facts then known.

Icon—An image, representation, or symbol. For example, an icon for electricity is a small lightning bolt.

Instantaneous electronic media—The transmission and reporting of events as they happen through the use of satellites and television.

Jurassic—The middle period (from 208-144 million years ago) of the Mesozoic Era. The name comes from the Jura Mountains of France and Switzerland where such rocks were first discovered.

Larynx—The human voice box located at the top of the throat and containing the vocal chords.

Legend—An explanatory caption for a map showing interpretive information such as symbols, color keys, and scale.

Ligaments—Tissue that connects bones.

Lyric prose—A type of expression in which the speech or writing is almost musical but does not have the artificial format of poetry.

Mesozoic—The middle of the three eras of geologic time (from 245-66 million years ago). The Mesozoic follows the Paleozoic and precedes the Cenozoic. *Mesozoic* means "middle life."

Microchip—A small slice of silicon crystal that contains the various electrical circuits that make computers work.

Molten rock—Rock made liquid by heat from the earth's center. Molten rock can erupt as lava from volcanoes.

Monocular—Having or pertaining to one eye.

North pole—The northern end of the earth's axis of rotation; 90 degrees north latitude. (Note: this is not where a compass points; a compass points to the magnetic north pole, or magnetic north.)

Oscilloscope—An electronic instrument that can transform wave energy into a visual display on the screen of a cathode-ray tube.

PVC pipe-A type of plastic pipe made from **p**oly**v**inyl **c**hloride.

Pangaea—The great continent believed to have been formed in the northern hemisphere by the union of the two supercontinents Laurasia and Gondwana approximately 250 million years ago.

Plate tectonics—A unifying geological theory incorporating the building of mountains, volcanoes, earthquakes, and structural relationships of large, floating pieces of the earth's crust.

Prediction—A determination of what will happen in the future.

Prime meridian—The line of zero degrees longitude that, by international agreement, runs through Greenwich, England, and separates the eastern and western hemispheres.

Sedimentation—The process in which solid material falls to the bottom of a body of liquid; for example, sand or mud settling to the bottom of a lake.

South pole—The southern end of the earth's axis of rotation; 90 degrees south latitude.

Strata—Layers or beds of sedimentary rock formed as material settles out of a liquid.

Tendon—Elastic connective tissue that attaches muscle to bone.

Trackway—Two or more consecutive footprints belonging to an animal moving in a given direction.

Triassic—The earliest period (245-208 million years ago) of the Mesozoic Era. The name comes from the three-part subdivision of the rocks of this period.

Vestigial—no longer functioning (applies to structures, often limbs or other body parts).

FAUNAL AND FLORAL GLOSSARY
(with pronunciation guide for dinosaur names)
(mya = millions of years ago)

Albertosaurus (al-burr-tow-**SOAR**-us)—A late Cretaceous carnivore similar to a *Tyrannosaurus* but less massive and with a longer skull. The name means "Alberta lizard" (for the dinosaur's place of discovery, Alberta, Canada). (90-66 mya)

Allosaurus (al-oh-**SOAR**-us)—An abundant late Jurassic North American carnivore approximately 36 feet (11 meters) long and weighing approximately 1.5 tons. The name means "different lizard." (190-75 mya)

Anchisaurus (**an**-ki-soar-us)—Early Jurassic light-framed, probably quadrupedal herbivores approximately seven feet (two meters) long and weighing approximately 60 pounds (27 kilograms). The name means "near lizard." (220-210 mya)

Apatosaurus (a-pat-oh-**SOAR**-us)—Often incorrectly called *brontosaurus*. A large 70-foot-long (21 meters), quadrupedal herbivore with long neck and tail. The name means "deceptive lizard." (160-66 mya)

Brachiopod (**brach**-ee-o-pod)—A marine bivalve (similar to a clam) that lives mostly on the ocean bottom. The animal's soft parts are enclosed by two shells of unequal size and different shape. The name means "arm foot." (560 mya to present).

Brachiosaurus (brach-ee-oh-**soar**-us)—A member of the family of dinosaurs that lived in the late Jurassic containing some of the largest and tallest herbivores—more than 50 feet (16 meters) high and 50 tons in weight. Brachiosaurs had nostrils high on the head and front legs that were longer than the hind legs. The name means "arm lizard." (160-135 mya)

Brontosaurus (**bron**-tow-saur-us)—See *Apatosaurus*. Name means "thunder lizard." Misnomer for *Apatosaurus*.

Camptosaurus (camp-tow-**SOAR**-us)—A massive bipedal or quadrupedal herbivore whose arms were much shorter than its legs. This late Jurassic/early Cretaceous herbivore was approximately 20 feet (six meters) long. The name means "bent lizard." (180-100 mya)

Coelophysis (see-low-**FY**-sis)—A small, slim-bodied carnivore that lived during the late Triassic and had a long neck and tail. It was approximately 10 feet (three meters) long and weighed 60 pounds (27 kilograms). The name means "hollow form" because the bones were light and hollow. (225-200 mya)

Compsognathus (komp-sog-**nay**-thus)—A small, slim-bodied, two-legged carnivore that probably moved very quickly. It lived during the late Jurassic and was one of the smallest dinosaurs, only two feet (60 centimeters) long and weighing approximately six pounds (three kilograms). The name means "pretty jaw." (150-140 mya)

Cycad (**SIGH**-cad)—A group of gymnosperm plants with a short trunk topped by a crown of palmlike leaves; first appeared during the Triassic. (245 mya to present)

Deinonychus (die-**NON**-ik-us)—A medium-sized, fierce carnivore known from the Cretaceous. It was approximately 10 feet (three meters) long, and its most conspicuous feature was a large claw on each foot. The name means "terrible claw." (144-66 mya)

Dimetrodon (die-**ME**-trow-don)—A fin-backed, large-jawed carnivorous reptile (not a dinosaur) from Permian times that was approximately 14 feet (11 meters) long. Its name means "two-measure tooth." (320-286 mya).

Dinosaur (**DIE**-no-soar)—Extinct (?) animals that lived from 230-66 million years ago. They are often considered reptiles and in 1841 were given the name that means "terrible lizard."

Diplodocus (dih-**PLOD**-oh-cuss)—A long (up to 87 feet [27 meters]), graceful, four-legged herbivore that lived during the late Jurassic and was marked by a very long, snakelike neck and tail. The name means "double beam." (160-66 mya)

Euoplocephalus (yoo-op-low-**SEF**-a-lus)—A massive, four-legged, armored herbivore from the late Cretaceous approximately 23 feet (seven meters) long and weighing two tons. The tail had a bony club at the end. The name means "well-armored head." (120-66 mya)

Exogyra (ex-o-**GY**-ra)—An oyster that lived during the time of the dinosaurs. It had a spiral-shaped shell and was approximately three to four inches (8-10 centimeters) long.

Ginkgo (**GING**-ko)—An order of tall trees with fan-shaped leaves. The order is first known from Permian times and is represented today by one species. (270 mya to today). The trees are unable to tolerate severely cold climates.

Glossopteris (gloss-**OP**-ter-us)—A unique fossil plant (seed fern) of Permian age with tongue-shaped leaves. Fossils are found in Australia, Africa, India, and Antarctica.

Hadrosaurs (**HAD**-row-sores)—A general name for dinosaurs that belong to one of two families. Hadrosauridae (big lizards—including the duckbill dinosaurs) and Lambéosauridae (lambés lizards). Both from the late Cretaceous. (105-66 mya)

Heterodontosaurus (het-er-oh-dont-oh-**SOAR**-us)—An early Jurassic bipedal or quadrupedal herbivore approximately four feet (1.5 meters) long, characterized by several different kinds of teeth. The name means "mixed-tooth lizard." (225-190 mya)

Hypsilophodon (hip-sih-**LOAF**-oh-don)—A small two-legged plant eater known from the early Cretaceous. It had long feet and short arms and was approximately six feet (two meters) long. The name means "high-ridged tooth." (170-70 mya)

Ichthyosaurus (ik-thee-oh-**SOAR**-us)—A carnivorous marine reptile (not a dinosaur) that existed from the Triassic into the Cretaceous. Size varied considerably, but the largest may have been 46 feet (14 meters) long and weighed 40 tons. Name means "fish lizard." (230-80 mya)

Iguanodon (ig-**WAH**-no-don)—One of the earliest known dinosaurs. A bipedal or quadrupedal herbivore approximately 30 feet (nine meters) long. The name means "iguana-tooth." (140-80 mya)

Lambeosaurus (lam-bee-oh-**SOAR**-us)—A large bipedal or quadrupedal herbivore approximately 50 feet (16 meters) long from the late Cretaceous. Named for its discoverer, Lawrence M. Lambe. (100-66 mya) (see *Hadrosaurus*).

Maiasaurus (my-ya-**SOAR**-us)—A bipedal or quadrupedal herbivore that lived in the late Cretaceous and was found near nests containing eggs. Approximately 30 feet (nine meters) long. Name means "good mother lizard." (100-66 mya)

Mesosaurus (mez-oh-**SOAR**-us)—A toothed, aquatic, early reptile of Permian age found in Brazil and Africa; 3-6 feet (1-2 meters) long.

Mollusk (also Mollusc)—Any of a large phylum of marine, freshwater, or land-dwelling invertebrates consisting of approximately 60,000 species that vary in length from a fiftieth of an inch (0.5 millimeter) to more than 53 feet (16 meters). Among the more common mollusks are snails, clams, squid, and octopuses. The name means "soft-bodied."

Mosasaurs (**mow**-zah-soars)—Large swimming, carnivorous lizards that lived during the late Cretaceous. They were contemporaries of dinosaurs but were not dinosaurs.

Pachycephalosaurus (pack-ee-seff-ah-low-**SOAR**-us)—A late Cretaceous bipedal herbivore with a high dome on the top of its skull. It reached a length of approximately 15 feet (4.6 meters). The name means "thick-headed lizard." (140-70 mya)

Parasaurolophus (par-a-soar-**AH**-low-fuss)—A late Cretaceous bipedal or quadrupedal herbivore with a long hollow tube (contained within the skull structure) that projected backward from its head. It reached lengths of 33 feet (10 meters). The name means "like *saurolophus*." (100-66 mya)

Plateosaurus (plate-ee-oh-**SOAR**-us)—A late Triassic bipedal or quadrupedal herbivore with a bulky body and small head. It reached lengths of approximately 26 feet (eight meters). The name means "flat lizard." (220-210 mya)

Plesiosaurs (**PLEE**-zee-oh-soars)—Long-necked, short-tailed, small-headed marine reptiles that may have swum like penguins or seals, catching prey in their long teeth. Name means "ribbon reptile." Not a dinosaur but coexisted with the dinosaurs. (225-66 mya)

Protoceratops (pro-tow-**SER**-a-tops)—A four-legged herbivore from the late Cretaceous with a large head and a parrotlike beak. It reached a length of approximately six feet (1.8 meters). The name means "first horned face." (85-75 mya)

Psittacosaurus (sit-a-co-**SOAR**-us)—An early Cretaceous bipedal herbivore with a parrotlike beak and grasping hands. It might have reached lengths of 6.5 feet (two meters). The name means "parrot lizard." (140-120 mya)

Pteranodon (ter-**AN**-o-don)—A large, flying carnivorous reptile with a wingspan of up to 24 feet (7.5 meters) that lived during the late Cretaceous. Name means "wings without teeth." Not a dinosaur but coexisted with the dinosaurs. (200-66 mya)

Reptile—Member of the class *Reptilia*. Reptiles share the following characteristics: they lay eggs with hard shells on land; they have scaly skin; they are ectothermic (cold-blooded); and they breathe through lungs. Common reptiles are snakes, lizards, turtles, alligators, and according to some, dinosaurs.

Stegoceras (steg-oh-**SER**-as)—A slightly built, beipedal herbivore from the late Cretaceous with a dome-shaped skull. It reached lengths of approximately 6.5 feet (2.5 meters). The name means "horny roof." (140-70 mya)

Stegosaurus (steg-oh-**SOAR**-us)—The largest plated dinosaur. A distinctive 30-foot (nine-meter) long, four-legged herbivore that lived during the late Jurassic. Name means "roof lizard." (180-95 mya)

Triceratops (try-**SER**-a-tops)—A late Cretaceous animal, it is the largest of the horned dinosaurs. It had three large horns that projected forward from its face, and a large, shieldlike bony frill at the back of its large head. It reached lengths of up to 30 feet (nine meters) and weighed six tons. The name means "three-horned face." (75-66 mya)

Tyrannosaurus (tie-ran-oh-**SOAR**-us)—A giant, bipedal, carnivorous dinosaur from the late Cretaceous with a massive skull and jaws and strong legs but small arms: the classic predatory dinosaur. It reached a length of 39 feet (12 meters) and a weight of seven tons. The name means "tyrant lizard." (90-66 mya)

Velociraptor (vell-**AH**-see-rap-tor)—An aggressive, bipedal carnivore from the late Cretaceous with sharp teeth, a straight, stiff tail, and large claws on its feet. It was approximately 6 feet (1.8 meters) long. The name means "quick plunderer." (144-66 mya)

Bibliography

Adams, Frank Dawson. *The Birth and Development of the Geological Sciences.* New York: Dover, 1954.

Alexander, R. McNeil. *Dynamics of Dinosaurs and Other Extinct Giants.* New York: Columbia University Press, 1989.

Aliki. *Digging Up Dinosaurs.* New York: HarperCollins, 1988.

American Heritage Dictionary, Second College Edition. Boston: Houghton Mifflin, 1982.

Bakker, Robert T. *The Dinosaur Heresies.* New York: William Morrow, 1986.

———. *Dr. Bob's Guide to Teaching Dino Science.* Chicago: World Book, 1994.

Baylor, Byrd. *If You Are a Hunter of Fossils.* New York: Charles Scribner's Sons, 1980.

Benton, Michael J. *On the Trail of the Dinosaurs.* New York: Crescent, 1989.

Berger, Melvin. *The Trumpet Book.* New York: Lothrop, Lee & Shepard, 1978.

Beyer, Barry K. *Teaching Thinking Skills: A Handbook for Elementary Teachers.* Boston: Allyn & Bacon, 1991.

Borror, Donald J. *Dictionary of Word Roots and Combining Forms.* Palo Alto, California: Mayfield, 1960.

Boyer, Barry K. *Teaching Thinking Skills: A Handbook for Elementary Teachers.* Boston: Allyn & Bacon, 1991.

Brown, Ruth. *If at First You Do Not See.* New York: Holt, 1992.

Collette, Alfred T., and Eugene L. Chiappetta. *Science Instruction in the Middle and Secondary Schools.* Columbus, Ohio: Merrill, 1989.

Czerkas, Sylvia J., and Stephen A. Czerkas. *Dinosaurs: A Global View.* New York: Mallard Press, 1991.

Desmond, Adrian J. *The Hot-Blooded Dinosaurs.* New York: Dial Press, 1976.

Dixon, Dougal. *Dougal Dixon's Dinosaurs*. Honesdale, Pennsylvania: Boyds Mills Press, 1993.

Echoes: A Guide to Dinosaur National Monument. Dinosaur, Colorado: The Dinosaur Nature Association, 1993-94.

Engel, Leonard. *The Sea*. New York: Time-Life Books, 1961.

Falk, John H., and John D. Balling. The School Field Trip: Where You Go Makes the Difference. *Science and Children* 17, no. 6 (1980): 6-8.

Farlow, James O. *On the Tracks of Dinosaurs: A Study of Dinosaur Footprints*. New York: Franklin Watts, 1991.

Ferrell, Nancy Warren. *Camouflage: Nature's Defense*. New York: Franklin Watts, 1989.

Gould, Stephen Jay. *Bully for Brontosaurus*. New York: W. W. Norton, 1991.

Hoffman, Mary. *Animals in the Wild: Zebra*. Milwaukee, Wisconsin: Raintree Children's Books, 1985.

Holmes, Arthur. *Principles of Physical Geology*. New York: Ronald Press, 1965.

Horner, John R., and James Gorman. *Digging Dinosaurs*. New York: Workman, 1988.

———. *Maia: A Dinosaur Grows Up*. Philadelphia, Pennsylvania: Running Press, 1989.

Kiefer, Irene. *Global Jigsaw Puzzle: The Story of Continental Drift*. Brattleboro, Vermont: The Book Press, 1978.

Lambert, David. *The Dinosaur Data Book*. New York: Avon Books, 1990.

Larrick, Nancy, and Wendy Lamb. *To Ride a Butterfly*. Dover, Delaware: Bantam Doubleday, 1991.

Lauber, Patricia. *Dinosaurs Walked Here and Other Stories Fossils Tell*. New York: Bradbury Press, 1987.

———. *Living with Dinosaurs*. New York: Bradbury Press, 1991.

Leet, L. Don, and Sheldon Judson. *Physical Geology*. Englewood Cliffs, New Jersey: Prentice-Hall, 1971.

Lockley, Martin. *Tracking Dinosaurs*. Cambridge: Cambridge University Press, 1991.

McClung, Robert M. *How Animals Hide.* Washington D.C.: National Geographic Society, 1973.

Moravcsik, Michael J. *Musical Sound.* New York: Paragon House, 1987.

Munsart, Craig A. *Investigating Science with Dinosaurs.* Englewood, Colorado: Teacher Ideas Press, 1993.

Murie, Olaus J. *A Field Guide to Animal Tracks.* The Peterson Field Guide Series. Boston: Houghton Mifflin, 1974.

Murphy, Jim. *Dinosaur for a Day.* New York: Scholastic, 1992.

National Science Resources Center. *Science for Children.* Washington D.C.: National Academy Press, 1988.

New Standard Encyclopedia. Chicago: Standard Educational, 1992.

Newman, William L. *Geologic Time.* Denver, Colorado: U.S. Geological Survey, 1991.

Norman, David. *The Illustrated Encyclopedia of Dinosaurs.* New York: Crown, 1985.

———. *Dinosaur!* New York: Prentice Hall, 1991.

Ommaney, F. D. *The Fishes.* New York: Time-Life Books, 1963.

Ostrom, John H., and John S. McIntosh. *Marsh's Dinosaurs: The Collections from Como Bluff.* New Haven, Connecticut: Yale University Press, 1966.

Palmer, Allison R. The Decade of North American Geology 1983 Geologic Time Scale *Geology* 11, no. 9 (1983):503-504.

Powzyk, Joyce. *Animal Camouflage.* New York: Bradbury Press, 1990.

Prelutsky, Jack. *Something Big Has Been Here.* New York: Greenwillow Books, 1993.

———. *The Dragons Are Singing Tonight.* New York: Greenwillow Books, 1993.

Psihoyos, Louie. *Hunting Dinosaurs.* New York: Random House, 1994.

Richards, Roy. *101 Science Tricks: Fun Experiments with Everyday Materials.* New York: Sterling, 1991.

Romer, Alfred Sherwood. *Vertebrate Paleontology.* Chicago: University of Chicago Press, 1945.

Rossbacher, Lisa A. *Recent Revolutions in Geology.* New York: Franklin Watts, 1986.

Sagan, Carl. *Cosmos.* New York: Random House, 1980.

Sowler, Sandie. *Amazing Animal Disguises.* New York: Alfred A. Knopf, 1992.

Stall, Chris. *Animal Tracks of the Rocky Mountains.* Seattle, Washington: The Mountaineers, 1989.

Tinbergen, Niko. *Animal Behavior.* New York: Time-Life Books, 1965.

To Ride a Butterfly. Delaware: Bantam Doubleday, 1991.

Vacca, Richard T., and Jo Anne L. Vacca. *Content Area Reading.* Glenview, Illinois: Scott, Foresman, 1989.

Walpole, Brenda. *175 Science Experiments to Amuse and Amaze Your Friends.* New York: Random House, 1988.

Webster, David. *Track Picture Book.* Newton, Massachusetts: Education Development Center, 1968.

Yolen, Jane. *Dinosaur Dances.* New York: G. P. Putnam's Sons, 1990.

Index

All activities in index are noted in **boldface**.

About the Authors

Craig A. Munsart

Craig A. Munsart is a former energy industry geologist, educational programs manager at a children's museum and middle school science curriculum writer. He has taught at the university, high school, junior high, and middle school levels and has talked extensively to elementary schools. He holds a Bachelor's Degree and Master's Degree in Geology from Queens College of the City University of New York, and a Bachelor's Degree in Architecture from Pratt Institute. He is presently an Earth Science educator in the Denver area and a secondary school science teacher in Jefferson County, Colorado. His first book, *Investigating Science with Dinosaurs*, received a "Top Ten Dinosaur Book" Award from the Dinosaur Society in 1994.

Karen Alonzi Van Gundy

Karen Alonzi Van Gundy has twenty-one years experience as an elementary teacher in the Jefferson County Schools. In addition to her elementary responsibilities, Karen is involved in teacher education through Colorado State University and the Colorado School of Mines. In 1990, Karen received Honorable Mention for Colorado Teacher of the Year.